THE ECONOMIC FOUNDATIONS OF GOVERNMENT

338.9
H699e

The Economic Foundations of Government

Randall G. Holcombe
Professor of Economics
Florida State University
Tallahassee

NEW YORK UNIVERSITY PRESS
Washington Square, New York

First published in the U.S.A. in 1994 by
NEW YORK UNIVERSITY PRESS
Washington Square
New York, N.Y. 10003

Library of Congress Cataloging-in-Publication Data
Holcombe, Randall G.
The economic foundations of government / Randall G. Holcombe.
p.   cm.
Includes bibliographical references (p.   ) and index.
ISBN 0–8147–3506–1
1. Social choice.   2. Economic policy.   3. Finance, Public.
I. Title.
HB846.8.H65   1993
338.9—dc20   93–16212
                                                       CIP

Printed in Hong Kong

To Lora, Ross, and Mark

Contents

Preface   xii

1 Introduction   **1**
Positive versus Normative   3
Normative Analysis and the Public Sector   5
Government as an Economic Institution   6
The Constitutional Foundation of Government   7
Protection for Tribute: The Fundamental Contract   8
Other Activities of Government   9
Conclusion   10

2 The Economic Theory of Rights   **11**
Positive and Normative Theories of Rights   12
The Benefits of Rights   13
The Origins of Rights   14
The Historical Origins of Rights   16
Rights without Government: The Case of Peru   18
A Semantic Issue Regarding the Definition of Rights   20
Positive Alternatives to the Economic Theory of Rights   21
The Utility of Altruism   23
The Economic Theory and Other Theories   26
Contractarianism and a Normative Theory of
    Economic Rights   27
Conclusion   29

3 Governments and Constitutions   **32**
The Exchange Model of Government   32
Agreement and Exchange in Anarchy   34
The Exchange of Protection for Tribute   35
How Well Does the Two-Person Model Extrapolate to
    Many People?   37
Government as Monopolist   37
Competition among Potential Governments   38
Constitutional Rules and Legitimacy   40
The Social Contract   41
Other Theories of the Social Contract   43

Normative versus Positive Aspects of the Social
  Contract   48
The Characteristics of Constitutions   50
Constitutions and Monopoly Government   51
Conclusion   52

4 A Model of Rights and Government   54
Opportunistic Behavior and Rights   54
Monitoring and Enforcement   55
Institutions Do Not Make Rights Unconditional   57
Institutions and Enforcement   59
Government and Rights   60
Military and Police Protection of Rights   61
A Model of Rights Structures   62
Comparative Statics   65
Competition and Exchange   69
Conclusion   70

5 Distinction between Clubs and Governments   72
An Economic Theory of Clubs   73
Clubs and Governments   74
What is a Government?   80
A Definition of Government   83
The Reason for Defining Government   86
Coercion   87
Constitutions and Mobility   89
Conclusion   89

6 Government as Monopolist   92
Competition, Monopoly, and Coercion   93
Natural Monopoly in Government   94
The Government Cartel   95
The Competitive Model of Politics   96
Competition and Special Interests   97
Barriers to Entry and Monopoly   98
Seniority as a Barrier to Entry   99
Political Competition   101
Government and the Profits from Government   102
Federalism and Cartels among Governments   103
Regulation   105
Corruption   106

The Secret Ballot 107
Conclusion 108

7 Institutions and Exchange **110**
Dictatorship and Democracy 111
Agreement in Politics and in the Marketplace 113
Lindahl Equilibrium and Agreement 113
Why is Compromise Necessary in Politics? 116
Cycles and Stability 119
Large and Small Number Settings 121
Stability in General Elections and in the Legislature 121
The American Constitution 124
Conclusion 125

8 Constitutional Evolution **128**
Constitutions as a Constraint on Monopoly Power 129
The Scope of Constitutional Rules 131
Constitutional Evolution 132
Constitutional Evolution and the Division of Labor 134
Enforcement, Evolution, and Revolution 137
Legitimacy and Enforcement 138
Factors that Reduce Legitimacy 139
Conclusion 140

9 Competition in Politics **142**
Government Exploitation 142
Intergovernmental Competition 143
Political Competition through Voting 145
Constitutions as Substitutes for Mobility 146
Constitutional Rules and Competition 146
War: The Health of the State 147
Government Growth and Decline 148
The Importance of Constitutional Constraints 150
Constitutional Design 151
Social Science and Social Engineering 152
Conclusion 153

10 The Concept of Agreement **155**
Agreement and the Operation of Government 156
Legitimacy 157

Legitimacy and Agreement   159
The Production of Legitimacy   160
Agreement and Coercion   161
Ideology   162
Positive and Normative Agreement   163
Problems with the Concept of Agreement   165
Implied Agreement   168
Implied Agreement in Law   169
Fictions   170
Conceptual and Implied Agreement   171
A Positive Application of Implied Agreement   174
Normative Application   175
Conceptual Agreement   178
Conclusion   178

11 Positive and Normative Theories of Government   **180**
Why Normative Theories Require Positive Theories   180
Contractarianism   182
Utilitarianism   183
Act versus Rule Utilitarianism   185
Distinctions Between Utilitarians and Contractarians   186
Disagreements about Facts and Values   188
Natural Rights   189
Natural Law   191
The Role of Fictions   192
Conclusion   194

12 Political Ethics and Public Policy   **196**
Rawlsian Agreement as a Heuristic Device   196
Wicksellian Agreement   198
Agreement as a Benchmark   199
Non-Pareto Superior Policy Proposals   200
Problems with Non-Pareto Superior Policy Proposals   202
The Wicksellian Model of Taxation   203
Desirability and Feasibility   204
Legitimacy and Agreement   205
The Importance of the Status Quo   206
Conclusion   207

13 Conclusion   **210**
The Exchange Model of Government   210

Clubs and Governments   211
Constitutional Rules   212
Constitutions and Competition   213
Competition and Monopoly in Government   215
Government by Agreement   215
Agreement and Public Policy   216
Desirable Political Institutions   217
Dimensions of Political Competition   220
Institutions and Outcomes   221
Building on the Foundations   223

Notes   224

Bibliography   259

Index   269

Preface

Governments are created for the purpose of securing the benefits of collective action. Thus, the foundations of government are explicitly economic. In an idealized setting, government might be formed by people who cooperate to draw up rules for their mutual benefit. Under other circumstances, some individuals use force to impose their rules on others. When rules are imposed by force on a reluctant population, one can easily imagine that most of the benefits of collective action will go to those who dictate the rules. Regardless, the purpose of government is to produce benefits through collective action that could not be produced by individuals acting independently. How those benefits are distributed is perhaps as interesting a question as how they are produced.

The latter part of the 20th century has seen an increasing interest among economists, political scientists, philosophers, and others in understanding the economic foundations of government. Led by scholars such as James Buchanan and John Rawls, the social contract theory of the state has been employed to understand how the underlying rules of a society can be developed, and what it might mean to say that people are in agreement with the rules. A new subdiscipline of constitutional economics is emerging to analyze the rules of society in an explicitly economic framework, so there is some indication that there will continue to be a growing interest in using economic tools to analyze the foundations of government.

The social contract theory of the state provides a starting point for much work in constitutional economics, but as depicted by Buchanan and Rawls, the social contract is based on the normative principle of unanimous agreement. In Rawls' *A Theory of Justice*, people agree behind a veil of ignorance. In Buchanan's *The Limits of Liberty*, people enter a hypothetical renegotiation of the rules from a position of anarchy. Regardless of the construction used, the underlying principle is that in some conceptual sense, everybody must agree to the terms of the social contract.

Certainly these models of the social contract can be accepted on their own terms, and they provide a great deal of insight into the economic foundations of government. However, governments are fundamentally coercive organizations, and the real impetus behind citizen conformance to government rules is force, not agreement. No matter how much people agree with the rules of their government, and no matter how much they support their government's actions and policies, the government still stands ready to use force to make people conform to its rules. It is force, not agreement, that makes a government. A purely positive model of government must recognize that while people do have the incentive to agree to rules that can enable them to reap the benefits of collective organization, those who have power can use it to alter the nature of the agreement.

Starting from the premise that there are potential gains from collective organization, one can analyze the types of institutions that are likely to arise when threats and force can be used as a part of the bargaining process. This provides a more realistic foundation than one in which unanimous agreement is required, but perhaps more importantly, it eliminates the normative elements from the contractarian model. Even without this normative foundation, many of the contractarian conclusions remain. Constitutional rules are an important part of the government's foundation, and even the most powerful governments have an incentive to create constitutional constraints on their power. One can easily see how constitutional constraints would be produced through a process where unanimous agreement to the rules is required, but these same constraints are produced without the unanimity requirement.

My interest in this topic goes back several decades. I was a graduate student at Virginia Polytechnic Institute and State University when James Buchanan was writing *The Limits of Liberty*, and there was considerable interest among both faculty and graduate students in applying the contractarian model to understand the economic foundations of government. In the years since, I have used a contractarian framework to argue points in some of my previous writing. Originally, I envisioned the contractarian model as a metaphor, but was not inclined to push the model too hard because I did not believe it would hold up under close scrutiny. By using it in my own writing, however, I was forced to consider just how much of a theory of government the contractarian foundation could support. This book is the result of my exploration of the contractarian framework.

I consider what appears in this book to be an exchange model of government, rather than a contractarian model. There are many references to the contractarian model, however, and even a claim that this exchange model of government can be extended into a model of a social contract. Such an extension would not be necessary, but is included for two reasons. First, it is worthwhile to see the relationship between this exchange model and prior developments of the contractarian framework. Second, my ideas developed out of the contractarian model, and it seems appropriate to acknowledge those origins.

My ideas on this subject have evolved over a period of two decades, so any list of acknowledgments is sure to leave out someone. Many chapters of this volume circulated as working papers, and among those who have read and provided helpful comments on parts of the manuscript are Bruce Benson, Donald Boudreaux, James Buchanan, James Gwartney, Walter Hettich, Tibor Machan, Robert Tollison, Gordon Tullock, Viktor Vanberg, Stanley Winer, and Leland Yeager. The advice of these individuals surely has improved the final product, but since most did not see the entire manuscript, and since there still remain some points of disagreement, I alone must retain responsibility for any of the book's shortcomings. Financial support for a portion of this work was provided by the Earhart Foundation, and I am grateful to them for enabling me to complete the book sooner than otherwise would have been possible. I also owe much thanks to my family, to whom this book is dedicated. Without the understanding, encouragement, and support of my wife, Lora, and my two sons, Ross and Mark, this book could not have been written.

RANDALL G. HOLCOMBE

1 Introduction

The institutions of government are the result of human design, but the operation of governmental institutions may differ from the intentions of their designers. One reason is that actions may have unintended consequences, so institutions designed to have one effect may end up having other effects in addition to – or at times instead of – their intended effects. Another reason why governmental institutions in the real world will never exactly reflect the preferences of any particular designer is because those institutions are the result of compromise. Public sector institutions are produced by a bargaining process in which the preferences of many individuals are aggregated to produce the institutional structure ultimately referred to as government.

Economic analysis has explored in great detail the unintended consequences and secondary effects of governmental activity. At times the analysis has proceeded as if the secondary effects are completely unintended, as for example, when individuals who genuinely want to help the plight of the poor propose a minimum wage law that has the secondary effect of increasing unemployment, which has the unintended effect of harming at least some poor individuals. At other times the analysis treats secondary effects as the intended, even if unstated, goals of governmental activity. An example here would be the depiction of the minimum wage law as a device politically supported by unions in order to raise the wage of nonunion labor in order to make nonunion labor less competitive with union labor. This strengthens the position of unions by increasing union employment at the expense of nonunion employment. Regardless of which model one uses, both of these lines of reasoning accept government institutions as given and take their analysis from that point.

This common ground makes both views an analysis of the effects of government activity. There is undeniable value in examining the effects of government activity, both for positive reasons, to understand how government works, and for normative reasons, to identify ways to improve the functioning of government. But this type of analysis stops short of a complete understanding of governmental institutions because it does not explain the origins of the institutions that allow government activity to take place. One might find that a particular policy is the result of a special interest using the government for its benefit at the expense of the general public interest, which is a good explanation of the particular policy. But what created the public sector institutions that allow this type of political activity to occur?

Analysis often stops at this point rather than incorporating a theory of the development of institutions, but there has been important work done by scholars such as Buchanan,[1] Nozick,[2] and Rawls,[3] who have gone further to look into a theory of the foundations of government. Rather than take the institutional structure as given, these individuals have attempted to explain the characteristics of government that would emerge from a bargaining process, and the types of governments that should emerge.[4] This type of analysis can provide some insight into the economic foundations of government.

The institutional structure that exists as government is not the product of any one individual's design, but rather is the result of a group of individuals who have bargained, traded off one provision for another, and through their negotiations have produced the complex web of rules and institutions called government. Government, in other words, is the outcome of a bargaining process and can be analyzed as such. The same economic tools that are used to analyze the results of bargaining in markets can be applied to government.

The use of economic tools to analyze government is not new,[5] but it is unusual to model governmental institutions themselves as the result of a bargaining process. The social contract theory of the state provides the best example, and the analysis that follows draws heavily on the social contract theory for its foundations. The social contract theory might be cast in either a normative or a positive light, depending upon whether one views it as describing the type of government people should have or describing an actual agreement among the citizenry to abide by the terms of the contract.[6] The theory could, of course, be seen in both ways, as a positive description as well as a normative recommendation.

The beginning of this book explores the contractarian theory of government in a positive framework. The first nine chapters develop a model of governmental institutions that arise through a bargaining process, without using external norms – such as a rule of unanimity, or a theory of natural rights – to limit or evaluate the process. The object is to model government as a set of institutions which are produced as the result of agreements that all participants view to be in their best interests. After this positive model is developed, later chapters discuss normative theories of government, ethics, and policy espousal in clearly normative terms. The positive foundation for the work, though, stems from the fact that governmental rules and institutions actually are the result of a bargaining process through which individuals have interacted and bargained with each other.

One could examine movie theatre complexes, drive-in windows at fast food restaurants, credit cards, and cable television as the creations of particular individuals or groups who designed and marketed them. While much insight might be gained this way, economists also step back to examine products of an economy as the result of a bargaining process – an interaction of supply and demand for goods and services. In the same way that these market institutions are a result of a bargaining process among individuals, so are public sector institutions like public schools, speed limits, the division of responsibility between federal and state governments, the right to free speech, the obligation to pay taxes, and even representative democracy itself. By drawing the parallel to market institutions, it is clear that much insight could be gained by modelling public sector institutions as the product of a bargaining process among individuals in a society. Indeed, it is through just such a process that the actual institutions were created.

Seen in this way, government has explicitly economic foundations. The economic foundations of government come from the fact that public sector institutions are the result of a bargaining process among individuals in a society, and as with any process of economic exchange, the tools of economic analysis can be used to understand the process. One goal of this book is to use economic analysis to model government as the result of a bargaining process, in much the same way that standard economic theory models private sector institutions as the result of a bargaining process.

Positive versus Normative

The later chapters of the book deal with explicitly normative matters, but the theory itself has the potential to rest on a completely positive base. This is because actual public sector institutions are the actual result of bargaining among individuals. Without placing any normative constraints on the bargaining process, the development of governmental institutions can be modelled as a product of exchange to see what types of governmental institutions would be produced as a result of bargaining and exchange among individuals.

The social contract theory of the state models government as the product of a contractual agreement among individuals, but the agreement as modelled by recent contractarians such as Rawls and Buchanan contains a normative element because terms of the social contract are those that receive unanimous agreement.[7] Institutions not unanimously agreed to are not a part of the social contract. Government is fundamentally a coercive institution, and while it is possible that people might agree with all of the actions their governments take, if they do not agree, they may be forced to go along anyway. By allowing bargains to take place in which everyone does not have to agree, the coercive element in government institutions can be modelled explicitly. Furthermore, it is possible to compare what might be produced if unanimity is not required with the types of institutions that would be agreed to under a unanimity rule.

For example, Rawls argues that just rules are those that would be agreed to from behind a veil of ignorance, where people had to bargain without knowing their actual situations in the resulting society. People would have no knowledge of their own personal characteristics, their abilities, their race or gender, their wealth, or any other characteristics. Behind this veil, rules that everyone would agree to would become the social contract. In the real world, people do have different characteristics that can affect their bargaining power. Thus, in the real world, government produced through bargaining and exchange would reflect the differential bargaining abilities of individuals. Individuals that could offer more in exchange – or were better able to threaten others – could expect to do better. A purely positive exchange model of government can examine the expected characteristics of a government produced through exchange, but does not pass judgment on the desirability of the resulting institutions.

The criterion of unanimity gives every individual veto power, since without everyone agreeing, no bargain can be made. Without the requirement of unanimity, individuals might be forced into a bargain simply because agreeing to go along would benefit the individual more than not participating in the bargain. This opens up the question of what constitutes coercion, which Chapter 5 considers in some detail. But again, the issue of coercion will be analyzed from a positive standpoint, without considering whether the outcomes of coercive institutions are desirable using some normative benchmark.

The model of government developed in the first nine chapters is purely positive. It starts with the idea that government institutions are a product of exchange and examines the likely results of the exchange process. But in one sense, there are always value judgments underlying the institutions of government. Because government institutions are the result of human choices, the values of those who are doing the choosing are a factor in determining what will be chosen. While seeing that this is true, the institutions themselves can be analyzed without the external imposition of value judgments. Just because the people in the model have values, and the institutions might be chosen based at least partly on those values, does not preclude a positive analysis of the institutions. Differences in religious institutions, for example, are largely the result of different values held by those in different religions, but it is still possible to do a purely positive study of religious institutions. The institutions are evaluated for what they are, without applying any outside values to judge their desirability.

Normative Analysis and the Public Sector

While the first nine chapters of this book remain firmly in the realm of positive analysis, normative analysis is especially relevant to any examination of the public sector. Government institutions are the result of the collective choices of individuals, and because people can choose their government institutions, it makes sense to establish some criteria for evaluating the desirability of alternative institutions. Chapters 10 and 11 use the positive model of government developed earlier to establish a framework for evaluating various theories of government, and Chapter 12 is directly concerned with evaluating the desirability of alternative government institutions.

In the abstract, people are free to assert that anything they might like would be desirable, but in the real world, a positive framework is necessary in order to make practical suggestions for public policy. Not every imaginable state of the world is actually possible, and positive analysis can help to limit normative recommendations to those that are consistent with individual behavior in the real world. In addition, if a positive theory can help establish the way that institutions really work, then the problems that have been identified with actual institutions can be the target of normative recommendations to improve them. Economic analysis often proceeds along these lines. For example, the normative recommendations to establish antitrust legislation were a result of the perception that big business was getting too powerful.[8]

A positive foundation for normative recommendations is helpful in several ways, then. First, it helps to identify problems that could be improved by institutional redesign, and second, it helps to limit normative recommendations to those that are actually feasible to implement.

Any normative analysis is based on value judgments, so the normative analysis that appears at the end of this volume does not strictly follow from the positive model of government. It appears nevertheless, because it is based on the exchange model of government that is developed earlier, and it is useful to see the connection between the normative and positive analysis within an exchange model of government. It also appears because any normative analysis of the public sector takes on a special significance in light of the fact that people choose their public sector institutions. What types of institutions should they choose? A framework to help answer this question will always be useful, even though any ultimate answer must be based on a value judgment.

Is there a conflict between the arguments that, on the one hand, institutions are the product of exchange, and on the other, that people choose their institutions? In the private sector, the economy can be viewed as the product of an evolutionary process, as Alchian has described,[9] and yet the specific products, firms, and ideas that have a chance to compete for their niche in the economy will be the result of individual entrepreneurial decisions, following Kirzner's model.[10] Surely Kirznerian entrepreneurs can exist in an Alchianeque evolutionary economy, although some entrepreneurial decisions will find their niche and multiply while others will be driven to extinction. The independence of these two ideas is even stronger when discussing the public sector, however, because the exchange process that produces public sector institutions can be influenced by coercion, and once established, new institutions do not compete with existing institutions on a level playing field. The monopoly power enjoyed by existing governments and existing institutions is the subject of Chapter 6.

Government as an Economic Institution

The premise upon which this analysis of government is built is that government is fundamentally an economic institution. Government is an economic institution because, first, government institutions are created as a means by which people can accomplish certain ends. The goal in politics is to produce a result that makes people better off, so the institution is economic in the same way that other productive institutions are economic. Clearly, governmental institutions can be used to make some people worse off, but the same could be said of manufacturing institutions. The point is that people interact with government institutions in order to improve their well being.

The second reason why government is an economic institution is that it is the product of the bargaining and exchange of individuals. People can make market exchanges for mutual gain, but sometimes beneficial exchanges involve specifying the rules under which individuals will interact over prolonged periods of time. If a beneficial exchange could be made involving the interactions of only two individuals, then a contract could be written to make them better off.[11] However, if the beneficial exchange involves the way that people in a society in general interact with each other, then some type of collective agreement must be reached. People would be interested in pursuing the possibility of such exchanges producing collective agreement if they thought that their welfare would be enhanced as a result. This bargaining and agreement among individuals that forms the foundation of governmental institutions has a fundamentally economic character.

The implication is not that every individual will benefit from every collective agreement, though. Individuals will pursue such agreements if they believe they will benefit, but the result might be institutions that lower the welfare of some individuals who do not agree. When leaving the group is not a viable option, government institutions can be coercive. This does not overturn the observation that the institutions are established because some people wanted them for their own self interests, or that the institutions are established as a result of exchange and agreement. Agreement must underlie institutions, although not everyone needs to be party to the agreement.

To set the stage for the exchange model of government, one must note that governmental institutions are established so that people can further their personal interests, and that exchange and agreement underlie the creation of those institutions. From this point, one can then examine the types of bargains that people would want to make to establish collective institutions, and model the types of institutions that would be likely to be produced through the bargaining process.

The Constitutional Foundation of Government

In the day-to-day operation of politics, political exchange can be analyzed in the same framework as market exchange. People trade when they find the opportunity for mutual benefit. But political exchange takes place within the institutional structure of government, and the institutions themselves are the result of political bargaining. The presumption underlying all of government is that the political institutions under which the government operates are of a semi-permanent nature. They can be changed if there is broad general agreement, but they will remain intact otherwise.

These institutions provide a stable environment that defines the terms under which individuals can interact. Because these institutions provide the incentive structure facing individuals, stable institutions are important for any type of long-term planning. In order to undertake any type of investment activity, individuals need to have some assurance that they will be able to reap the benefits in the future of the investment and its associated foregone consumption in the present. Stable institutions that protect property rights and limit the government's power to tax provide this assurance. The government can and does take peoples' property, but it does so in a predictable and well-defined manner that gives individuals a clear incentive structure within which to work.

Consider, for example, the allegation that taxation is theft. Regardless of whether the allegation is true, there is an important difference between the government's taking of one's property through taxation and a thief's taking one's property. People would be reluctant to invest if they believed that their property was likely to be stolen from them in the future. But the government taxes according to well-defined rules that give investors the assurance that even though the government will share in their profits, the individuals making the profits will also be able to keep a share. One difference between taxation and theft is that taxation is institutionalized in the form of a well-defined rule that retains an incentive for productivity.[12]

The protection of rights in general falls under this same principle. Rights to contract with others, rights to use property in certain ways, and rights to engage in certain political activities are all a part of the long-term constitutional framework of a society. Thus, constitutional rules in this framework refer to those long-term rules that are recognized as established and legitimate in a society. This may include a written constitution, as in the United States, but even in the United States includes much more of the general institutional framework, including the common law and well-established norms.[13] The general framework of rights that people will have in a society will be the result of a bargaining process that produces these constitutional rules. This bargaining process is discussed in more detail in the next three chapters.

At the outset, it is important to recognize the difference between agreements on the rules of interaction in a society and agreements that are made under those rules. In the first case, a constitution is developed which has the promise of stability through time, which is different from agreeing to an exchange that carries no implications once the exchange has been made.[14] Bargains to establish constitutional rules take on special significance in the next several chapters, and differentiate an exchange model of government from more general models of economic exchange.

Protection for Tribute: The Fundamental Contract

This model of government as the product of exchange builds upon the exchange of protection for tribute as the fundamental exchange in the contract. Governments do many other things than protect their citizens, but the exchange of protection for tribute is the basis for all other exchanges.

The government gets its income from taxing its citizens. While citizens may like their governments and want to contribute, the government still forces them to contribute and gives them no choice. Most people agree to go along with this exchange, but perhaps only under duress because the government threatens unpleasant consequences for tax resisters. But given that the government receives its income from the productive activity of its citizens, it then has an incentive to protect its citizens, because in so doing, it is protecting its source of income. Thus, the exchange of protection for tribute is a natural one. Again, one might consider the allegation that taxation is theft. Regardless of whether it is true, once the government finds a steady source of income from its citizens, it has an incentive to protect them in order to protect its income.

Other Activities of Government

A government that establishes its claim to protect the rights of its citizens establishes a monopoly position for itself. The government uses force to protect rights if necessary, but protecting the rights of individuals entails preventing them from using force against each other. As the protector of citizen rights, government gains the monopoly right to coercive activity.[15] The fundamental contract of protection for tribute generates monopoly power for government.

If governmental institutions are depicted as the result of exchange, and if the government is a monopolist in the exchange, then government should be expected to act like any other monopolist, and in particular, should be expected to sell its protective services at monopoly prices. Furthermore, it might use its power to produce other goods and sell them at monopoly prices, in a manner similar to the way in which monopolists might try tie-in sales, all-or-nothing sales, price discrimination, and so forth to enhance their profits. The government has an advantage in gaining monopoly power in that it can make competition against it illegal. Governments can either run monopoly businesses themselves, or they can grant monopolies to others and sell the right to be a monopolist in exchange for a share of the monopoly profits.

Once a general model of government is developed within an exchange framework, Chapter 6 looks directly at the issue of government as monopolist. What advantage is there to running a government based on the exchange of protection for tribute? And once this exchange is established, why would the government branch out into other areas besides the production of protection? The answer is that the government can receive monopoly profits by virtue of its unique position. From the standpoint of citizen welfare, the control of the monopoly power of the government is an important issue, and Chapter 9 looks directly at competitive forces in politics that can control the monopoly power of government.

People are ready to compete for the right to run the government, whether through democratic means or through force, because running the government entails the capture of monopoly profits. Within the exchange model of government, the origin of this monopoly power can be explored, and methods of controlling it through the use of competitive political institutions can be examined.

Conclusion

The basic model of government that will be developed in the following chapters is one where bargaining and agreement produce a government that exchanges protection for tribute. Individuals have an incentive to bargain to produce a society that is organized under well-defined rules that protect individual rights, and the result of the bargain is government. Once established, the government has monopoly power, and this monopoly power provides monopoly profits to those who run governments.

This lure of monopoly profits provides an incentive for others outside government to challenge the position of those who run the government. In democratic nations, there is a well-defined institutional structure through which to mount a challenge. This being the case, there is less incentive in a democracy to try to overthrow the government by force, since resources can be used to enter the political process instead. In dictatorships, the use of force may be the best alternative. In either case, the degree to which the existing government is threatened is the degree to which competitive influences naturally affect the government and reduce its monopoly power.

The bargaining process whereby protection is exchanged for tribute establishes the basic rights of citizens, but not all citizens are in equally powerful bargaining positions. Without some outside constraint, such as a method of enforcing a unanimous decision rule, individuals may not be able to bargain for the same rights. The next chapter deals with the issue of rights directly, by using the exchange framework to develop an economic theory of rights.

2 The Economic Theory of Rights

A right is a claim by a specific individual, which is honored by other individuals, that some specific treatment is due him.[1] How is an individual able to make such a claim, and why are others willing to honor it? The answers to both of these questions are the same. An individual will claim a right because he believes that having the right will make him better off. Likewise, others will honor the claim because they believe they are better off honoring the claim than not honoring it. The first step in developing a theory of rights is the recognition of the fact that people honor the rights of others because those honoring the rights believe it is in their self-interest to do so.

The rights that individuals claim for themselves and the rights of others that individuals honor are very much affected by the constitutional rules established and enforced by the creation of government. Individuals are able to claim more rights for themselves if the institutions of government back them up; likewise, they will find it in their self interest to honor more rights of others if the institutions of government enforce those others' claims of rights. One might argue that individuals' rights are those that the government says it will enforce, or that there are natural rights that exist independent of government. But in the real world, people may not be able to exercise some of their "natural" rights, or even some rights that government claims to grant. These are rights that people, by some definition, should have, but are not necessarily the rights they are able to exercise. This chapter discusses the rights that people actually do have, rather than the rights they should have. This a purely positive theory of rights.

For example, people might claim to have the right to life, either because it is a natural right or because it is a right granted by government. However, there are some neighborhoods in the United States where it is dangerous to walk after dark, and people recognize that in those areas, one's right to life is not unconditional. That right is not a guarantee, and a murderer could take one's right to life. From a positive standpoint, dead people no longer have the right to life, independent of any normative claim that they should have the right to life. As another example, one might claim the

11

ownership right over a bicycle, but in many places, leaving an unlocked bicycle in a public place almost guarantees that it will be stolen. Does the individual have the right of ownership to the bicycle? Regardless of one's natural rights or government-granted rights, the owner recognizes that if the bicycle is left unlocked, the right to ownership will almost surely be forfeited. Locking up the bicycle is an attempt to enforce the claimed right of ownership, but one has an ownership right over the bicycle only as long as others observe the right, regardless of the claims of the original owner.[2]

The theory of rights developed in this chapter is motivated by individual self-interest. Individuals find it in their interest to claim rights, and find it in their self-interest to observe the rights of others. There are other possible alternatives to appealing to self-interest as a foundation of the theory of rights. This chapter begins by discussing them, in order to justify the approach taken here, before developing a theory of rights based purely on self-interest and exchange.

Positive and Normative Theories of Rights

Theories of rights can be either positive or normative, and the economic theory of rights is a purely positive theory. The economic theory of rights attempts to explain the rights that people actually have the power to exercise, and does not consider the normative question of what rights people should have. The positive theory of rights is very relevant to any normative theory, however.

If normative theories are intended as blueprints for rights structures that actually could be implemented in real-world societies, then there must be a close connection between any normative theory of rights and an underlying positive theory of rights. A normative system of rights could not be implemented unless it is consistent with feasible rights structures in a positive sense. One might desire, for example, as some sort of ideal normative goal, to see the lions lie down with the lambs, but one of the positive facts of natural science is that lions are carnivores and must eat meat to survive. Normative goals that are inconsistent with the positive facts of reality cannot be implemented in the real world.

There are laws of social science, just as there are laws in the physical and natural sciences. The laws of social science govern the way that people interact, and societies cannot be designed to violate these social laws. Any attempt to impose normative standards on a society that are inconsistent with the laws of social interaction must fail. Thus, if normative theories of rights are espoused as goals for implementation, it is reasonable to question whether those normative theories are consistent with the positive laws of social science. It makes little sense to try to devise social systems that give certain rights to people without seeing that those rights are consistent with the laws of social interaction.[3]

Several normative theories of rights are discussed later in the chapter, using the positive analysis as a foundation. Meanwhile, in defense of some of the material that follows, there are two key things to note. First, a normative theory of rights cannot be used as a basis for critiquing a purely positive theory such as the one developed in this chapter. The model developed here simply attempts to identify the way in which actual systems of rights are developed and maintained without reference to any value judgments. Second, a positive theory of rights is an important foundation for any normative theory; therefore, the positive theory of rights developed here is very relevant to normative theories of rights, but normative theories of rights are not relevant to the development of a purely positive theory.

An alternative to the economic theory of rights would be a theory based on some normative principle. However, even if one takes a strongly normative approach to the theory of rights, the positive approach taken here is not only justified, but important as a foundation to understanding the normative theory in a social context.

The Benefits of Rights

There is an extensive literature explaining why people are better off living in societies that recognize rights for their citizens, and this section provides an overview of that reasoning. Thomas Hobbes is an antecedent to the contemporary literature on the subject. Without some structure of rights, Hobbes argues, "every man is Enemy to every man,"[4] and without any security, individuals have no incentive to be productive. People would not produce any more than they could immediately consume, because any excess would be subject to predation, and the production of capital goods would be out of the question because there would be no way to protect them from theft. In this state of nature, Hobbes's famous appraisal is that life would be "solitary, poore, nasty, brutish, and short."[5]

The discussion in Chapter 3 will extend this argument to show that the development of a well-defined structure of rights makes sense for all individuals in a society. Starting from a setting of anarchy, even the most powerful people will benefit from the granting of rights because ultimately they could trade for more in a productive society than they could steal in an unproductive one.[6]

If no rights are observed, it will always be possible to create a structure of rights such that everyone is better off. This principle underlies the economic theory of rights. If everyone could be better off when rights are observed, then the foundation is laid for individuals to bargain in order to create a mutually beneficial structure of rights.

The Origins of Rights

In contemporary theories, building on a Hobbesian foundation, rights are produced by creating an institutional structure that makes everyone better off. The exchange model provides a foundation. Buchanan builds a model around the benefits of developing social rules that improve the well-being of individuals when compared to a state of anarchy. In Buchanan's model, people envision the type of society that might emerge from a bargaining process starting at anarchy, and a social contract is the product of the agreement that results from this bargaining process.[7] Nozick's model of rights emerges from a bargaining process among individuals also, which results in a minimal state (and, perhaps, more) which observes and enforces a structure of rights.[8] These models provide not only a precedent for an exchange model of rights but also the foundation for a structure of rights as beneficial to those in a society.

The prospect of mutual gain gives every individual an incentive to participate in establishing a structure of rights, but it does not by itself establish what types of rights people would have. In a pure bargaining environment, there is every reason to anticipate that some individuals will end up with more rights than others. Starting from anarchy, for example, there is no reason why threats as well as bribes would not be used, and a Pareto superior move could be made which might make the least powerful individuals a little better off while making the most powerful individuals much better off. Those in a more powerful bargaining position should be able to appropriate more of the gains from trade.[9]

The contractarian model of rights is based on an exchange model of government, but uses unanimous agreement of all members of a society as a normative benchmark for evaluating rights.[10] In a pure economic theory of rights, rights are produced by agreement, but there is no requirement that everyone agree. Some individuals might not be a part of the bargaining process, and a large group might decide to exclude some minority group from bargaining on an equal footing. In the pre-civil war

South, the rights of slaves were determined without their entering into the bargaining process, and in the segregated South after the civil war, citizens of African descent were not accorded equal status in the bargaining process. Within the contractarian model, the civil rights movement can be viewed as an attempt to renegotiate the social contract because the requirements of agreement were not met.[11]

The point is that a purely positive exchange model of rights does not presume any sort of equality in the bargaining process. People will have whatever rights they can bargain for, and some people would be expected to be in a more powerful bargaining position than others. A purely positive theory of rights would have to be consistent with slavery, for example, because slavery is one of the rights structures that has existed. In the pure economic theory of rights, one would have to bargain just to be included in the bargaining process.

The creation of rights where there are no rights to begin with can easily be imagined as a product of bilateral exchange. For example, in a primitive setting, food could be obtained by gathering it oneself or stealing what others have gathered. Because it would allow for inventories to be stored, it is easy to imagine that everyone would benefit from agreeing not to steal the food gathered by others. By the same token, it is also easy to imagine that a few powerful individuals are able to steal without retribution while other less powerful individuals are likely to be injured or killed by their targets if they are caught stealing. The powerful individuals must expend effort to find inventories to steal while less powerful individuals must expend effort trying to hide any inventories they are able to accumulate. Here, an exchange can be made where the less powerful individuals agree to exchange a share of their income with the more powerful individuals, and in return, the more powerful individuals agree not to harm the less powerful individuals or to take more than the agreed-upon share. Everyone is made better off, although inequality is produced since some individuals have the right to take the production of others.

In order to have rights, one must come into the bargaining process with something to exchange. Powerful individuals can offer not to steal from others in exchange for goods, which automatically gives them an incentive to protect the producers of those goods. Very productive individuals can offer a smaller proportion of their production to be included in the bargain, whereas less productive individuals, who have less to offer, would expect to receive less in return. This provides the foundation for an exchange model of rights by describing the endowments that individuals have available to trade. But unlike models where property rights are assumed to be protected, individuals can bargain with threats or promises. Thus, the greater one's ability to use force against others, or the greater one's potential to produce goods that can be consumed by others, the larger will be an individual's endowment that can be exchanged for rights.

Casual observation seems to confirm that higher-income individuals are extended more rights, and those rights are more extensively protected, than lower-income people. Other applications of the principle that people obtain rights to the extent that they can bargain for them suggest themselves as well. For example, the rights of handicapped people are being extended as the economy develops. Today, productive work requires less in terms of physical abilities and at the same time technology makes it easier for handicapped people to be more productive. This places physically handicapped individuals in a better bargaining position because of their increased potential for productive work. The same advances are not apparent for the mentally handicapped. As physically handicapped individuals are gaining rights, most noticeably in the form of access to public buildings and transportation, mentally handicapped individuals are losing rights. The increasingly visible problem of homelessness in the United States is due at least partly to mentally handicapped people who at one time would have been under public care now having to fend for themselves.

The rights of children and animals are interesting peripheral issues. Animals and children are not in a good bargaining position, so are accorded fewer rights. People in more secure bargaining positions can bargain for the rights of children, animals, or any other group, but the observation of limited rights for children and animals is consistent with the idea that people have rights to the extent that they are able to bargain for them. It is interesting to note how much more humanely the law considers dogs and cats, whose company people enjoy, than chickens and pigs.

If aliens from outer space landed on this planet, would we accord them rights? Only if they were willing and able to bargain for them. Otherwise, we would consider them as enemies (if they were like the aliens in many science fiction movies) or as property (if they were more docile). Aliens might be very valuable to circuses, zoos, and museums, as well as to the scientific community.

The Historical Origins of Rights

In a purely positive framework, this idea of the origin of rights is straightforward. There are benefits available to everyone from the observation of rights, so rights are established to make a Pareto superior move. The rights accorded to any particular person within this exchange paradigm will depend on the person's bargaining position. Models such as those by Buchanan, Nozick, and Rawls are based on an exchange model, but consider the evolution of rights in an ahistorical context. This is reasonable, first, considering the normative aspects of each model, and second, because rights have been observed since the beginning of recorded history, making the actual origin of rights a matter of conjecture. Observing packs of animals hunting together, and observing the way that a pecking order is established among groups of animals, it must be the case that primitive rights structures predate the origins of man.

While it is not possible to reconstruct the first observance of rights, it is possible to see how rights are accorded new individuals in a society, and how rights structures can change. Following this line of reasoning, in a truly historical context, rights arise in two ways. Individuals may be accepted into a group and accorded the rights of others in that group, or one group may use force to establish a set of rights which treats that group differentially better than the group over which it uses the force.

In primitive societies, the observation of rights must have started with families. These family–societies tended to be relatively small in size, and were patriarchal. While family members could participate in the decision-making process, final decision-making authority was vested in the eldest valid male descendent.[12] While primitive, this type of rights structure contains a powerful mechanism for maximizing the wealth of the society. Since ultimate ownership and authority is vested in a single individual, that individual's private wealth-maximizing decisions should also maximize the wealth of the family. Because societies were small, there would be low transactions costs among the members of society, which would enable individuals to work out externality problems, property rights problems, and other disputes, always being able to appeal to the patriarchal leader.

The history of political ideas begins with the assumption that individuals are politically united solely because they have descended from a single common ancestor.[13] As societies grew, the common ancestry that was obviously true in the case of the family was assumed to be true for larger political groups. In larger societies, leaders found their powers limited by the concept of natural law.[14] Like the modern common law, natural law evolves slowly, using the fiction that each decision is an application of existing law, even though existing law is not recorded anywhere. From the efficient patriarchal society, then, rights evolve through natural law, through a bargaining process where those that have more to offer are able to command more rights than those with less to offer. Rights developed in this way would tend to be relatively equal, since their origin is through the family.

This relatively equal bargaining setting in which rights evolve finds a parallel in the contractarian models of rights. In contrast, the structure of rights can also be a product of force. Relatively powerful groups can prey upon weaker ones, taking their accumulated wealth. There are potential savings to both predator and prey in this setting if the weaker group simply agrees to pay tribute to the stronger one in exchange for being allowed a peaceful existence. The fundamental relationship in this type of rights structure is force. The group accorded differentially more rights must retain the ability to use force against those with less rights in order to maintain the relationship. Otherwise, there is nothing to stop the group with less rights from demanding to be treated equally, or even rebelling and ruling over their former rulers. This element of force is not adequately treated in the contractarian model.[15]

Considered in a historical setting, rights are produced through two different processes. A cooperative process most closely captured by the way in which family members accord each other rights leads to a type of social contract within a group. But there is also a coercive process whereby groups, still in an exchange setting, attempt to bargain for differential rights. The actual use of force is inefficient, so bargaining arises when the more powerful group offers not to use force, or offers to use force only as an agent of the less powerful, in exchange for tribute. The powerful group says, "Share your output with me and I will not hurt you," or "In exchange for a share of your output, I will protect you from others."

In the economic theory of rights, the amount of bargaining strength an individual has will determine the extent of the individual's rights. More bargaining strength translates into more rights. Bargaining strength comes from two sources: economic productivity, and the ability to use physical force. Economic productivity conveys bargaining strength because it provides the ability to give more in exchange, whereas the ability to use force conveys bargaining power both because it enables an individual to use threats, and because it enables an individual to promise protection. Sometimes there is a thin line between the two.[16]

Rights without Government: The Case of Peru

As defined here, rights exist only when a person claims them and when others observe them. In contemporary societies, the rights that people are able to exercise closely parallel those that governments grant and protect. However, when people can agree upon rights that governments attempt to declare illegal, rights can be established and generally observed despite government prohibitions. An example is the existence of black markets for goods and services the government tries to outlaw.[17]

Hernando de Soto, in his book, *The Other Path*, provides more startling evidence on the emergence of rights in defiance of government, using Lima, Peru, as a case study.[18] Despite much unused land around Lima, as the city's population grew the government placed great obstacles in the way of real estate development. While there was a government-sanctioned market for existing housing, receiving approval to purchase and develop land for new housing was difficult at best, as was obtaining building permits. Because development was almost impossible to undertake legally, people simply seized land, built homes on it, and claimed it as theirs. Gradually, the occupants were granted increasingly secure property rights to the land they had taken. The process is referred to as an invasion by de Soto, and the term is descriptive.

A group of settlers would decide that they want to create a development on a piece of land, and agree on a plan to move in and occupy it one night. The next day, lots are staked out and the land is occupied by a large group of people that would have to be forcibly removed to overturn the invasion. If the land is owned by the government prior to the invasion, it may not be immediately noticed, and in any event no individual has a strong incentive to act against the invaders. If the land is privately owned, it typically has relatively little value to the legal title holder, and the nominal owner must decide whether it is worthwhile to fight the invaders. Sometimes the invasion is overturned, but usually the invaders are able to hold on to the property they now claim to own.

Because the settlement is established illegally, the invaders must define and protect property rights, establish infrastructure, and in general provide those services that government provides to legal settlements. De Soto refers to the resulting institutions as the informal sector of the economy. In addition to the informal sector in housing, de Soto discusses at length the informal business sector that exists because of all the bureaucratic red tape that must be navigated to establish a business. It is prohibitively costly to try to start a small business legally in Peru. The same thing is true in transportation, where over 95 percent of public transportation is illegally provided through the informal sector.

While the informal sector provides a way that economic activity can occur despite the prohibitively costly obstacles that government erects for legal activity, Peru would be much better off if this informal activity were accorded the full benefit of government law. Without it, property rights evolve only slowly, with resulting inefficiencies. For example, it may be impossible to sell a house in an informal settlement because firm property rights are not legally in place. De Soto reports that it takes about 20 years before those occupying the property have the same rights of ownership as other legally recognized property owners.[19]

For present purposes, the Peruvian case is interesting because it illustrates how rights are established outside of the governmental legal system. In Peru, people claim rights, and if they are able to enforce those claims, in time people recognize them as legitimate. Invaders who establish a residential settlement or business people who establish a business are prepared to meet challengers, and they may fail in their attempts to establish the rights they claim. If they are successful, their claims establish increasing legitimacy over time and are less likely to be challenged. The Peruvian case provides a clear example where rights are established because some people claim them and others honor them.

A Semantic Issue Regarding the Definition of Rights

Rights, as described in this chapter, refer to the claims that individuals make, and that others honor, regarding the treatment of the individual. If others allow an individual to say anything she wants, then she has the right of free speech. If others do not steal the bicycle she claims as hers, then she has the right of ownership over the bicycle. But the word is used in at least two other very legitimate ways.

Sometimes the word rights is used to refer to those activities that the government claims to protect for its citizens. However, these government-granted rights can be violated with such regularity that the individual is not actually able to exercise them. Chapter 3 examines in more detail the relationship between government guarantees and rights; meanwhile, simply as a definitional matter, rights that individuals nominally have because the government says so are not considered actual rights for present purposes if individuals cannot exercise them.

The term rights also is used to refer to the actions individuals should be free to undertake, whether they actually can or not. For example, some theories of rights argue that individuals should have the right to freedom of speech. If their governments prevent free speech, they would still have the right, following this line of reasoning, but be prevented from exercising it. For the purposes of this chapter, people are considered only to have rights they can actually exercise.

For some purposes, this semantic issue is more than just a trivial matter of definition. From a normative standpoint, one might want to argue that oppressive governments violate peoples' rights, but rights can be violated only if people have them. Using the terminology in this chapter, one could not say that a government violates its citizens' rights to free speech; rather, one would have to say that the citizens of that government do not have the right to free speech. People who live under a government that routinely and randomly kills its citizens would not have the right to life – regardless of whether they should – and the government could not be accused of violating rights that people do not have.

I am very sympathetic to the normative issue that this raises. In a normative sense, governments can violate the rights that people should have, and it may be giving up too much not to be able to say that people have unambiguous rights that can be violated by governments or other individuals. Using the present terminology, a normative recommendation would have to say that people should have a right to life, not that their right is violated. Using rights as the word is used here, a defender of an oppressive government could argue that nobody's rights are violated; that people in that nation do not have the right to free speech, private property, or even life. My response would be that they should have those rights, but I am sympathetic to the argument that the word should be used normatively to refer to the rights people should have, regardless of whether they actually are able to exercise them.[20]

The argument works in the opposite direction as well. Governments might grant people privileges that go beyond any normative definition of rights, and these privileges might even infringe upon the normative rights of others. As the word is used in this chapter, such privileges are considered rights, and if those normative rights that others should have are infringed upon, they lose them if they cannot enforce them.

This chapter will continue to call something a right only when the individual has the power to exercise it, while recognizing that the word does have a legitimate normative meaning and can refer in other contexts to rights that people are prevented from exercising. In Chapters 11 and 12, this normative connotation of rights will be discussed again for the purpose of considering ways in which the rights people should have can be determined.

Positive Alternatives to an Exchange Theory of Rights

The economic theory of rights is a direct application of the exchange model of government. Individuals claim rights when they view it in their self-interests to make such claims, and individuals honor the rights of others when they view it in their self-interest to honor those rights. In this model of rights, individuals obtain rights by making mutually beneficial agreements. Rights are generated by exchange by self-interested individuals. Other purely positive models of human behavior could be used as a foundation for a theory of rights, and this section considers the appropriateness of the exchange model as a foundation for a theory of rights.

While there is no limit to the number of alternate behavioral hypotheses that might be used as a foundation for a positive theory of rights, one alternative presents itself most frequently. People observe the rights of others because they view it as in the best interest of the society to do so. The observation of rights might sometimes violate the narrow self-interest axiom, but people observe the rights of others anyway, to further the public good.

There are at least three variants of this public interest concept of rights. First, people act in the public interest because there are sanctions for deviating from public interest behavior, and people want to avoid those sanctions. Second, people act differently in public and private settings. In their private affairs, they pursue their own self-interests, but in public matters they behave in a public-spirited way. And third, people receive utility from acting in a public spirited manner. They want to cooperate with others, and feel they are better off cooperating with the group than acting in an opportunistic way by following their narrow self-interests.

The first hypothesis about public interest behavior is easily dealt with because it is actually an extension of the narrow self-interest model. People observe the rights of others because they are afraid of the possible consequences if they do not. The simplest implication of this view of public interest behavior would require a system of monitoring and enforcement of rights extensive enough that people have an incentive to observe the rights of others. Some work in law and economics follows this reasoning by suggesting that penalties for violations equal the social cost of violations adjusted for the probability of detection, or that public officials be compensated in excess of their opportunity costs by an amount sufficient to give them an incentive to act in the public interest.[21] Organized religion can also fit into this category, for even if it is not detected by other mortals, bad behavior must be paid for on judgment day.

The self-interest view of public interest behavior undoubtedly is important. If it were not, the elaborate police and legal institutions that are a part of society would not be necessary. This does not rule out the other explanations, however.

The second variant of the argument for public interest behavior is that people behave differently in their private and public dealings. People set aside their self-interested behavior in public settings and act altruistically.

Such an explanation is inherently unsettling to economists, who want to explain all behavior as the product of a single underlying utility function.[22] There is no reason to believe that people would have different expectations and motivations in their public sector dealings than in their private sector dealings.[23]

The third variant of the public interest concept of rights argues that people behave altruistically because they derive utility from doing so. They are willing to sacrifice some amount of narrow self-interested behavior in exchange for the good feeling they get from acting in the public interest. This variant is the most persuasive, and perhaps the earlier two arguments were merely straw men; sophisticated adherents to either of them really perceive their argument as extending here. The self-interest explanation means that people get utility from public-spirited behavior, and the public-private behavior dichotomy means that people derive utility from their public-spirited actions. Thus, the above discussion should not be taken as a criticism of any particular individual's argument, but the problems with those two lines of thought at their most naive can help to steer the discussion about altruistic behavior as utility-enhancing.

The Utility of Altruism

People derive utility from acting in ways that enhance the well-being of others, even when those actions might be against the narrow self-interest of the actor. Such behavior in families is apparent enough that it needs no support, but individuals engage in behavior that is personally costly to enhance the well-being of strangers who they may never see again. In shopping malls, people will hold open doors so that mothers with baby carriages can pass through. Why should people be willing to bear costs to help these mothers care for the children they chose to have? Drivers will pause to allow other drivers to enter congested roadways. Why should drivers extend such courtesies, especially when that places one more car in front of the courteous driver on an already congested road? People have been known to make great sacrifices for others in times of need, such as accidents and natural disasters, but the behavior described above is of people helping others go about their ordinary business in life in cases where they could manage without the help.

In the above examples, people are making small sacrifices for others, and there is likely to be a limit to the extent that people are willing to sacrifice. A person who would phone for help for someone whose car had broken down would be less likely to loan his car to that person, or help the person with the broken car pay for repairs. Marginal analysis applies, and it is useful to consider the factors that would cause someone to be more willing to help another. For example, if two men who had never met discovered that they both went to the same school, or were in the same fraternity, they might be more inclined to help each other out. They both identify with the same group. Courteous and pleasant behavior also increases the inclination of others to offer help. Could this be because such behavior suggests a willingness to help others in the group should the occasion arise?

Group identification is important in altruistic behavior. People are more inclined to behave altruistically to those from the same country, the same school, or the same club. The utility from altruism may come from the group identification, since people choose to identify themselves with groups simply for entertainment purposes. Social clubs may provide other benefits, but how would one explain being the fan of a particular baseball team except that one gets utility from identifying with the group? If cooperative behavior does come from identification with the group, then success in producing cooperative behavior depends upon the creation of group identification. This issue will be explored further momentarily.[24]

One possible explanation for cooperative behavior rather than narrow self-interested behavior is that people might perceive that it is in their long-run self-interest to behave cooperatively. The first lesson of economics is that people benefit from cooperation and gains from trade.[25] Thus, what appears to be altruistic or cooperative behavior really might be self-interested behavior from a longer-run perspective. Economists are concerned with the free rider problem that can arise when cooperative behavior is necessary for optimal resource allocation, but the earlier examples suggest that cooperative behavior is more widespread than would be expected from narrow self-interested action. One explanation is that cooperative behavior is in the long-run best interest of individuals. Axelrod, for example, reports results of a tournament held within a prisoners' dilemma setting, and finds that with repeated plays cooperative participants fare better than those who try to act in their narrow self interest.[26] If this is the case, then the argument falls back to self-interest, which justifies building a model of rights using the underlying assumption of self-interested behavior.

The issue of cooperative behavior with a group with which one identifies raises the most plausible alternative to purely self-interested behavior. While it might be argued, as above, that this behavior is really just self-interested behavior from a broader perspective, this objection will be left aside to focus on the idea that people will behave altruistically toward members of a group with which they identify.

An important component to this aspect of cooperative behavior is that individuals exhibiting the behavior identify with the group toward which they behave altruistically. People do not behave altruistically toward everyone, but rather behave altruistically toward others with whom they identify. Thus, in order to evoke altruistic behavior, the group must somehow convince its members that they have an interest in the group's well-being.

Douglass North discusses this under the heading of ideology.[27] Following North's ideas, ideology gives individuals a commitment to pursue certain principles without those principles being in the narrow self-interest of the actor.[28] But in order for individuals to be willing to behave in this way, they must identify with the group. There is an extensive literature on group consciousness, but the bottom line is that unless people are convinced to identify with the group, they will not behave in a cooperative manner. Margaret Levi develops a model of revenue maximizing government and notes the importance of developing identification with the group in order to encourage voluntary cooperation.[29] The monitoring costs would be prohibitively costly if people could not be counted on to act in the group interest on their own much of the time.

Murray Edelman explains how the political process is designed in order to convince citizens of the legitimacy of their governments so that they will cooperate with the government without having to be coerced.[30] Regardless of the motivations that one sees for altruistic behavior, that behavior will only occur toward individuals and institutions that individuals feel warrant cooperation. Therefore, the institutions must be viewed as legitimate and beneficial institutions if individuals are to cooperate without being coerced.

People do behave altruistically, but not unconditionally. People will behave altruistically only to those institutions and individuals who they believe deserve it. Thus, one cannot simply develop a theory of rights based on altruistic behavior without explaining how those whose rights are being observed have earned the benefits of altruism. The answer must be through some type of exchange process. People benefit from cooperation, so will cooperate with others when they feel they are being fairly treated in the bargain. What constitutes fair treatment – or even the perception of fair treatment – is a legitimate question that will be dealt with later.[31] At this point, it is sufficient to see that altruistic behavior requires something in return, which points directly to the exchange model.

When the foundations of altruistic behavior are considered, none of the explanations for altruistic behavior can stand without individuals believing that they receive something in return for their cooperation. Thus, when developing a theory of rights, even though people may behave altruistically, the observance of rights occurs only in exchange for something. In this way, the observation of the rights of others is not charitable activity, where rights are observed and nothing is expected in return.[32] From a positive standpoint, the only reasonable foundation for a theory of rights is exchange among self-interested individuals.

The Economic Theory and Other Theories

The economic theory of rights places the emphasis on the process by which rights emerge rather than focusing on the outcome (and resulting individual rights) that emerge from the process.[33] Unlike other procedural theories of rights, however, there is no assumption about constraints on the process. The exchange model of government is one of the fundamental building blocks of public choice. The economic theory of rights continues in the tradition of the exchange model of government to develop a theory explaining individual rights. Unlike most theories of rights, the pure economic theory of rights developed here does not rely on any external condition to evaluate rights, does not make any normative judgments, nor does the theory determine when rights are violated. The pure economic theory of rights explains what rights people are able to exercise, not what rights they should have.

Seen in this way, the economic theory of rights has more in common with theories about the evolution of social institutions than with other theories of rights.[34] Theories of rights tend to have normative foundations, sometimes based on religious principles, and sometimes based on other criteria for producing desirable social institutions. Yeager discusses utilitarianism, natural rights, and contractarianism along these lines.[35] Utilitarianism suggests the aggregation of individual welfare into some type of social welfare function which would then be maximized,[36] which uses the criteria of economic efficiency and interpersonal utility comparisons as normative criteria. Economic efficiency places the society on its production possibilities frontier, and interpersonal utility comparisons are required to choose one among the many efficient allocations. The economic theory of rights would tend toward efficient allocation, following the criteria of utilitarianism, but would tend to weight the social welfare function toward those with more bargaining power, as described above. Utilitarians do not agree on the criteria that should be used in the social welfare function; the economic theory of rights implies that the social welfare function will be designed in accordance with the desires of those with greater bargaining power.[37]

Natural rights theory argues that individuals inherently have certain rights, but as a normative principle, while recognizing that in the real world individuals can have their natural rights violated.[38] In the economic theory of rights, individuals have rights to the extent that they have bargaining power. This does give "natural" rights to anyone who can provide something valuable in exchange, but from a positive standpoint, does not extend rights beyond this point.

The economic theory of rights is closest in approach to the contractarian model of the state as developed by Buchanan and Nozick, and to a lesser degree Rawls. The Buchanan and Tullock foundation of politics as an exchange process is clearly evident.[39] But whereas the public choice approach has placed a heavy reliance on the rule of unanimity on issues related to rights, the limits of government, and so forth, the unanimity benchmark is not used in the pure economic theory of rights.[40]

Buchanan and Tullock say "Our theory of constitutional choice has normative implications only insofar as the underlying basis of individual consent is accepted."[41] In this model of rights, that underlying basis is not used. With the Buchanan and Tullock foundation of individual consent, individuals can implement constitutional rules if *they agree* that the rules make them better off. By contrast, in the economic theory of rights, individuals have no say in their rights unless *others agree* to observe the rights.

Contractarianism and a Normative Theory of Economic Rights

The preceding discussion has established a positive framework describing the structure of rights in a society as the product of a bargaining process. However, normative extensions to the theory can be made in a manner similar to the normative extensions that exist in the discussion of the operation of competitive markets. There does appear to be an invisible hand leading societies toward more efficient rights structures because there is more surplus available with more efficient rights structures. The normative implications of the pure economic theory of rights are the same as the normative implications wrapped up in the efficiency of a competitive equilibrium, and it is the same type of bargaining process that leads to Pareto superior moves and an optimal structure of rights. Efficiency in the economic theory of rights is generated along the lines suggested by Coase; in the absence of transaction costs, rights will be accorded to those who value them most.[42]

Like Coase's model, the value referred to here is market value. Thus, using value in this way, a slave would be said to value freedom more than the slave owner values owning the slave if by being free the slave could generate enough income to compensate the owner for the loss of the slave. The example suggests a source of inefficiency when transactions costs are present because it is easy to conceive of a slave who values freedom more but cannot structure a contract in such a way as to guarantee compensation to the former owner once the slave is freed.

Another potential source of inefficiency is the possibility of monopoly power being exercised in the bargaining process, which opens up the possibility that all changes in the rights structure may not lead to efficiency or that some possible efficient changes will not be made. Thus, to make sure that a structure of rights is efficient, there must be some additional guarantee. This is the role played by the rule of unanimity in the contractarian model of the state.

A rule of unanimity promises that Pareto superior moves will be made, thereby promising that changes will be in the direction of efficiency.[43] This is consistent with the economic theory of rights, but goes one step further by entering an explicitly normative criterion in the form of the unanimity requirement. Thus the pure economic theory of rights could be considered as a possible positive foundation for the social contract theory developed by Buchanan and Rawls, who go beyond a purely positive contractarian model.

There are some distinctions that might be noted also, however. For the rule of unanimity to yield efficient changes in institutions, individuals must be able to foresee the effects of the institutional changes that they approve. Otherwise, the possibility arises that individuals might unanimously approve institutional changes that unintentionally make them worse off. In the short run, even unanimous approval is not sufficient to guarantee efficiency considered from the vantage point of an omniscient observer. Over the long run, however, efficient institutions will generate more surplus, so in an evolutionary setting will tend to dominate.[44]

This distinction in the normative implications between the contractarian model and the pure economic theory of rights deserves some emphasis. An efficient rights structure could be expected to emerge in the economic theory of rights through a process of natural selection, whereby more efficient rights structures produce more productive societies that displace less productive societies.[45] In the contractarian model, efficiency is generated by Pareto superior moves that are the product of the rule of unanimity. This requires that people be able to forecast the effects of various decisions on their own well-being, and it is not difficult to imagine that when selecting among things as abstract as constitutional rules, people in the real world may not have a good idea about the ultimate effect of certain rules. If perfect knowledge is assumed, then unanimous agreement will make everyone better off. If people are unable to forecast the effects of constitutional rules on their own future well-being, then people could unanimously agree to rules which, with hindsight, make them worse off.

As a conceptual device, the unanimity required by the contractarian model is useful because, first, it suggests changes that will be efficient (subject to information constraints), and second, because it suggests changes that will be politically possible because everyone should agree with them. In the real world, the benefit of identifying politically feasible changes – or side payments that can make proposed changes politically feasible – is important. But information constraints may be great enough that real-world people do not have the same ability to discern optimal constitutional rules as conceptual people, which can erode the unanimity rule's claim to efficiency when applied to the real world.

The pure economic theory of rights contains an invisible hand mechanism that causes the structure of rights to tend toward efficiency, but efficiency at any point in time is not guaranteed. Furthermore, there is nothing implied about equality of rights, and there is no supposition that if a vote were taken there would be unanimous agreement, or even majority agreement, with the rights structure. Lack of agreement could coexist with an efficient and stable structure of rights.

Conclusion

The economic theory of rights places the emphasis on the process that produces the rights that people are able to exercise, rather than focusing on the outcome (and resulting individual rights) that emerge from the process. Unlike other procedural theories of rights, however, there is no assumption about constraints on the process. There are no natural rights, and there is no presumption that unanimous approval is necessary to establish rights. Rather, rights are the result of a bargaining process, and a right exists only if an individual is able to make an agreement with others to observe that right.

The economic theory of rights is consistent with Mises's idea, expressed in the first pages of *Human Action*, that institutions cannot be designed to cause people to violate the laws that govern social interaction. There are laws in social science, just as there are laws in physical science, that govern the way that people interact, and societies cannot be designed to violate these social laws. Thus, it makes little sense, *a priori*, to claim that people should have certain rights without seeing that those rights are consistent with the laws of social interaction.

This chapter has concentrated more on a foundation for an economic theory of rights than on actually identifying the resulting rights structure, but note that the economic theory of rights described here is not inconsistent with a doctrine of natural rights, or any other normative rights doctrine, because the pure economic theory of rights is a theory of the rights that people actually will have rather than the rights that they should have. In the economic theory of rights, there are no absolute rights and nobody is guaranteed any right. This does not imply that people should not have rights, but reflects the purely positive nature of the economic theory of rights. Normative theories of rights are considered more extensively in Chapter 11, after the positive theory of government is developed more fully.

The purpose of this chapter is to develop a foundation for investigating rights from a purely economic perspective. The contractarian model of government does this in a manner similar to what is suggested here, but relies on the unanimity rule in a way that a pure economic theory of rights does not. The model developed here pushes the contracting process one step further back to the point where people have to bargain even for the right to be included in the bargaining process.

One might, in a normative analysis, say that people should have the rights that would be unanimously agreed upon, or that would be contracted for under hypothetical circumstances, but the economic theory of rights does not go this far. People have rights only if others observe them, and others observe them only if those others benefit. Indeed, any normative criterion for rights that is inconsistent with the positive laws of social behavior could not be successfully implemented, so a positive theory of rights is an important foundation for serious analysis of any normative theory.

Using this foundation, a natural extension is to explore in more detail questions about the variation in rights structures among countries and over time in the same country. Is there a natural progression of rights structures that parallels economic development? Why has overt slavery, once a common institution, now disappeared? Would it be possible to eliminate the relative freedom and equality enjoyed by citizens of today's advanced economies without at the same time destroying the economy?[46] Applications naturally extend into law and economics as well, as rights structures can be analyzed in terms of what threats or promises were exchanged as a foundation for existing rights. The erosion of some rights can be viewed as the result of a reduction in bargaining power for the group losing the rights.

In the next chapter, the economic theory of rights is used as a foundation for a model of government. While many rights are recognized informally, important rights are often sanctioned and protected by government. This implies that government is more than a trivial determinant of the rights people have. Chapter 3 builds on the economic theory of rights by using an exchange model to develop a theory of government, constitutions, and a social contract. That chapter then extends the economic theory of rights to some of the questions regarding why particular structures of rights exist, and what factors cause relative equality or inequality of rights.

3 Governments and Constitutions

The previous chapter developed a theory of rights that showed how, in an exchange setting, people would find it in their interest to claim rights and how others would find it in their interests to observe them. A structure of rights and of social interaction could thereby arise purely as a result of exchange. Even in the most primitive of societies, individual exchange accounts for only a small fraction of the rights that people can exercise. Most rights are dictated by social and governmental institutions that specify which people are entitled to what rights. These institutions are the outcome of an exchange process like that described in the previous chapter. This chapter extends the exchange model to describe how governments are established, how the rights of various individuals are determined, and how constitutions are developed as an integral part of any government.

The development of a model that depicts government as a product of exchange among individuals in a society suggests the economic foundations of government. The economic nature of decisions regarding the productive and redistributive activities of the state is clearly evident. However, there is also an economic foundation to decisions that do not explicitly deal with resource allocation, such as what rights will be extended to citizens and what limits will be placed on government power.[1] This chapter continues the line of reasoning from the previous chapter to illustrate how individuals can engage in rational self-interested exchange to produce a government. The chapter illustrates that a well-defined set of constitutional rules is essential to the success of any government.

The Exchange Model of Government

The fundamental model of government in this chapter is Hobbesian. Hobbes surmised that in a situation of anarchy, life would be nasty, brutish, and short.[2] In Hobbesian anarchy, even those who are best off would have a relatively low standard of living. Consider the simplest case of a two-person society where one person is physically strong and the other is weak. In such a setting, the strong person could take everything the weak person produced. How well off would the strong person be in this case? Not very, because the weak person has no incentive to produce things that he knows will just be stolen from him later.

One possibility would be for the strong person to enslave the weak one and force the weak person to work for her. The strong person is the residual claimant in this case, but once again the weak person has little incentive to be productive. Slavery will be most productive when slaves can be assigned clearly defined tasks and when shirking is easy to monitor. Slavery obviously will be unproductive in cases where shirking is hard to monitor, but also will be relatively unproductive when productivity requires individuals to make independent decisions about how to allocate resources.[3]

Another possibility from the starting point of anarchy is for the strong person to agree to take only a predetermined share of the weak person's output. For example, if both people agreed that that weak person would give the strong one-third of his output, both could be better off.[4] The weak person now has an incentive to produce, knowing that he will be able to keep two-thirds of his output, and the strong person gets one-third of the weak person's output. Under anarchy, the weak person would be unlikely to produce anything that could be taken by the strong, reducing the output that could be consumed by both persons. The two-person society is more productive, and both people are better off under the agreement that the weak person shares a specified percentage of his production with the strong.[5]

Such an exchange creates a structure of rights, as discussed in Chapter 2, when the strong person establishes a right to a share of the weak person's income. Note that the right is mutually beneficial only if it is agreed upon in the form of a rule that will persist through time, since the weak person has an incentive to be productive only if there is a rule limiting the amount that the strong person can take. The agreement must have the promise of some permanence, because accumulation of productive assets by the weak person in this example requires an assurance that those productive assets will earn a return in the future. An agreement to establish a rule that endures through time gives the rule a constitutional character.[6] At least in this case, there is a link between rights and constitutional rules. Later in the chapter, a more definitive link will be drawn.

This domination of the weak by the strong establishes a setting for the formation of constitutional rules. Both people agree to the income-sharing rule over an extended period of time because it makes them both better off, but note that the agreement here is substantially different from that in Buchanan and Tullock or Rawls.[7] There is no externally imposed requirement for unanimous agreement, but the weak person knows that if an agreement is not reached, the strong person can use force. This threat of force distinguishes agreement in a purely positive exchange setting from agreement in a normative setting where, under the rule of unanimity, any one person can exercise veto power. In this purely positive model, there is no such equality in the bargaining process.

Agreement and Exchange in Anarchy

The idea that people might be threatened into agreeing is unsettling enough that it warrants further discussion. Typically, when economists talk about agreement and exchange, they do so within the context of a system of clearly defined property rights. People have the right to exchange what is theirs, have no right to claim what belongs to others, and can always retain their property unless they explicitly agree to exchange it or give it away. In this framework, if a robber takes someone's wallet at gunpoint, saying "Your money or your life," one would be hard-pressed to argue that the holdup victim was simply engaging in an exchange, and agreed to give up his wallet in exchange for his life. The key is that the person who has the wallet has a recognized right to it, and the robber does not. This simple state of affairs does not exist in anarchy, where no rights have been established.

Consider some hypothetical examples. Assume that with the present system of rights, person A trespasses onto person B's property and picks apples from person B's apple trees. The contemporary legal system would view that situation as being a case of theft, where person A stole person B's apples, and the apples rightfully would belong to B. If B then confronted A and took the apples from A (perhaps with the help of the police), B's taking apples from A would not be theft, but rather the return to B of apples which B rightfully owned. Now consider the same situation in anarchy. A has a stock of apples and B takes them. Is this theft? If B has some claim to the trees from which the apples came, then the answer is no, but in anarchy, clear rights are not established.

As a similar example, in a situation of anarchy individual A cuts some trees and builds a log home. Person B then forces A out of the home and lives in it himself. Have A's rights been violated? In the present society, if the trees which were cut were on B's land, and if the house was built on B's land, then A would have no right to it, but in anarchy, no clearly defined rights have been established. Thus, A and B must bargain to see who has what rights, and if B is stronger or has some other bargaining advantage, then A may lose the house he built. But the hypothetical example shows that the same might happen in contemporary society with a well-defined rights structure, if B was considered the owner of the land and raw materials out of which the house was built.

If rights are clearly established, then one can discuss agreement and voluntary exchange in the context of those rights, but in the absence of any agreed-upon rights, it is not clear who owns what property. Still, exchange and agreement could take place if individuals consent to institutions which would make everyone better off. One would not want to argue that agreement can take place only if rights are well-defined; indeed, agreement is often a way to settle disputes of rights. If one party to an agreement has a bargaining advantage, then that party is likely to get an outcome the weaker party might envy, but the bargain could still be agreed to by both parties, and could still improve the welfare of both parties.[8]

This idea is echoed by James Coleman, who argues, "What is right is defined within the system itself, by the actors' interests and relative power in that system. The theory implies that moral philosophers searching for the right distribution of rights are searching for the pot of gold at the end of the rainbow."[9] People can use or exchange only those things over which they have rights. In a situation in which no rights are defined, the bargaining involved in defining those rights might include threats as well as promises, but by definition would not include any violations of individual rights. Without rights having been previously defined, the individual who threatens, "Your money or your life," might be considered to have the right to the money in the same way that individual B has a right to the apples A possesses, but which came from B's tree. Without a well-defined structure of rights, what constitutes a threat is not entirely clear, since it is not clear who has what rights. Indeed, the whole purpose of defining rights is to establish boundaries what actions individuals can legitimately take in their interactions with others.

The Exchange of Protection for Tribute

This exchange model of government can easily be extended from a two-person model to a model with many persons. As is the case with only two persons, the strong can prey on the weak, so the weak have no incentive to produce anything more than they can immediately consume. The standard of living for both the strong and the weak will be low in this setting.

In a many-person setting, there is the incentive to strike the bargain described above. The weak can form an agreement with the strong to turn over a fixed share of their output in exchange for the promise that the strong will allow the weak to keep the remainder of what they produce. As above, this agreement benefits both the strong and the weak. The coalition of strong people in this model can be labeled government, and the weak people can be called citizens of the government. This model of government is intended to be theoretical, but note its relationship to the historical and empirical origins of government. Most governments throughout history have been imposed by force, as a physically stronger group conquered and ruled over those they conquered.[10]

One complication arises in the model with many persons. An agreement that the citizens turn over a share of their production to the government might be written among a subset of persons, but when there are many strong people who can prey upon the weak, there is the possibility that others who are not party to the agreement will steal from the government's citizens. The government has an incentive to prevent others from taking the production of their citizens, because the government receives its income from the production of its citizens. Thus, a natural exchange situation is created where citizens write a contract with their government to trade protection for tribute.

The exchange of protection for tribute benefits both citizens and their government. The government benefits because it receives income from the production of citizens, and the citizens benefit because the government promises to protect their right to keep part of what they produce. In a setting of Hobbesian anarchy without government protection, everything they produced could be stolen from them. In the two-person model where the weak person pays the strong not to steal anything more than the payment, the exchange looks like extortion. In a large number setting where citizens pay their governments, governments have an incentive to provide protection and the exchange is not so obviously coercive. Coercion is clearly present, however, because the government attempts to punish those who try not to participate.

This exchange model of government isolates several important characteristics of government and the government's relationship to its citizens. (1) The government establishes its right to govern through the threat of force. (2) Citizens agree to be taxed by their government through well-defined tax rules because both the citizens and the government will be better off when there is a limit to what the government can take. (3) Because the government receives its income from the production of its citizens, government has an incentive to protect them. By protecting its citizens, government also protects its income. Thus, the fundamental characteristic of government is that it exchanges protection for tribute.

How Well Does the Two-Person Model Extrapolate to Many People?

In the two-person model, it is straightforward to see that both people can benefit from establishing constitutional rules that allow the strong person the right to a predetermined share of the weak person's production, in exchange for the promise to take no more than that share. A Pareto superior move is made. It is reasonable to question whether a two-person model extrapolates to a many-person setting. In this case, the many-person setting adds a motivation for exchange that is not present in the two-person setting, so the argument is strengthened when extended from two to many persons. Because the government has an incentive to protect its source of income, and because citizens will have to provide for protection from potential aggressors in any event, citizens receive a benefit from the exchange that they would have to somehow replace if the exchange were not made.

In the two-person case, the weak person would be unambiguously better off by killing the strong person or escaping the strong person's domination in some other way. In the many-person case, a citizens escaping the government would lose the government's protection, so somehow would have to provide for their protection in another way. Protection is costly, and the exchange of protection for tribute between citizens and governments is likely to be the most effective way for most people to protect themselves from potential predators. The exchange characteristic of the many-person model, not present in the two-person model, makes the two-person exchange model of constitutional rules even more plausible in an environment with many people.

Government as Monopolist

The previous sections have outlined a purely positive exchange model of government where both the government and its citizens have an incentive to enter into a well-defined agreement to exchange protection for tribute. In a competitive setting, citizens would be purchasing protection in much the same way as they purchase other services, but the very nature of the exchange gives government the characteristics of a natural monopoly.[11] In market exchange, there is the presumption that firms will charge monopoly prices and earn monopoly profits whenever the opportunity arises, and this presumption should also apply to government just as strongly as to participants in a market. In a natural monopoly setting, the government will charge monopoly prices for its protective services.

Historically, governments have also used force to establish monopolies in areas other than the production of protective services. Postal delivery, utilities, and mass communications are other areas over which the government has established monopolies in various countries at various times. In addition, it has also used its force to allow private sector firms to be monopolists in exchange for tax revenues or other political support.

The government's exercise of monopoly power will be considered in detail in Chapter 6, but for present purposes it is sufficient to note that those in government are in a position to earn monopoly profits because of, first, their natural monopoly in the exchange of protection for tribute, and second, their ability to use force to enforce monopoly production in other areas. These monopoly profits make governing an attractive activity, which entices potential entrants. Thus, adding to the earlier list of characteristics of government, (4) governments can earn monopoly profits for their activities.

Competition among Potential Governments

Competition among potential governments takes many forms, including wars, revolutions, and elections. This competition could be beneficial to citizens because if citizens have anything to say about who will govern them, they can evaluate competing offers and select the government that benefits them the most. In the limit, such competition for the right to be the monopoly government can produce results identical to the competitive outcome.[12]

Citizens do have some ability to choose their governments. Governments are dependent upon tax revenues from their citizens for their continued operation, and while the threat of force against those who do not comply with the tax laws helps the government to raise revenues, governments do not have sufficient resources to force every individual to pay. Only if most people comply with the government's laws is it feasible for the government to use force against those who do not. Governments do use force to get their citizens to comply with laws, but force is useful as a threat to coerce people to comply, rather than as a tool that can be used against every citizen.[13]

Any alternative to an existing government must have the strength to overcome the existing government. No government wants to give up its monopoly power voluntarily. For dictatorships with no constitutional method of changing governments, this means amassing the military force to violently overthrow the existing government. In democracies, the police power of the state is insulated from the government's leaders so that existing leaders will find it difficult to use the police power of the state to retain office. Rather, electoral strength is used in democracies. Essentially, voters on all sides line up behind their candidates, and with the military effectively insulated from the electoral process, it is not to fanciful to imagine voters on the winning side view their strength in numbers as indicating that if the conflict came down to a show of force, the majority could overpower the minority.

With wars and revolutions, the same process occurs, but with more at stake. The existing government needs the tax revenues of its citizens to survive, so if a challenger mounts a credible enough show of force and offers citizens an attractive alternative to the current regime, they can transfer their tax revenues to the challenging government, and can physically fight for the challenger as well. Governments need the support of their citizens in order to survive.

Governments do rely on the threat of force to foster cooperative behavior from their citizens, and the established power structure of an existing government gives the incumbent a competitive advantage. Without this advantage, the government would be unable to extract monopoly profits. But in a competitive setting, governments must retain the support of their citizens in order to continue receiving the monopoly profits from government. Governments can force some degree of citizen compliance, but have only a limited power to make people comply.

The argument can be extended at this point to examine the types of governmental institutions that allow the government to earn more or less in the way of monopoly profits. Chapter 9 considers competitive forces in politics. But without developing the argument further at this point, this section adds to the previously made points that (5) competition among potential governments restricts the monopoly profit that existing governments can earn, (6) the existing power structure gives incumbent governments an advantage in that competition, and (7) because of potential competition, governments must retain the support of their citizens to continue in power.

Constitutional Rules and Legitimacy

The concept of the legitimacy of government has been explored more by political scientists than by economists. Yet in a setting where there is competition among potential governments, the existing government must retain the perception of legitimacy among its citizens in order to retain power. As already noted, the government can use force to get citizens to follow its mandates, but the more legitimate the government's actions are perceived to be, the greater will be the degree of voluntary compliance. Voluntary compliance lowers the resource cost of compliance to the government, but more importantly, it provides the government with security against potential competitors.

Douglass North explores this idea under the heading of ideology.[14] While economists have explored the concept of ideology from the standpoint of questioning whether legislators might vote their own political views instead of the interests of their constituents,[15] North takes the concept of ideology a step further and considers it to be a loyalty that citizens have for their governments. If governments can foster an ideological commitment from their citizens, then citizens will view the government's activities as legitimate and will be predisposed to cooperate. The free rider problem is not completely eliminated, but citizens with an ideological commitment want to cooperate with their governments rather than actively resist them.

One way for the government to establish legitimacy is for it to operate under clearly defined rules. This is an extension of the earlier argument that explained fixed taxation schedules. In exchange for the government's right to a share of the citizens' incomes, and perhaps other clearly defined obligations, the government agrees to give citizens certain rights and to protect those rights. Totalitarian governments tend to have a larger list of obligations and to extend a smaller set of rights to their citizens than democracies, but as long as citizens follow the government's rules, the government stands ready to protect the agreed-upon rights of its citizens. Arbitrariness erodes the perceived legitimacy of government, while predictability enhances it.[16]

Working within constitutional rules conveys legitimacy to governments, and by so doing generates popular support that helps the existing government to maintain its position in the face of potential competing governments. If it is followed, the constitution provides a sure set of rights and obligations between citizens and their government. The promises of potential competitors cannot always be believed, particularly if citizens have no actual experience with the potential competitors. Therefore, (8) constitutional rules provide legitimacy to existing governments, which helps them to maintain their power and continue receiving the monopoly profits that governments are in a position to collect.

The Social Contract

The constitution, as described above, is a social contract. The fundamental agreement between a government and its citizens is the exchange of protection for tribute. By providing protection, the government allows its citizens to be productive while substantially reducing the risk that the results of their productive activity will be taken from them. Citizens pay tribute to the government in exchange. This payment serves the function of giving the government an incentive to protect its citizens, who are the source of the government's income. This outcome is a result of an exchange that makes both the government and the governed better off. Just as an exchange between two private individuals constitutes a private contract, the outcome of this exchange model of government is a social contract.

Other constitutional rules are an extension of this fundamental exchange in the contract. The government promises to extend and protect certain rights for its citizens, and the citizens agree to pay tribute to the government in return. This is not a hypothetical contract, but a description of the actual operation of constitutional rules. The exchange of protection for tribute and other well-defined rights and obligations of the government and its citizens are a contract that fundamentally differs little from a home mortgage or an employment contract.

As already noted, the government's ability to use force gives it a bargaining advantage in determining the terms of the contract, but it is also true in markets that one party could have an advantage over another. In the United States, the antitrust laws attempt to remove the bargaining advantage of economically stronger traders. The existence of such laws illustrates that a bargaining advantage can exist; just because a bargaining advantage exists does not mean that bargains cannot be made. Governments bargain from a position of strength when negotiating the terms of the social contract, but the bargain still takes place.

Some people might choose not to participate in the bargain. This would be expected in a large group of people. Opportunistic behavior is possible, as some people see that if others follow the rules while they violate them, the opportunistic violators can gain an advantage. More fundamentally, some people may not accept the legitimacy of the terms of the social contract. Just because some people are not party to the social contract does not mean that everyone is not. A social contract still can exist that binds most members of a society together in agreement. Governments are bound by certain procedures in the contract when dealing with violators. However, it is noteworthy that governments typically uphold their end of the social contract even when dealing with individuals who do not.

In the United States, murderers and tax evaders are dealt with following specified procedures as the government upholds its part of the contract. This adds to the legitimacy of the government. Even in the former Soviet Union, where dissidents were sometimes dealt with by committing them to mental institutions, this treatment was well-known around the world and a part of the social contract. Ordinary citizens did not have to worry about being committed to a mental institution if they followed the rules, but they knew that if they engaged in visible protest against the government, they could be committed. All governments do not extend their citizens the same rights. But even in very repressive regimes, governments follow constitutional rules that guarantee their citizens that if the citizens obey the rules, the government will protect them. This is part of the exchange of protection for tribute.

The social contract theory developed here is a purely positive theory. In it, the social contract is an agreement between the government and its citizens that if the citizens follow certain rules, including the payment of tribute to the government, then the government will protect them. The government has an incentive to do so because it gets its income from its citizens. Because there are alternative governments that can be produced through war, revolution, election, emigration, constitutional convention, and so forth, the social contract is the agreement the current government offers its citizens with the hope that they will not act to seek an alternative government. The current government has an advantage because it can use the threat of force as a bargaining tool, and because its well-defined constitution is an option to the promises of alternative governments that may not be willing or able to keep their promises if they were to gain power. The current government does have a bargaining advantage, but this does not make the exchange of protection for tribute any less of a contract.

Citizens do exchange protection for tribute with their governments. This is a purely positive statement derived from the exchange model of government. The terms of this exchange constitute the primary provision of the social contract. Thus, looking at the actual relationship between citizens and their government, a social contract exists in the positive sense, for just the reason stated by Hobbes. Without it, there would be a war of all against all, and life would be nasty, brutish, and short. When citizens agree with their governments to abide by constitutional rules, a social contract is created that benefits both citizens and the government.

Therefore, (9) a society's constitutional rules are a social contract. The social contract is an agreement between the government and its citizens that defines the rights and obligations of all parties. The exchange of protection for tribute is a contractual agreement in a purely positive sense, so the social contract theory of the state can be developed without recourse to any normative principles.

Note that because no normative principles are involved, there can be no claim that the terms of this social contract are desirable. The next chapter considers the rights that citizens might have in more detail, but again, this contract is simply an evolutionary product of an exchange model of government, with no claims made about its desirability.

Other Theories of the Social Contract

The social contract theory of the state has a long history, and the most recent developments of the social contract theory provide the foundation for much of the work in the relatively new area of constitutional economics. Therefore, it is worthwhile to compare the social contract theory presented in this chapter with earlier formulations of the theory. The major differences lie in the way government is incorporated into the theories, the role of differential bargaining power and coercion, and the use of the unanimity rule to draw up terms of the contract. There is some interrelationship among these items, but this section will analyze them independently.

The Role of Government

A major difference between this formulation of the social contract and other contemporary formulations is the role played by government. For purposes of discussion on this point, contemporary theories can be ranked from Rawls's *A Theory of Justice* and Buchanan and Tullock's *The Calculus of Consent* to Buchanan's *The Limits of Liberty* to the theory in this chapter. In Rawls's formulation, there is not a government involved in drawing up the provisions of the social contract, although a government might be the result of agreement behind his veil of ignorance. Drawing on a blank slate, individuals behind the veil decide on the constitutional rules that will define a government. There is not a preexisting government – or preexisting individuals who will become government – as a part of the bargaining process. Behind the veil, nobody knows what position they will take in society, so the resulting government is an outcome of a bargaining process among equals, and government itself is not involved in drawing up the social contract.

The same is true in Buchanan and Tullock's *The Calculus of Consent*. In their theory of constitutions, constitutional rules are the product of unanimous agreement among individuals, so all individuals have veto power over any constitutional rule. As in Rawls, governments are the result of the bargaining process, not one of the bargaining parties.

Buchanan's *The Limits of Liberty* describes a different process where individuals evalutate existing (or proposed) institutions to decide if they are (or should be) a part of the social contract. In Buchanan's model, individuals envision a renegotiation of the social contract from a state of anarchy, and judge whether the institutions would be a likely outcome of the bargaining process. If individuals judge that they would be, then Buchanan is willing to say that they are a part of the social contract. If not, then the institutions do not meet Buchanan's test of agreement, and they are not a part of the social contract.[17]

In Buchanan's model, the existing government and potential competitive governments can play a role in the expected outcome of renegotiation from anarchy. Just as in the model in this chapter, the strong are in a good position to impose a government upon those less strong, meaning that in renegotiation from anarchy, individuals must take their own particular circumstances into account in a way not present in Rawls's veil of uncertainty model. A person's expectations in the renegotiation process would be affected by the presence of an individual or group that would be in a superior bargaining position in a situation of anarchy. While a government itself is not explicitly a part of Buchanan's bargaining process, the same forces leading to government that are in this chapter's model are also present in Buchanan's renegotiation from anarchy.

At the other extreme from Rawls is the model in this chapter where some individuals find themselves in a position to dominate others before the bargaining begins. They become the government by negotiating a contract with those in an inferior bargaining position. Thus, the social contract established in this chapter's model is one that is negotiated between citizens and government.

This is closer to the Hobbesian vision of the social contract than models where a social contract is made among individuals prior to the establishment of government. In order to avoid the war of all against all that Hobbes envisioned would occur in anarchy, he proposes that a government be formed, which is common ground with other contractarians. Hobbes argues, "The only way to erect such a Common Power, as may be able to defend them from the invasion of Forraigners, and the injuries of one another, and . . . that . . . they may nourish themselves and live contentedly; is, to conferre all their power and strength upon one Man, or upon one Assembly of men, . . . and therein submit their Wills, every one to his Will, and their Judgments, to his Judgment."[18]

In the ideal state of affairs, following Hobbes, every person would promise to all others, "*I Authorise and give up my Right of Governing my selfe, to this Man, or to this Assembly of men, on this condition, that thou give up thy Right to him, and Authorise all his Actions in like manner*"[19] (original emphasis). This social contract, according to Hobbes, is a contract among all citizens to recognize the rights of the government, and the government is not directly involved in the Hobbesian contract except as the object of allegiance for its citizens. But it is clear that in the Hobbesian vision of a social contract to avoid the problems of anarchy, there are two classes of individuals: those who are citizens, and those who are government. This is in contrast to the Rawlsian contract where everyone bargains in a state of equality behind the veil.

The social contract theory developed here treats government and citizens of government distinctly, which is more in line with Hobbes's vision than the contemporary social contract theory. In a purely positive setting, this is more descriptive of the way that constitutional rules are actually drawn up than imagining a bargaining process among individuals without a preexisting government.

Differential Bargaining Power and Coercion
The social contract theory presented here gives differential bargaining power to those who are in government. The quotations from Hobbes just cited clearly show this to be Hobbes's vision of the resulting contract. Hobbes argued that creation of the government implies authorizing all of the government's actions. Such authorization is not implied in the model in this chapter, nor in the work of 20th-century contractarians, but again there are differences.

In a strict unanimity voting setting such as behind the Rawlsian veil of ignorance and in Buchanan and Tullock's *The Calculus of Consent*, every individual has veto power over any constitutional provision, so no individual can exercise more power than any other in the formulation of constitutional rules.[20] The same is not true with Buchanan's *The Limits of Liberty*, where individuals are considered to be in agreement with the social contract if they view the existing constitution as within the expected bounds of renegotiation from anarchy. Thus, an individual who would be a weak bargainer in anarchy would expect less in any renegotiation from anarchy. Buchanan's model is close to the one in this chapter with regard to assigning people differential bargaining power in agreeing to the social contract. Following the implications of Buchanan's renegotiation from anarchy, it seems evident that people who are physically weak or who do not have the potential to be productive cannot expect the same amount of bargaining power as those who are strong or productive.

The strong and productive can offer output and protection – or can threaten others in the bargaining process – in order to gain differential power in drawing up the terms of the constitution. In imagining renegotiation from anarchy, this would seem possible in Buchanan's model just as it is possible in the model in the model developed here.

Unanimity Rule

The place where 20th-century contractarian theory finds the most common ground is with regard to the unanimity rule. While Buchanan's *The Limits of Liberty* has an unusual conception of what it means to be in agreement, the models of *The Limits of Liberty, The Calculus of Consent, A Theory of Justice,* and Nozick's *Anarchy, State, and Utopia,*[21] all use the concept of unanimous agreement in some way or another to determine appropriate constitutional rules. In the model developed in this chapter, a social contract can be the result of agreement of only a subset of individuals.[22]

At the outset, there is the practical question of what determines who is in the group that agrees to the social contract. In the models of the contractarians listed above, a closed group is considered, so membership in the group is determined before those in the group bargain to determine the terms of their contract. In a broader model, persons who do not agree with one group might join another, much as Tiebout described intergovernmental competition, but Tiebout-type competition falls outside the bounds of contemporary contractarian models.[23] Contractarian models require unanimous agreement from everyone in the group and do not consider the possibility of dissenting individuals joining another group.

If actual unanimous agreement is required in the real world, the holdout problem develops. An individual could opportunistically refuse to agree to a proposal which would benefit everyone, hoping that by holding out, the group will give something more to the holdout to win the holdout's vote. Wicksell[24] dealt with this problem by requiring approximate unanimity, and Rawls handles it with the requirement that bargaining be done behind a veil of ignorance. Actual unanimous agreement does not appear to be a practical alternative to developing constitutional rules in the real world, so contractarians who adhere to the principle of the unanimity rule as a criterion for judging constitutional rules must develop some sort of conceptual unanimity criterion so that conceptual unanimous agreement can be reached even when actual unanimous agreement would not be possible.[25]

Having recognized the holdout problem and its implications for unanimity, the rest of this discussion will ignore the holdout problem to concentrate on the problems of reaching unanimous agreement when there are real differences of opinion. Rawls deals with this problem by invoking the veil of ignorance. Behind the veil, everyone has an equal probability of being anyone after the veil is lifted. Since all people behind the veil are essentially identical, there can be no differences of opinion. Buchanan, in *The Limits of Liberty*, deals with the problem by saying one is in conceptual agreement if the current outcome is within the bounds that would be expected in a renegotiation from anarchy. People may not agree in fact, but if they would not expect to be any better off after renegotiation, they are in conceptual agreement. And Nozick, in *Anarchy, State, and Utopia*, deals with the problem by having a constitution evolve from a series of individual agreements. Everyone agrees in all bargains they make as individuals, and they do not have the opportunity to disagree with other peoples' bargains.[26]

Unanimous agreement may be hard to produce because of legitimate differences of opinion. The issues would be distributional, since in theory, it would be possible to compensate someone for unfavorable terms in the contract. However, people may disagree about what would be fair compensation. Some might in principle think that a few should not be compensated to agree, while those few might refuse to agree without compensation.

In the real world, people are sometimes forced to agree to things because unanimous agreement is not required. If unanimity is required, everyone has veto power, so nobody is forced to agree. If unanimity is not required, then a dissenting individual has the option either of going along with the rest of the group or of remaining in the minority. Since going along is often less costly than remaining in the minority, it is possible to obtain unanimous agreement with a less-than-unanimous decision rule more readily than if unanimity is required.[27] Following the earlier discussion on differential bargaining power and coercion, people may agree to go along because of the threat of negative consequences if they choose not to.

What about people who still do not agree to cooperate with the con-stitutional rules agreed to by most others? Hobbes argued that "because the major part hath by consenting voices declared a Soveraigne; he that dissented must now consent with the rest; that is, be contented to avow all the actions he shall do, or else justly be destroyed by the rest."[28] This is consistent with the approximate unanimity argued by Wicksell. If most people agree to a social contract, then others who want to remain a part of the group are required to go along with the rules that are accepted by most as legitimate.

The model developed at the beginning of the chapter defines what it means to say that most people agree. In that exchange model, there is no voting rule. Rather, citizens agree that they are better off exchanging protection for tribute with the government than not being a party to this exchange. Governments must retain their legitimacy in order to have the popular support necessary to survive in the face of alternative governments, and the legitimacy that enables the government to survive constitutes agreement. In a world with many governments, a government may allow dissenters to leave, or may require that they abide by the rules of the state or "be destroyed," to use the words of Hobbes.

Governments in the real world and governments in this chapter's model do not have unanimous approval in anything but the most abstract sense. Yet in most cases there is a general agreement that constitutes a social contract. Citizens have an ideological commitment, in the sense described by Douglass North, to their countries, and try to work within the system to effect change. The peaceful change in Eastern Europe in 1989 is an example of how governments can be replaced when they lose ideological commitment and the appearance of legitimacy; governments that rule without the general aura of legitimacy – Uganda under Idi Amin might be an example – are rare and usually short-lived.

Many 20th-century contractarian models use the rule of unanimity as a criterion for establishing constitutional rules within a social contract, but the model in this chapter uses the concept of ideological commitment and legitimacy instead. A social contract exists in this model if the citizens in general view their government as a legitimate party to an exchange of protection for tribute. As noted earlier, some people may not agree and yet the government can still be viewed as legitimate, and the bargain may take place in a coercive setting. Whether a government is viewed as legitimate can depend not only on the specific terms of the agreement between the government and its citizens, but also on what alternatives its citizens have to the status quo.[29]

Normative versus Positive Aspects of the Social Contract

The social contract present in this model of government is a purely positive concept that explains why government actions are viewed as legitimate, and why people abide by government edicts when they are not absolutely forced to. The answer is that government makes an exchange with its citizens: the government grants certain rights to its citizens and acts to protect them in exchange for citizens agreeing to abide by the rules and pay their taxes. The terms of this exchange constitute a social contract.

Because this social contract is couched in a purely positive setting as the result of an exchange, it offers no more normative guidance than the result of any other exchange. Economists frequently argue that their job is simply to analyze and predict the results of economic activity, and not to pass judgment on the desirability of the outcomes produced by the activity. In the same way, constitutional rules within the social contract are the result of an agreement, and are not subject to evaluation of their desirability without some additional normative criteria.

All social contract theories share this characteristic. The very use of the word contract indicates that the terms of the contract are the result of an exchange. However, some social contract theories go further by using some explicit normative criteria to evaluate the terms of the contract, and the unanimity rule is often the criterion of choice. By adding the requirement that constitutional rules be unanimously approved within some specific (sometimes hypothetical) decision-making process, the desirability of real-world constitutional rules can be evaluated using that criterion.[30]

In the model in this chapter, some people are in a better bargaining position than others, and those in a weak bargaining position could be forced to go along with the strong or be excluded from the group. If the unanimity requirement were imposed on this model, everyone would have veto power, imposing greater political equality among individuals, and possibly resulting in different constitutional rules from those produced without the unanimity requirement. Surely, a positive model can be evaluated using normative criteria. There is nothing inconsistent with social contract models that want to judge the desirability of certain states of affairs, as opposed to simply modeling the results of a bargaining process.

But the fact that the present model does not contain any normative criteria does not make it any less a social contract theory of the state. This model simply looks at the contracting process to see what terms would be expected to emerge from an actual bargaining situation, as opposed to looking at hypothetical bargaining situations or trying to evaluate the outcome of the bargain.

The Characteristics of Constitutions

By depicting constitutional rules as the result of a bargaining process – the terms of a social contract – it is possible to analyze the bargaining process to explain the expected results of the bargain. This is in principle no different from the economist's analysis of rent controls to predict shortages in the housing market, or Niskanen's analysis of the bargaining process between a bureau and its sponsor to explain the characteristics of bureaucracy.[31]

In this exchange model of government, the government's legitimacy is established as the outcome of an agreement between the government and its citizens. The citizens agree to pay tribute to the government and abide by certain government rules, and the government agrees to protect certain rights of its citizens. The key point is that because the government receives its income from its citizens, it has an incentive to protect them. Productivity requires durable assets, and for this reason, a long-term contract is required between the government and its citizens. Daily exchanges, as might occur in a marketplace, are insufficient; individuals who sacrifice to produce durable assets today will do so only if a long-term agreement exists that promises a future pay-off for those who choose to invest in the present.

The social contract is more than a metaphor; it is the essential relationship between a government and its citizens. For a government to be anything more than a thief, it must be viewed as being both willing and able to ensure the protection of well-defined rights both now and in the future. This perception by its citizens gives the government legitimacy. This model of government suggests the expected characteristics of actual constitutions.

(A) Constitutions grant citizens a well-defined set of rights. The government will not modify this set of rights except by using a well-defined procedure. This is necessary for the government to be viewed as legitimate by its citizens.

(B) Constitutions require citizens to fulfil a well-defined set of obligations. The government will not modify this set of obligations except by using a well-defined procedure. These first two characteristics of constitutions provide a general outline for the exchange model of government.

(C) The result of the exchange between government and its citizens is a long-term contract that cannot be modified except by the consent of both parties. The long-term nature of the contract and its relatively fixed rules differentiate government from the market provision of similar services. For example, this differentiates government police from private security guards.[32]

(D) Every constitution must provide for the protection of its citizens. Governments exchange protection for tribute. This must include protection from physical harm as well as economic protection. Physical protection means that the government will try to protect the individual from harm as long as the individual obeys the government's rules. Economic protection means ensuring a way to earn an income in exchange for productive activity.

(E) Every constitution must provide for a clearly defined mechanism whereby the government collects its tribute. Constitutional limits on its taxing power provide citizens with a guarantee that they can retain some of what they produce. This incentive to be productive benefits both the citizens and the government that receives its income from the productivity of its citizens.

(F) From the standpoint of those in government, government is a way to reap monopoly profits. Constitutional rules define the extent to which the government can produce monopoly profits. Just as in other industries, the extent to which the government can generate monopoly profits is a function of the alternatives available to the consumers of government services.

This section has outlined some general characteristics that one would expect to find in all constitutions, if constitutions are a product of the exchange model of government. But while the exchange model of government suggests features common to all constitutions as social contracts, the final characteristic (F) also suggests reasons why constitutions differ among nations.

Constitutions and Monopoly Government

In an ideal setting, such as behind a Rawlsian veil of ignorance, no individual will be at a bargaining disadvantage in the process of producing constitutional rules. In the exchange model of government developed here, citizens are at a disadvantage relative to government because the government bargains from a position of monopoly power. While the previous section argued that all constitutions would have certain common elements, differences among constitutions will be the result of differences in the monopoly power of governments. Constitutional rules would give government more monopoly power when citizens have fewer alternatives to the existing government. This provides the foundation for understanding differences among constitutions.

If an existing government can be replaced at low cost, then it would have less monopoly power than one that could be replaced only at higher cost. Democratic governments should be able to exercise less monopoly power over their citizens than dictatorships. Within democratic governments, increased security for incumbents and a more entrenched government bureaucracy makes it more difficult to replace government. These trends in the United States suggest increasing government monopoly power.[33] A government that allows emigration has less monopoly power over its citizens than one that does not. In general, more open borders reduce the monopoly power of government. Thus, the monopoly power of government can be enhanced by erecting trade barriers and increasing international hostilities, including the starting of wars.[34] Mutlinational corporations enhance international mobility, and so reduce the monopoly power of government.

Chapter 6, on monopoly government, and Chapter 9, on competition in politics, more fully explore the implications of this model of government, but this section indicates that the exchange model of government developed here suggests, in a purely positive framework, both similarities and differences that would be expected to exist in constitutions across countries. Normative implications could be developed as well simply by accepting the premise that monopoly power is undesirable.

The point of this section is not to draw out every implication of this exchange model of government, but rather to illustrate that it can produce testable implications about similarities and differences in constitutional rules among nations, and can be used as a foundation for a normative analysis of constitutional rules as well. This section outlines some implications that can be developed further.

Conclusion

The primary purpose of this chapter is to illustrate the economic foundations of government. Governments exist because those who operate under the rules of government believe that they are better off abiding by the government's rules than not. This could only be the case if the citizens of government believe they get something in exchange for what the government extracts from them. Frank Knight said that "to say a situation is hopeless is the same as saying it is ideal."[35] People abide by the rules of their government because they view it as preferable to the alternatives. As the model in this chapter illustrates, those in government have a bargaining advantage, so the exchange that produces government does not give citizens a strong position from which to bargain.

The exchange benefits citizens because government provides an environment under which they can be productive, and they are better off with some guaranteed rights than in a situation of anarchy where anything they produce can be taken from them by others who are stronger. Thus emerges the fundamental exchange that produces protection for tribute. This chapter illustrates that no matter how oppressive a government, both citizens and those in government are better off with a well-defined set of constitutional rules that outline the rights and obligations of all parties, and that provide a procedure for modifying the rules. These constitutional rules are a social contract.

The economic foundations of government are apparent in the institutions that define property rights, collect taxes, and produce public works. Governments do other things, though, such as protecting human rights and providing justice. These other things are a part of the social contract and a product of exchange just as much as the more obviously economic aspects of the constitution. The next chapter develops this model further by modeling rights and government in a more formal setting.

4 A Model of Rights and Government

According to the economic theory of rights, individuals have rights to the extent that they are able to bargain for them. In the real world, significant rights might sometimes be bargained for on an individual basis. When does the teenager have the right to take the family car? Rights of family members within the family setting are clearly subject to negotiation, but the same is true outside of the family setting. What often is referred to as corruption is the outcome of an exchange process that accords some individuals more rights than others.[1] Even in societies that espouse equal rights as a public policy, factors such as corruption and special interest legislation create a setting where some people have more rights, or more securely enforced rights, than others.[2] Differential rights can be created by individual bargaining, but can also be the result of group action, where one group is able to impose a rights structure that gives them advantages over others.

This chapter begins by considering how the bargaining processes described in the previous two chapters produce an institutional structure with well-defined rights for individuals in a society, and how that structure might evolve over time. The relationship between government and rights is also discussed, because the two will go hand-in-hand. Then, a model is developed to describe rights structures with special reference to the relative equality of rights that will exist in a society. The model identifies several factors which will create conditions more conducive to relative equality of rights. An important problem in the implementation of any structure of rights is developing a method for ensuring that rights are honored. One could hardly claim to have a right, except in some abstract sense, if others do not observe it. The chapter begins by considering this problem.

Opportunistic Behavior and Rights

In any exchange promising mutual gain, one problem is to make sure that the terms of the agreement are carried out. For example, an individual who agrees to buy a loaf of bread at the grocery store enters into a mutually beneficial exchange where the grocer is better off with the money and the customer is better off with the bread. What if the customer takes the bread from the store without paying? A landlord and tenant can mutually benefit from exchanging the right to live in an apartment for rent. What if the tenant occupies the apartment but refuses to pay the rent? There are mutual benefits to living in a society that respects the right to life. What if a person, sensing an opportunity for gain, kills another?

The issues here are matters of degree. In each case, despite the possibility for mutually beneficial exchange, opportunistic behavior can benefit an individual, and in each case, the question is one of observing the rights that another person claims. In retail transactions, retailers try to protect their claim to rights over the items they sell by trying to prevent their customers from leaving their establishments until the customers have paid for the merchandise. Rights are protected by simultaneous exchange. Because the landlord-tenant relationship involves less of a simultaneous exchange, provisions are made to prevent opportunistic behavior. Written leases, monetary deposits, and so forth, coupled with the police protection of the state, are designed to prevent opportunistic behavior. Leases typically give the landlord the right to inspect the property periodically, to evict a non-paying tenant, and so forth. These provisions are examples of methods for monitoring and enforcing the provisions of an exchange when the two parties do not tender the objects of exchange simultaneously.[3] The less simultaneity there is in an exchange, the more carefully the agreement must be designed in order to monitor and enforce its provisions.[4]

Rights are no different from any other object of exchange, when viewed in this context. Since there is rarely a simultaneous exchange outside of market transactions, there are many occasions to engage in opportunistic behavior. One can steal unattended property, and may be able to kill others without being detected. What prevents such opportunistic behavior? Often, it is not prevented. Property is stolen, and people are killed. Claiming a right is not sufficient to have the right; it must also be protected. Market exchange, political exchange, and the observation of rights all share the similarity that some people will behave opportunistically if the opportunity arises. For this reason, people who claim rights must be able to monitor and enforce those claims if they want their claims to be respected.

Monitoring and Enforcement

While people might agree to a rights structure that is Pareto superior to the status quo, it is likely that individuals could further enhance their welfare through opportunistic behavior. Rights structures have the characteristics of a prisoners' dilemma, where each individual would benefit from violating the agreement, but everyone is better off if the agreement is kept by all. Therefore, rights structures will typically be accompanied by some institutions that attempt to monitor and enforce the rights structure.

Criminals are people who do not observe rights that the legal system accords people. Criminals engage in criminal behavior because they believe that they will be better off by not observing peoples' claims to rights. The legal system in general and the criminal justice system in particular exists to give people the incentive to observe the rights of others. The legal system is a solution to a prisoners' dilemma game because it provides – for most people – an incentive to cooperate in the observation of rights which, as noted earlier, makes everyone better off.

The prisoners' dilemma situation that arises in observing the rights of others is depicted in Figure 4.1, which shows two people, A and B, who must decide whether to observe the rights of others. In each cell, the payoff for A is in the upper right corner and for B is in the lower left. Thus, if both observe the rights of each other, a payoff of $5 results, but either can violate the rights of the other and receive $7 if the other continues to observe rights. Regardless of the strategy taken by the other person, both individuals have an incentive to violate the rights of the other, resulting in a payoff of only $2 each instead of the $5 that would result if they cooperated and observed each others' rights.

One possibility is that individuals would voluntarily cooperate with each other, which in the long run would even be in the narrow self-interest of each person, if others could monitor the person's behavior,[5] but in a large society some individuals will behave opportunistically, which could cause cooperative arrangements to degenerate. The role of monitoring and enforcing institutions is to detect noncooperative behavior and to make it more costly not to cooperate with others than to cooperate and observe each others' rights.

Within the framework of Figure 4.1, an institution could be developed which penalizes each individual $8 for violating the rights of the other, which modifies the Figure to look like Figure 4.2. Adding in the $8 penalty, it now pays each individual to observe the rights of the other regardless of what the other person does.[6] The logic of establishing institutions that delineate well-defined rights with well-defined penalties for violation is that such institutions reduce opportunistic behavior that results from the prisoners' dilemma nature of a system of rights.

Note that such institutions do not guarantee the rights of individuals. Rights specified by the legal system are violated regularly. Individuals

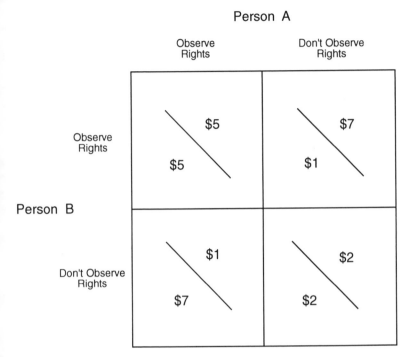

Figure 4.1   The Prisoner's Dilemma of Observing Rights

recognize that they do not have an absolute right to their property or their lives by buying locks, by avoiding dangerous neighborhoods, and according to the National Rifle Association, by carrying weapons for their own protection. Efficiency losses arise because people have to protect their rights in this way,[7] but these efficiency costs are a manifestation of the fact that rights are not absolute: individuals have only those rights which they can protect.

Institutions Do Not Make Rights Unconditional

Even the institutionalized legal system often recognizes that rights exist only if they are enforced. A person crossing the property of another is guilty of trespassing, but if the person has a history of crossing the property on a regular basis, the legal system will recognize an easement which will allow the crossings to continue to occur. Likewise, squatters who begin as trespassers can develop rights to the property they occupy. Activities

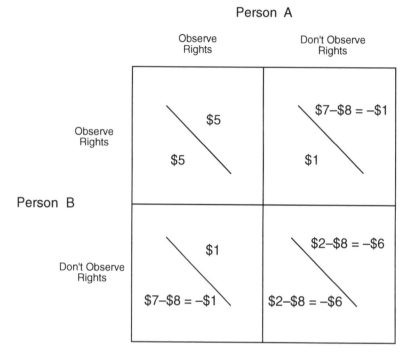

Figure 4.2   Enforcement to Avoid the Prisoner's Dilemma

that are violations of the law the first time they occur eventually become activities that are protected by the law. Even in institutionalized legal systems, rights are not absolute and people can lose the rights they do not enforce.

From an efficiency standpoint there is a reason to adopt institutions that protect rights when the cost of collective monitoring and enforcement is less than the cost of individuals undertaking monitoring and enforcement themselves. The right to life is not qualitatively different from other rights. Police protection, the court system, and even the death penalty itself can be viewed as institutions geared toward helping individuals maintain the right to life[8] and other rights. These institutions help solve a prisoners' dilemma problem since everyone would be better off respecting everyone else's right to life, but there will be cases where a particular individual would benefit from opportunistically taking the life of another. While legal institutions attempt to solve this problem, there always will be a trade-off between protecting life and pursuing other goals. In a world of scarce resources, a corner solution is unlikely to be optimal, so efficient institutions will not completely guarantee everyone's right to life, or any other right.[9]

Any positive theory of rights must recognize that individuals have to take some responsibility for their own safety, and that no real-world rights structure can unconditionally guarantee rights. This is an application of the idea individuals have rights only because others find it in their self-interest to honor them. Legal institutions provide incentives by attempting to monitor and enforce rights, but they do not provide unconditional rights.[10]

Institutions and Enforcement

There is no unconditional guarantee of any right; people have rights only to the extent that others observe them. In order to have rights, people must, first, claim them, and second, be able to enforce their claims. A structure of rights could arise simply through individual contracting among all members of society, but in a large society where people interact with many others, and often will have only the most superficial relationships with those they interact with, organized institutions provide the basic rights structure. The legal system spells out basic rights accorded to individuals and provides the monitoring and enforcement of those rights.

The legal system might provide different rights to different classes of people, and some rights (or some peoples' rights) might be enforced more than others, but the basic structure is institutionalized through the legal system. Because there are economies of scale in monitoring and enforcing rights, resources are saved by having this monitoring and enforcement provided to the group through centralized institutions. Otherwise, individuals would have to constantly be checking for violations of their claimed rights.

A model along these lines is developed by Nozick, who described how individuals would hire firms to protect their rights, and eventually a single large monopoly firm would protect all rights.[11] Nozick's model conveys the reason why rights would be institutionalized, but he paints an optimistic picture of peaceful negotiations that would occur to produce the structure of rights. In reality, rights are likely to be the product of threats as well as promises, producing a structure of rights different from that described by Nozick.

The point here is that although rights are the product of bargaining and exchange, the basic structure of rights will be insitutionalized to economize on monitoring and enforcement costs. From this basic structure, individual negotiation can alter the rights that any particular individual will have.

People can lobby legislators for special interest laws to benefit them, they can bribe officials for differential treatment, and they can negotiate with their neighbors for rights. For example, consider A and B, living in adjoining apartments, and A likes loud music on the stereo while B likes peace and quiet. Person A might be able to intimidate B by playing the stereo, thus getting the right to play loud music, B might intimidate A by banging on the walls, threatening to damage A's car, or the like, or they could work out an agreement so that A plays the stereo at predetermined times when B is not home. The point is, while the institutional structure defines rights in a general sense, a person's specific rights are still subject to negotiation.[12]

The rights framework in a society will be institutionalized even though the rights specific individuals have will very based upon negotiations they have made. Institutionalization takes advantage of economies of scale in monitoring and enforcement, and the resource savings gives an advantage to those societies that have institutionalized monitoring and enforcement of rights. Government is the institution that monitors and enforces rights, and the next section considers how rights are produced through bargaining in the exchange model of government.

Government and Rights

Government control over the monitoring and enforcement of rights is a natural extension of the economic theory of rights because of the potential efficiency gains from institutionalizing the basic rights framework. Within a contractarian setting, this could mean that individuals would get together to agree on institutions that define the rights of individuals. In a less egalitarian setting, this also means that if someone were to impose an institutionalized rights structure on a group by force, the resulting society would have the potential for greater efficiency than one in which rights were observed only by individual contract, without a central enforcer.

Rights arise through exchange, but bargains can be struck on the basis of threats as well as promises. Historically, the structures of rights that have existed in most societies most of the time have been the result of an elite group forcing the masses to accept their institutions. Powerful individuals can agree not to harm those less powerful in exchange for payment. Unless they can fight back, productive people have an incentive to agree. They will be better off producing and keeping some of their output rather than having no incentive to produce because everything they produce will be taken from them. Thus, actual structures of rights are produced as a result of a bargain that makes everyone better off. Powerful people are better off with an institutional structure that transfers some wealth from others to themselves, and productive people are better off agreeing to pay a portion of their production to powerful people rather than having to fight off the attacks of those people if there were no agreement.

Early tribes raided other tribes, killing and stealing, and then returned home with the gains from their plunder. Later tribes learned to extract tribute in exchange for a promise not to raid. In this situation, government arises as a way of consolidating gains from military conquest; in other words, to extract tribute from conquered peoples. Even though the rights structure favored the conquerors, the conquered realized they were better off agreeing to the arrangement than trying to fight it.

Military and Police Protection of Rights

In order to maintain their position, those with more rights must display to others with less rights that they have the ability to use force to maintain the status quo should anyone resist. As a result, military and police protection go hand-in-hand with the institutionalization of rights. There is the prisoners' dilemma problem to overcome with the monitoring and enforcement activities of police power, and overcoming the problem creates an efficiency gain. Those with the power are able to obtain the largest share of the efficiency gain precisely because they have power. Military and police power therefore go with greater rights. Those who use these rights to take income from others must use some of this income to produce military and police power, which gives them the ability to use coercion to maintain their differential status.

In order to maintain their position, those in power will have to devote some of the resources they extract to the production of coercive institutions, such as police and military forces. These forces are produced as a part of the exchange of protection for tribute – they are the protection – but also have the function of being available to those in government to force reluctant citizens to pay the tribute that government demands. Government specializes in protecting the rights of its citizens, but the same coercive power that it can use to protect its citizens can also be used to coerce those same citizens to agree to a structure of rights that might not be agreed to if all individuals had veto power, as for example, under a rule of unanimity.

A Model of Rights Structures

While there is mutual gain for individuals living in societies where rights are observed, any particular individual's rights will be a function of the individual's power and productivity. The individual's power has a clear direct relevance to the ability to obtain and protect rights, and the individual's productivity is relevant because the individual can exchange the output produced, which gives others an incentive to share in the gains from trade.[13]

By giving the ground rules for cooperation, any rights structure will increase productivity over a state of anarchy. Individuals can choose to produce within the existing rights structure or can choose not to cooperate within that framework, for example by revolting in order to replace the existing rights structure with another one. Since an individual could not unilaterally replace the structure of rights, individuals would choose not to accept the existing rights structure only if they believed that under the existing structure they were worse off than they would expect to be if the structure of rights were to be renegotiated.

The individual's willingness to accept the current rights structure could be depicted in the following way. If the existing rights structure were eliminated, individuals would be thrown into a state of anarchy, from which Pareto superior moves could be made by agreeing to observe certain rights. Individuals have some expectation about the result of this bargaining process, and if they view that the existing structure of rights leaves them worse off than they would expect to be with renegotiation, they have the incentive to renegotiate.

This process for two individuals is depicted in Figure 4.3, which shows the utility of individual X on the horizontal axis and of individual Y on the vertical axis. In a state of anarchy, individuals would expect to have relatively low levels of utility, depicted by the point A in Figure 4.3. The observation of rights enables the society to be more productive, so the two individuals could reach a point on the utility possibilities frontier C, between points c and c'. Exactly where they might end up on the utility possibilities frontier depends upon how the gains from cooperation are shared.

Assume that the individuals expect that if they were to bargain from anarchy, they would end up somewhere between a and b. In that case, as long as X had at least utility level X_a and Y had utility level Y_b, they would accept the existing rights structure as within the bounds of renegotiation, so would not have the incentive to try to replace the existing rights structure. Without those utility levels, they would not be willing to observe the

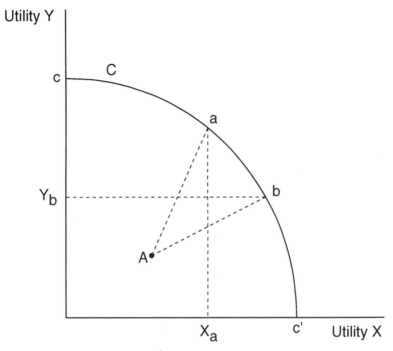

Figure 4.3　The Benefits of Rights

existing rights structure. Rights structures can vary, and a system of rights favoring individual Y would locate the group closer to a while a system favoring X would place the group nearer to b.[14]

The dashed lines that connect points a and b to A show the expected bounds of renegotiation from anarchy,[15] and the angles at which the lines move from A to a and b indicate the expectations of individuals regarding the outcome of the bargain to produce a social contract. For example, if when renegotiating from anarchy individuals expected only that a Pareto superior move would be made, leaving them at least as well-off as in anarchy, the lines would depart point A at a 90-degree angle, and point a would be directly above A, while b would be directly to the left of A. If, at the other extreme, individuals expected the utility gains from contracting to be split exactly evenly between them, the dashed lines would come together as a 45-degree line from point A, and points a and b would coincide on the utility possibilities frontier.

As they are drawn in Figure 4.3, each individual expects some utility gain from the social contract, but recognizes that one individual might gain relatively more than the other. This seems to be a reasonable way of depicting individuals' expectations. It would be reasonable to expect that in a bargaining situation, the gains from trade may not be shared completely equally, but at the same time, the outcome of any bargain would be likely to leave all parties to the bargain with some of the gains from trade. If Figure 4.3 is taken to be descriptive, then if individual X was only as well off as would be expected in anarchy at point A, then individual X's well-being would fall outside the bounds of expected renegotiation between the dashed lines. Individual X would therefore not be in agreement with the social contract, and would attempt to renegotiate.

As depicted in the diagrams in this chapter, individuals X and Y have symmetric expectations, but this would not necessarily have to be so. Assume, for example, that individual X would expect to get little or nothing from a renegotiation of the social contract, but that Y would expect to get half or more of the utility gains. In this case, a 45-degree line would connect points a and A, while point b would be directly to the right of A, connected by a horizontal line. The effects of changes in the locations of points a and b are discussed below. The locations of those points are determined by the expectations of individuals regarding a renegotiation, and it is plausible that changes could occur which would affect those expectations.

Within this framework, consider two general classes of rights systems, which for lack of better terminology will be called cooperative and caste. Cooperative rights structures are characterized by equality of rights, private property, and market exchange, so that individuals have an incentive to produce the most valuable output to exchange for the valuable output of others. Caste rights structures are characterized by unequal rights. The upper caste controls productive resources and forces the lower caste to work for them. The lower caste does not get to keep its marginal product, although some provision for sharing output with the lower caste will have to be devised to give that group an incentive to continue to observe this rights structure.

The cooperative rights structure will be more productive since everyone has an incentive to maximize the value of their output. Under a caste system, the upper caste must monitor the output of the lower caste to try to keep them from shirking, but monitoring cannot be perfect, and members of the lower caste have an incentive to shirk because they do not get to keep their marginal product. Caste systems would include slavery, feudalism, and any system where there are economic advantages that accrue to royalty. The complex differences among systems will be assumed away to focus on the differences between simple cooperative and caste systems.

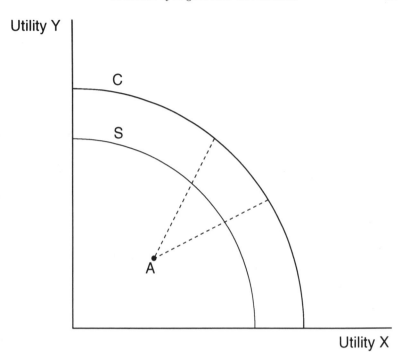

Figure 4.4 Two Rights Structures

At any point in time a cooperative system will have a utility possibilities frontier beyond that of a caste system because of the shirking
problem under a caste system. Figure 4.4 extends the model from Figure
4.3 to include these two types of systems. Utility possibilities frontier
C represents the cooperative system, while frontier S represents utility
possibilities with the shirking that occurs in the caste system. As before,
the dashed lines show the expected outcome of a renegotiation of rights
from anarchy.

This model can be used to illustrate why different rights structures will
tend to emerge, and how exogenous factors can influence the structure of
rights.[16]

Comparative Statics

To show how the model can be used, Figure 4.5 illustrates a situation
where cooperative rights would emerge because everybody is better off

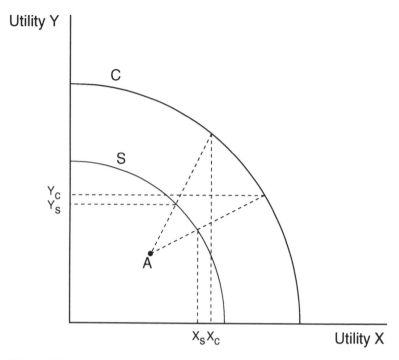

Figure 4.5   The Incentive for Equal Rights

under cooperative rights than with a caste system. Under a caste system, the highest utility levels that either individual could expect would be X_s and Y_s, which would make them less well-off than the worst that they would expect to do under a cooperative system. This situation provides the incentive for cooperation and a structure of relatively equal rights because everyone would be better off cooperating with others rather than trying to oppress them by forcing them into a lower caste.

In the situation depicted in Figure 4.5 there is the unambiguous incentive for a cooperative rights structure because every person must have a higher utility level under cooperation than with a caste system, assuming that the outcome remains within the bargaining range. This situation will produce greater equality of rights than a caste system, and some comparative statics can help to illustrate the conditions which are more favorable for equal rights.

Some changes are easy to visualize by looking at Figure 4.5. For example, if shirking were easier to prevent, the S curve would shift out toward C, and it is easy to visualize that as S shifts out, X_s and Y_s increase and eventually will become larger than X_c and Y_c. At that point, it is conceivable that a person could be better off under the most favorable conditions with a caste system than under a cooperative system. Thus, as it becomes easier to prevent individuals from shirking, more powerful individuals have a greater incentive to attempt to institute a caste system, placing themselves in the upper caste. This can be stated in the form of a proposition:

PROPOSITION 1: The less costly it is to monitor and enforce the productivity of others, all other things equal, the more likely it is that a caste system of unequal rights will exist.

A type of society implied in utility possibility frontier S will have more aspects of a command economy in order to allow the upper caste to take resources from the lower. The society implied in frontier C will be more market oriented, and individuals will have more autonomy over the resources they work with. This leads to increased productivity because each individual can make maximum use of the knowledge that would not be available to others, as described by Hayek.[17] Assuming that a caste system relies on existing technology while a cooperative society is better able to take advantage of new technology to improve productivity, an increase in productivity would shift C outward but would not affect S. Looking at Figure 4.5, it is easy to visualize that as C shifts out while S remains stationary, X_c and Y_c will move out while X_s and Y_s do not change, making making a cooperative rights structure more likely. Thus:

PROPOSITION 2: Increases in productivity make cooperative rights structures with more equality of rights more likely, all other things equal.

The next exercise in comparative statics pictures the bargaining range, represented by the angle at A, becoming narrower. Again, a look at Figure 4.5 enables the result to be visualized. From the standpoint of X, a narrowing of the bargaining range pulls the upper arm of the angle down, which increases X_c, and pushes the lower arm up, which lowers X_s. Cooperative structures become more attractive while caste structures become less attractive, so a narrower bargaining range should increase the likelihood of more cooperative rights structures. Therefore:

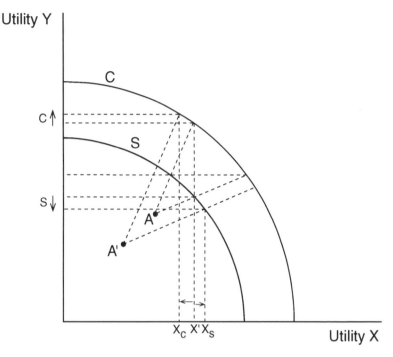

Figure 4.6   A Change in the Anarchistic Equilibrium

PROPOSITION 3:   A narrower bargaining range, all other things equal, will produce more cooperative rights structures and more equality of rights.

The final exercise in comparative statics is to see the effect of a change in the point of anarchistic equilibrium. This change may be harder to visualize without additional lines in Figure 4.5, so is shown in Figure 4.6. At anarchistic equilibrium A, the best individual X can do under a caste system and the worst X could do under a cooperative system are both X'. If the point of anarchistic equilibrium moves toward the origin, all else (including the angle representing the bargaining range) remaining the same, the diagram shows that the individual could do better under the caste system but could do worse under cooperation; thus for individuals who might be in the upper caste, there is an incentive to attempt to move to a structure of more unequal rights.

With a wider bargaining range, there is also the possibility of doing better under the cooperative structure, as shown by the arrow marked c on the

Y axis, and the possibility of doing worse under a caste system, as shown by the arrow marked s. However, the individual shown on the X axis, who would be in the upper caste of a caste system, has more of an incentive to attempt to impose an unequal rights structure; therefore, a caste system is more likely. This implies:

PROPOSITION 4:   The closer anarchistic equilibrium is to the origin, the more likely inequality of rights will be observed, all other things equal.

In a primitive society, per capita output is not very high, but individuals are also close to being self-sufficient. In more advanced societies, individuals rely more on others for their survival. Thus, if societies were to degenerate to anarchy, it is likely that a member of a primitive society would be better off than a member of a complex advanced society. Thus, the process of economic development itself opens the opportunity for more unequal rights, as suggested in Proposition 4, because development moves the point of anarchistic equilibrium toward the origin.

Competition and Exchange

If the assumption that cooperative rights structures with more equality will be more productive, then there will always be an incentive for cooperative rights structures because by moving to a higher utility possibilities frontier, the gains to the gainers would always be sufficient to compensate the losers and leave everyone better off. Unequal rights would exist only when some barrier to exchange prevents the lower caste from paying the upper caste for equality. This is nothing more than an application of the Coase theorem.

There are some potential barriers to exchange. First, the value of equality for the lower caste may exceed their present wealth, requiring future payments to be made in order to complete the transaction. There may be no way that the lower caste can assure that future payment actually will be made. For example, imagine how a slave could promise future compensation in exchange for present freedom in a manner that would convince the owner that the payment actually would be forthcoming. Second, if the benefit of being in the upper caste of a caste system is greater than the lower bound of expectations under a cooperative system ($X_s > X_c$, using the notation from above), then an unstable situation could arise where after relinquishing their power, another group would have an incentive to try to install themselves as the ruling caste in a new caste system. Thus, the propositions in the previous section above suggest the conditions under which more unequal rights structures would tend to be observed, but there is always an incentive to institute the most productive rights structure if the transactions costs can be overcome.

The upper caste in a caste system can be viewed as a monopoly. A monopoly market produces less total value than a competitive market, but the monopolist receives more profit than the competitors in a competitive market. Just as it would be possible to pay a monopolist to divest and become a competitive industry, it would be possible to pay the upper caste to agree to equal rights. But in both cases, it may be difficult to find a feasible and enforceable bargain that could be struck in the real world.[18] Despite this imprecision, the model does provide a framework within which rights structures in the real world can be analyzed.

Conclusion

The economic theory of rights provides a purely positive foundation from which one can analyze the extent to which individuals have rights that actually are observed, and can analyze the degree to which equality of rights will be observed in societies. The theory of rights explored in the past three chapters is an implication of the general exchange model of government. The observation of rights is the outcome of an exchange process whereby people claim rights when they view it in their self-interest to do so, and people observe the rights of others when they view that they benefit from observing those rights. Others observe a person's rights to the extent that the person claiming the right makes it beneficial for the rights to be observed.

Two factors that can enable a person to convince others to observe that person's rights are the degree of force that the individual can use to protect the claimed rights and the potential of offering mutually beneficial exchanges in return for the observation of rights. In anarchy, one can use physical strength to persuade others to observe one's rights, and with governments, control over the organized force of the state's police and military powers, or state power in general, can convey rights. Control of productive resources also can convey rights because others will observe a person's rights in exchange for being able to trade with productive individuals. Individuals who are strong and productive will have more rights.

While individuals can negotiate individually for rights, a structure of rights will be incorporated as a part of the society's constitutional rules.

These constitutional rules will broadly define the rights that individuals might expect, although the rights of particular individuals will differ from one another. This chapter has brought together the ideas of rights generated by constitutional rules and rights generated by individual bargaining by showing how an overall social structure of rights can be produced in which all individuals do not have the same rights. In the process, the chapter illustrated factors that can affect the types of rights that different individuals will have.

There are no implications in this analysis regarding what rights individuals should have. The model considers only what rights individuals would be expected to be able to exercise as a result of a bargaining process under various conditions. One might want to draw some normative implications for the types of rights societies should have, but to do so first requires an understanding of the underlying processes of social interaction. This discussion of government and rights lays the groundwork. The next chapter continues the discussion of government by considering what factors differentiate governments from voluntary organizations.

5 The Distinction between Clubs and Governments

The economic model of government is based on exchange. Individuals find it in their mutual self-interests to create constitutions that define individual rights and the limits of government power, and to grant governments the means to monitor and enforce the structure of rights defined by the constitution. While based on exchange, the model differs from what has sometimes been referred to as the exchange model of government because threats as well as promises could be used to encourage the observation of rights, so the resulting government could be forced upon some individuals.[1] The use of the word force is not unambiguous in this context, however, especially in light of the contractarian model of the state. In what sense might people be said to be in agreement with the constitution under which they are governed? Looked at in another way, clubs might be thought of as institutions that their members voluntarily agree to join, whereas people are forced to abide by the rules of their governments whether or not they agree. What distinguishes a club from a government?

The answer to this question is not completely obvious, as the remainder of this chapter suggests, but it is reasonable to ask what difference it makes. What is the benefit of grouping collective organizations into the categories of clubs and governments? From a strictly positive standpoint, there is little reason to make the distinction. There is an extensive literature explaining why people can be better off producing some goods and services collectively rather than individually, and collective decision-making can be studied independently of whether the decision-making unit is a club or a government. Many of the same principles apply in either case.[2] From a normative standpoint, however, there is a difference. If clubs are fundamentally voluntary organizations, then one can have little reason for wanting to interfere with the club's activities. People who do not like the club's activities do not have to join. If governments a fundamentally coercive organizations that force people to abide by the government's rules, then everyone in the group has an interest in the government's activities. Normative issues extend to matters of the public interest rather than just to the private interests of the club's members. From a normative standpoint, then, there is a reason to be concerned with the characteristics that differentiate a club from a government.

The issue of what constitutes the use of coercion will also be considered in this chapter. Governments are coercive organizations, but government activity and coercion are not synonymous. While defining coercion may be of limited interest from a positive standpoint, like the definition of government it is of more interest for normative purposes. For example, a social contract might allow the government to engage in coercive activities – to collect taxes, for example – but might prohibit the coercion of some citizens by others. What would be covered? Would an armed robber be engaging in coercive activity? Would a monopoly seller be engaging in coercive activity? Constitutional rules based on logically consistent concepts will be more enduring because they provide a logical foundation for precedent in extending the constitution to unforeseen circumstances. Within a constitutional framework, a precise understanding of coercion is worthwhile.

Not all government activity is coercive, and not all coercive activity is government. The distinction between clubs and governments will be considered before trying to pin down the definition of coercion.

An Economic Theory of Clubs

James Buchanan's article, "An Economic Theory of Clubs," enjoys a prominent position in the public choice literature, and justly so.[3] By looking at the collective provision of public goods in a club setting, the article suggests an analogy between clubs and governments. Buchanan's later work on the contractarian model of government further suggests the parallel between clubs and governments. Few people would be willing to argue that the government is nothing more than a large club, but the exact distinction between these two forms of collective organization is more difficult to identify.

Government activity is often associated with coercion, but coercion can sometimes take place independently of government. Indeed, sometimes the government even protects citizens against coercion, as, for examples, when police apprehend a thief or when courts convict a murderer. What is the distinguishing feature of government that sets it apart from other coercive activities? What differentiates, for example, taxation from theft? Even if one regards taxation as theft, one would hardly say that a thief becomes a government as a result of his thievery.

After considering the differences between clubs and governments, this chapter will propose a definition of government. This is more than just a matter of semantics, because a complete understanding of the definition of government requires that careful thought be given to the characteristics that make an institution a government. Such an understanding is essential if a society is to have any hope of controlling the power of government. Regardless of one's views on the appropriate role of government, precisely articulated views on the role of government require a precise understanding of the nature of government. Along the way toward a definition of government, the chapter will carefully consider the characteristics that make government what it is.

The chapter begins by exploring the continuum from clubs to governments. There is a natural tendency to want to say that either an institution is a government or it is not, yet according to common notions about what constitutes a government there is a continuum that runs from clubs to governments. Following the discussion on the continuum from clubs to governments, a definition of government will be discussed. The chapter concludes that the power to tax is the characteristic that defines government.

Clubs and Governments

This section examines the idea that there is a continuum between clubs and governments. This notion is controversial for several reasons. First is the natural tendency to want to be able to identify an institution as either a government or not a government. Another reason for controversy is that by drawing a parallel between clubs and governments there might be the tendency to justify the existence of government by arguing that it is really nothing more than a type of club. This justification is objectionable if clubs are fundamentally voluntary organizations while governments are coercive. But even here, the concept of coercion needs to be defined. Some examples later in the chapter will allow the reader to demarcate the line between clubs and governments, but the notion about voluntary agreement with the government's activities should be examined further.

The notion that citizens are in voluntary agreement with the actions of their government finds its intellectual roots in the social contract theory of the state. The social contract theory can trace its roots at least back to Locke and Roussseau,[4] but is a continually developing theory with recent contributions by contemporary scholars such as James Buchanan[5] and John Rawls.[6] Social contractarians argue that while there is not an actual contract between citizens and their governments, there is nevertheless some conceptual agreement that binds citizens to the terms of government.[7]

In its simplest form the contractarian argument of agreement does not depict the actual formation of governments through coercion.[8] This concept of agreement is examined more fully in Chapter 7. However, there is an element of truth to it in that in many countries – the United States, for example – citizens are in general agreement with their government even though they may disagree with some specific activities of the government.[9] Note that this would be true of a club too, however. Members may in general support the club while disagreeing with some specific club activities. There is no need to digress further into a discussion of contractarianism. The point here is that there are similarities between clubs and governments, and that collective organizations seem to fall on a continuum between privately organized groups and governments. Rather than discuss the theoretical differences further, some examples can illustrate the continuum.

Bridge Club
Consider first a bridge club, which is an organization that most people would agree is a club and not a government. The hypothetical bridge club in this example consists of four members and agrees to meet once a week, rotating meeting places among the homes of the club's members. The member at whose house the club meets for the week is responsible for providing refreshments for the entire group.

The game of bridge provides a good example of a collective activity because the game is played by four individuals, so the club will be unable to pursue its stated purpose of providing bridge games for its members if one of the members does not show up for a meeting. Since all members must be present for the club to function, this hypothetical club has a rule that if a member misses two meetings for any reason within a year's time without providing a substitute player, that member will be dismissed from the club and a new member will be found. Further assume that the members have agreed ahead of time that the rules of the club can be changed if three of the four members agree to the change.

While most people do not consider bridge clubs to be governments, note the similarity in this hypothetical example. The bridge club taxes its members by requiring that they pay for refreshments every fourth week. There is also a certain amount of work involved in hosting the group, such as setting up a place to play, preparing refreshments (or at least shopping for them), and cleaning up afterwards. This forced labor is similar in concept to a miliary draft, even though the military draft is far more demanding of the individual. Furthermore, the club has rules that must be obeyed and has established penalties for disobeying. A member could be expelled from the club, for example, for missing too many meetings. Thus, if the individual wishes to remain in the club, the club can force the individual to obey its rules. The club has also established a voting rule so that a majority can institute new rules that might impose costs on a minority.

The purpose of this example is not to argue that the bridge club is a government. It is a club, of course, and the example's purpose is to look at the bridge club and decide why it is a club rather than a government. It can force its members to contribute income and direct labor to the organization, it can change the rules without the consent of all of the members, it can place penalties on the members, and so forth. However, it is also true that the individual can quit the bridge club at any time that the club appears to be imposing more costs on the individual than it generates benefits. Rather than look for more in this example, consider another example of a club.

Swimming Club

The hypothetical swimming club in this example will be similar to the bridge club, so needs little discussion. Members voluntarily join and pay dues, which are then used to provide a swimming pool and associated facilities to the members. Officers of the swimming club are elected from the membership to oversee the club. Like the bridge club, members can quit any time they want. Clearly, the swimming club is not a government either.

Neighborhood Association Pool

The neighborhood association pool in this example is not hypothetical, but is drawn from an actual case in a subdivision near Washington, D.C. The subdivision was once a farm and was bought by a developer who divided the farm into individual lots and built houses on the lots. In the center of the subdivision the developer built a neighborhood pool and tennis courts. When the developer sold the houses, they were sold with a covenant attached that gave the homeowner part ownership in the pool, courts, and some surrounding land. In addition, the homeowner is responsible for paying a share of the maintenance expenses. The exact dues are determined by a majority vote of the homeowners in the subdivision. Furthermore, the homeowners elect individuals in the subdivision to serve as officers to oversee the operation, maintenance, and financing of the facilities. In this example, members pay dues that look suspiciously like taxation, and are subject to the decisions of a majority of the members.

The neighborhood association also has the power to expand its powers.

For example, some of the homeowners wanted to build additional tennis courts on the collectively owned land next to the pool, and a vote was taken to determine whether they would be built. While the vote failed, it might have been passed, in which case the majority would have been able to impose the extra costs for the new courts on the minority, some of whom might not even play tennis. This organization seems to be closer to the boundary between club and government. It has many of the characteristics of the swimming club in the previous example, in that the members pay dues and elect officers, and that a majority of the members can vote to impose costs on the group that may make a minority worse off. However, a homeowner cannot simply quit this neighborhood association because a restrictive covenant, agreed to by the homeowner at the time of purchase of the home, requires that the homeowner be a member of the organization as long as the homeowner owns the home. Is this association a government?

Even though the administering group does not call itself a government, it appears to be similar in many respects. Rather than consider the boundary between clubs and governments right now, consider another example.

Municipal Pool

Many municipalities have municipal pools paid for by the taxpayers in the municipality. Elected officials oversee the municipal pool, so that the municipal pool is financed and governed much as the neighborhood pool in the previous example. What is the difference between the municipal government in this example and the neighborhood association in the previous example?

Surely the answer cannot be related to coercion. Both the neighborhood pool organization and the municipal government have the ability to force its residents to contribute to its coffers. In both cases the individual cannot escape the organization without moving away, but in both cases it is possible to move away. Many towns are small enough relative to the general area where they are located that that there are other alternatives, ranging from living in another town to living outside the city limits of any town. Therefore, in many cases anyway, one can live in the area and choose to live in one of several municipalities or can choose to live outside the boundaries of any municipality. In such cases, nobody is forced, by circumstance or otherwise, to be subject to a city government. One can move only a few miles to be outside the city boundary.

Is a municipality government? Most people would agree that it is, but why? What makes it different from the neighborhood association discussed above? In both cases individuals are forced to be members if they live in the area, but can leave the area and quit the organization. One suggestion might be that municipalities have their own police forces while the swimming clubs do not. However, the city of Loachapoka, Alabama, which is admittedly a small town, is one example of an organization that collects taxes and has a mayor and town council, but has no police force. Is Loachapoka run by a government? Most people would say it is, but why? What is the difference between this organization, the swimming club, and the bridge club? The question will be considered after a few more examples.

State and Federal Governments

State and federal governments are quite obviously governments. One characteristic of this series of examples is that in each instance there is a bit more coercion than in the example before. The bridge club and swimming club are certainly clubs, even though they have the ability to coerce their members who want to remain in the organization. The neighborhood association has greater powers of coercion since a member must move in order to escape the organization. Simply stating "I quit!" would not be sufficient. The same is true of the municipality, although the individual still can move out of the municipality's jurisdiction. Yet the coercive powers of the municipality will generally be greater than that of the neighborhood pool organization.

It is less feasible to move away from a state or federal government, and even if one moves from one state, one must move into another state. Thus, while it is possible to escape municipal governments altogether, it is not possible to escape the jurisdiction of government at some level. Because the citizen has little alternative, the coercive power of a national government is clearly greater than the coercive power of a municipal government from which one can more easily move. The point here is that there is a continuum between a club and a government. A bridge club is a club and the U.S. Government is a government, but there are many ways in which the government of Loachapoka, Alabama is more similar to the bridge club than to the U.S. Government. Is there some clear dividing line? Before considering the question, one more case will be presented.

Restrictive Covenants

A restrictive covenant is a legal restriction that is attached to a piece of property and then remains with the property. The neighborhood association example above illustrates an extreme case, but this section will consider more common instances. For example, when an area is divided into lots for residential homes, a restriction may be attached to the lot that only a single family home may be built on the lot, that the home must be at least

1500 square feet, and that the house must be built at least 40 feet back from any road. Covenants can also stipulate that no signs can be erected on the property, that no commercial activities can take place on the property, and even that no boats or boat trailers are allowed to be parked on the property.

Covenants such as this are legally binding, and Houston, Texas provides an interesting case of a city that has no zoning laws.[10] Land use may still be restricted in a manner with effects similar to zoning, by attaching restrictive covenants to the property that states that it may not be used for multifamily housing, commercial establishments, and so forth. Note the difference between this type of covenant and a covenant which requires contributions to the neighborhood pool. This type of covenant disallows certain activities on the land whereas the neighborhood pool requires a contribution to a collectively consumed good. This distinction will be considered significant later in the chapter.

Summary
There is a continuum between clubs and governments, with some organizations having more of the characteristics of government than others. A municipal government, for example, forces its citizens to contribute to its upkeep, but a club also forces its members to contribute dues. One can move out of the municipality and not be subject to any municipal government, just as one can quit a club. The bridge club and the federal government are at opposite ends of the club-government continuum, but the point of these examples has been to show that indeed there is a continuum between clubs and governments.

Consider the examples given above. The bridge club is similar to the swimming club, which is similar to the neighborhood pool association, which is similar to the municipal government, which is similar to the state government, which is similar to the federal government. Where is the dividing line between club and government, and why?

The continuum between clubs and governments does not mean that governments are clubs, however. Despite the continuum there is an important distinction between clubs and governments. Considering the examples just presented, the reader might want to pause at this point to consider just what that distinction is. How could one define government in such a way that it would include those institutions one believes are governments but exclude those that are not? The purpose of this discussion is to illustrate the complexities involved in identifying the characteristics that make something a government. The next section will identify some issues that need to be considered in developing a definition of government.

What is a Government?

Many readers will already have an idea of what constitutes a good definition of government, so a good beginning for this section would be to look at some existing definitions of government. Robert Dahl correctly notes that the term can be used to describe the decision-making apparatus of voluntary organizations, and uses the word "state" in the same way this chapter uses government. Dahl says, "The distinctive characteristic of the state is supreme authority. Authority is the right to command and the right to be obeyed."[11] Following this definition, Dahl goes on to justify coercive activity on the part of the state, thus reinforcing the idea that the right to use coercion is the hallmark of government.[12] Elsewhere, Dahl defines *the* government as "any government that successfully upholds a claim to the exclusive regulation of the legitimate use of physical force in enforcing its rules within a given territorial area."[13] This definition is adapted from Max Weber's definition as having a "monopoly of the legitimate use of physical force in enforcing its order within a given territorial area."[14]

Ayn Rand defines government in the following way. "A government is an institution that holds the exclusive power to *enforce* certain rules of social conduct in a given geographical area." (original emphasis)[15] Rand's definition, like Dahl's, clearly is based on Weber's. Weber's definition and its derivatives focus on the government's monopoly over the use of force, and also specify that the monopoly extends only over a given geographical area.[16]

Carl Joachim Friedrich, after discussing various forms of governmental organization, says, "Government may therefore in its most general sense be defined as an institutionalized pattern of stabilized power, or rule."[17] The surrounding discussion makes it clear that Friedrich uses the term government as it is used in this chapter, and as Dahl uses state,[18] but Friedrich's definition does not do a good job of distinguishing clubs from governments in the continuum described earlier. Like Weber's definition and its derivatives, the concept of coercion comes through as a defining characteristic of government.

All of these definitions leave open the possibility that some institutions not normally considered governments would fit the definition, while some characteristics normally associated with government seem to be in conflict with the definition. Thus, as definitions, they are not very useful in actually identifying the defining characteristics of government. Some examples will be useful in pointing out some shortcomings in these definitions.

Some restaurants require that their male patrons wear jackets while dining in the restaurant. This is a rule of conduct, following Weber's definition and its derivatives, and an institutionalized pattern of stabilized power, or rule, as in Friedrich's definition. It is enforced by the restaurant because any male not wearing a jacket will not be served, so no other enforcement agency is needed.[19] The restaurant has the exclusive power to enforce its dress code, and the rule applies in a given geographical area – namely, the restaurant. The restaurant with the dress code seems to fit Weber's, Dahl's, and Rand's definitions of government perfectly, and also fits within Friedrich's definition, yet few would argue that the restaurant actually is a government.

Numerous similar examples could be developed. Teachers in a school impose rules on their students (for example, no cheating) and impose penalties in the form of lower grades or expulsion to enforce the rules within the geographical bounds of the school. The bridge club member requires that other members not smoke in his house, and enforces the rule by refusing to play otherwise. The point is that many institutions are able to enforce certain rules of conduct within certain geographical bounds, and not all of them are governments.

Another problem with Weber's definition is that a government may not have the exclusive or monopoly right to enforce a rule, because other governments might exist that have the right as well. For example, the federal government has rules for automobile exhaust emissions, but many state governments also have rules regarding auto emissions. Therefore, both the state and federal governments have the power to enforce rules regarding auto exhaust emissions, so neither one has the exclusive right. This is not merely a linguistic twist, but a problem with any definition of government which argues that government has a monopoly over the use of force. There cannot be two institutions with monopolies over the same thing, nor can two institutions hold the exclusive power to do something, so Weber's definition and other definitions of government that try to define government as a monopolist in the use of force imply that only one government can exist in a given area at a given time.

In fact, with a federal system of government, an individual can simultaneously be subject to city, county, state, and federal governments. Since only one monopolist could exist, a government cannot be defined as a monopolist as long as it is possible that one could be subject to multiple governments. Dahl's idea of government as the supreme authority seems to rule out multiple governments in one area also. One might argue that different governments enforce different rules, but the example of the auto emissions was designed to show that two governments can enforce the same rule. Since there seems to be no reason why all state rules could not also be federal rules, this is another problem with Weber's definition.

Again, this is not a semantic quibble. Since more than one government can govern an area at the same time, the essence of government is not that it has the monopoly power to do anything, or that it is the supreme authority in some way. One might try to twist Dahl's and Rand's use of the word exclusive to fit the concept of government, or twist Dahl's use of the word supreme, but why try when governments really do not have exclusive powers, but seem eminently able to share powers with other governments? Put plainly, monopoly is not a defining characteristic of government, since many governments can exist in a given area at a given time. Governments can exert monopoly power in particular markets, however.

Yet another problem with Weber's definition and its derivatives is that it seems to limit the government's use of force to a certain geographic area. In fact, there seems to be no geographic limit to the area in which governments will try to enforce certain rules of social conduct. For example, the United States government seems to have a predisposition toward democratic political institutions, and has used military force to try to enforce democratic rules of social conduct in Japan, Korea and Grenada (successfully), and Vietnam and Lebanon (unsuccessfully). Also high on the political agenda of past U.S. leaders has been the issue of human rights in the former Soviet Union. The U.S. government is powerful, but not particularly aggressive by world standards. Yet it would seem that the use of force to further rules of social conduct is limited only by the coercive power of the government, not by any geographical boundaries.

Again, this is not a matter of semantics. Governments have more power to enforce social rules within their own boundaries than outside them, but they can and do enforce social rules without geographic distinction. Consider, for example, the former Soviet Union's power to enforce rules of conduct in Eastern Europe prior to 1989. Since governments can enforce rules of social conduct wherever they have the power to do so, without regard to geographic area, this aspect of Rand's definition again does not seem to capture the essence of government.

The intention here is not to pick on the above-cited definitions of government specifically, but rather to take some representative definitions as a starting point for analysis. This discussion has identified three significant problems that are not overcome by any of the above definitions: (1) institutions other than governments have the exclusive power to enforce certain rules of social conduct in a given geographical area, (2) multiple governments can and do have the power to enforce the same rules of conduct in a given area, so a government does not necessarily have the exclusive power to do anything, and (3) governments enforce rules of conduct without regard to geographic area, if they have the power and inclination to do so.

The concept of government that appears clear at first becomes more elusive when one examines the continuum between clubs and governments, and when one realizes that many institutions enforce rules, yet with multiple governments even the governments themselves do not have exclusive powers of enforcement. Some, such as the city government of Loachapoka, Alabama, do not even have police departments to enforce their rules. The chapter up to this point has raised questions and identified some issues with regard to the nature of government. The remainder of the chapter will consider some answers.

A Definition of Government

The previous section was, perhaps, overly critical of the definitions of government that it analyzed, because they do encompass two of the major identifying characteristics of government. First, government has the power to enforce certain rules, as all of the definitions recognize, and second, governments are identified as existing over a given geographical area, as is clear in Weber's definition. Murray Rothbard has also considered the defining characteristics of government, and a quotation from Rothbard's *The Ethics of Liberty* lends some insight into Rothbard's ideas. Rothbard argues:

> For there is one crucially important power inherent in the nature of the State apparatus. *All other* persons and groups in society (except for acknowledged and sporadic criminals such as thieves and bank robbers) obtain their income voluntarily: *either* by selling goods and services to the consuming public, *or* by voluntary gift (e.g., membership in a club or association, bequest, or inheritance). *Only* the state obtains its revenue by coercion, by threatening dire penalties should the income not be forthcoming. That coercion is known as "taxation," although in less regularized epochs it was often known as "tribute."[20] (emphasis original)

Rothbard goes on to supply a definition of government himself.

> The State may therefore be defined as that organization which possesses either or both (in actual fact, almost always both) of the following characteristics: (a) it acquires its revenue by physical coercion (taxation);

and (b) it achieves a compulsory monopoly of force and of ultimate decision-making power over a given territorial area.[21]

Rothbard's concept of taxation as a crucial characteristic of government adds something to the concepts included in the earlier definitions because it specifies the activity in which the government forces people to participate. Perhaps, following Rothbard, a government could be viewed as an institution which forces people to contribute toward its support, or that has a monopoly over decision-making in a given area. There are some problems with this definition, though. In his first quotation above, Rothbard specifically exempts criminals from the realm of government, but on what basis? How, exactly, does one distinguish a band of criminals from a government?

One possible definition of government is: Government is an organization that has the ability to finance its activities by compulsory contributions from all individuals in a given geographic area. In this definition, the use of force within a given geographic area is critical, but the application of force that defines government is the forcing of individuals within the area to contribute toward the financing of the government's activities. Consider this definition within the context of the issues developed earlier in the chapter.

Robin Hood took from the rich to give to the poor, which is also the ambition of most contemporary governments, but Robin Hood was the leader of a band of merry men, not the leader of the government. Why not? Following the definition set out above, if Robin Hood was able to extract compulsory contributions from all individuals within a given geographic area, Robin Hood would have been the leader of a government. Because Robin Hood did not have the power to extract payment from everyone in the area, he was a robber of those from whom he could take, rather than a government over all individuals in the area.

Note that the definition does not require that the government actually extract payment from everyone, but only that it have the power to do so. Some individuals might be exempt from taxation. Also note that there is no requirement that the contributions be in the form of money. Governments often require other types of contributions, as would be the case with a military draft where compulsory contributions are made in the form of forced labor.

Following this definition, the use of force that identifies government is the ability to force individuals within an area to contribute to the support of the government's operation. What defines an individual's presence in an area? Residence is obviously one factor, and property taxes and income taxes are levied on this basis. But income taxes, sales taxes, import duties, and the like are also levied on individuals who engage in transactions within an area even if they are not physically present. However, the geographic area that is relevant to the definition of government is the area over which the government has the power to tax and not the area over which the government uses force. As noted earlier, governments exercise force on a regular basis outside of the jurisdictions that they tax.

The definition proposed above admits of the possibility that a government will use force outside of its geographic bounds. It also admits of the possibility that others (such as criminals, school teachers, restaurants with dress codes, and the like) will use coercion within the bounds of a governmental jurisdiction. Further, it allows the possibility that more than one government could exist at the same place at the same time, as long as they have the ability to force those in a defined geographical area to contribute to them. In short, this definition clearly distinguishes between governments and others that use force, it does not assert that the government has a monopoly over anything (although governments often do), so in general clears up the ambiguities that exist with some other definitions.

Now consider the continuum from club to government listed earlier in the chapter. While there is a continuum there is also a clear dividing line. The bridge club and the swimming club are not governments because while they may be able to tax their members, they cannot force contributions from people within a given geographical area. The neighborhood association, the municipality, and the federal government are governments because in each case they can force people in a given geographical area to contribute to them.

The neighborhood association in the earlier example is not normally considered to be a government, but falls on the government side of the dividing line, so warrants additional consideration. The underlying principle is that while the organization may have been formed voluntarily, everyone in a certain geographical area is required to contribute to the support of the pool, so the contributions are no different from any other type of tax, and the organization is in fact a government. While such an organization is not usually called a government, this definition would assert that when financing of the neighborhood swimming pool was made compulsory for everyone in the neighborhood, a new government was formed. If someone bought an existing house in the neighborhood, for example, that person would have to pay tribute to the neighborhood association just as surely as city taxes.

One might object that the rules of the neighborhood can only be enforced by the courts (and police) of some other government, but recall the city government of Loachapoka, Alabama, that has no police force of its own. The city is able to collect taxes even though violators would have to be pursued by an outside enforcement agency, since the city itself does not have one. If Loachapoka has a government without a police force, then so can the neighborhood association. Both are able to rely on the enforcement arms of other governments.

The neighborhood association in the above example was established by restrictive covenants attached to the property in question. What about restrictive covenants such as those requiring only single family homes, no boat trailers on the property, and so forth? These are different in character because they do not require contributions from the residents. Because there is no revenue generating ability implied in these restrictive covenants, they are of a different character than a covenant that says that a majority of the residents of an area can agree to tax everyone in the area.

This definition could be defended at greater length, but the discussion probably has been sufficient to make the point.[22] The proposal of this chapter is that government be defined as an organization that has the ability to finance its activities by compulsory contributions from all individuals in a given geographic area.[23] The exchange model of government developed in previous chapters identified the exchange of protection for tribute as a fundamental activity of government. This definition of government distinguishes government from others who sell protection.

The Reason for Defining Government

After defining government, it is worth commenting on why one should be interested in the definition. First, precise definitions are desirable at any time so that people understand the same thing when they use a term. Second, from a contractarian perspective, the definition sheds some light on what type of activity is unique to government, and why clubs and governments are different types of organizations. Also, if one ever wants to draw conclusions about government in general, rather than democracies, dictatorships, and so forth, there must be a general definition that determines when an institution is considered to be a government.

The normative analysis that appears later in the book depends upon a definition of government because in recommending desirable institutions, one might argue that individuals in their private arrangements should be allowed to organize their collective activities as they choose, while the government should be designed to minimize government intrusion on the lives of its citizens. As voluntary organizations, clubs should not be constrained in the rules they adopt, but the rules of governments should respect and protect the rights of their citizens. If this is the case, then being able to distinguish a club from a government is crucial because, in this normative framework, clubs can make any rules they want, whereas governments need to be constrained.

The key identifying feature of government in the definition of this chapter is that government can force people to contribute to it unless they move from the government's jurisdiction. Others may be able to refine (or replace) this definition, but it seems to capture the essential features of government more accurately than other definitions. Coercion is used outside of government, but government coercion is difficult to escape because of its geographical base.

Coercion

Governments engage in coercive activities, and taxation is one example. Individuals acting independently of government can also engage in coercive activities, of which armed robbery is one example. What is it about these activities that makes them coercive? The protection of individual liberty is often considered a desirable goal of government. This section considers the definition of coercion with the goal of determining when one individual infringes on the liberty of another by coercive activity.

Coercive activity can be looked at from two different perspectives: that of the individual being coerced, and that of the individual doing the coercing. Coercion is difficult to define when considered from the standpoint of the coerced individual. Consider some examples. Is the bridge club member who will be ejected from the club if he does not provide refreshments every fourth week being coerced? Does a blackmailer use coercion? How about the child who says "share your ice cream with me or I won't be your friend?" What about the employer who says that secretaries must make coffee to keep their jobs? Is the monopoly supplier coercing customers since there is no other alternative for the good?

Activities appear more coercive to the individual being coerced if there are fewer alternatives. What choice does the parched traveller lost in the desert have but to buy water at the asking price from the only person who is selling it? What choice does the secretary who wants the job have but to make coffee? If alternative jobs are available, then the secretary is in a better bargaining position and seems to be less coerced.

People may have limited alternatives for many reasons, some of which could be the result of their own previous actions. The parched traveller lost in the desert is likely to be in that situation as a result of previous risky choices which have now left the individual with limited alternatives. If the owner of the water in the desert had no part in creating the predicament of the lost traveller, then perhaps it is unreasonable to argue that the monopoly supplier of water is able to coerce the traveller because the traveller has no alternative but to buy the water at the price its owner asks. Similarly, if only one employer will offer the secretary a job, it seems unreasonable to argue that the employment is coercive.

Coercion is better understood as an action taken by the individual doing the coercing rather than from the standpoint of the coerced individual. Coercion can be defined as the stated willingness to harm someone if that person does not do what the coercing individual wants. Thus, the owner of water in the desert does not coerce the parched traveller by charging a monopoly price for the water. The traveller can agree to an exchange or not, but the owner of the water will not interfere with the traveller if the traveller decides not to make the exchange. While it may be true that the traveller would be better off if an exchange were made, and would be better off if the water were sold at a lower price, this is true for any market exchange. If the exchange is not made, the traveller is no worse off than if the owner of the water did not exist.[24]

Contrast this situation with taxation – a coercive activity. Government states its willingness to use resources to impose costs on delinquent taxpayers. Unlike the traveller trying to buy water, if a citizen decides not to pay taxes the government demands, the government asserts that it is willing to harm the citizen. This threat of harm if the taxpayer does not do as the government asks is what makes taxation coercive.

Following this definition of coercion, market exchanges are never coercive. Individuals can either trade at agreed-upon terms, or not trade if no agreement can be reached. Bribery is not coercive because an individual can always choose not to take the bribe and be no worse off. Blackmail is coercive because the blackmailer demands payment, or else will do something to harm the person being blackmailed.

The distinction between clubs and governments, discussed above, coincides with the distinction between dues and taxes as suggested by this discussion on coercion. In the swimming club, the bridge club, and so forth, individuals can choose to end their memberships and no longer pay dues. With taxes, an individual cannot choose not to pay in exchange for not receiving the services in question. Thus, governments use coercive means to finance their activities, while clubs do not.

Constitutions and Mobility

The reason why governments can coerce people is that it is costly for people to escape the power of the government. In the Tiebout model of local governments, governments compete with each other for residents by offering potential citizens desirable bundles of local goods and services.[25] For the Tiebout model to work perfectly, people must be able to move costlessly from one local government to another. In such a setting, governments that do not offer their citizens the goods, services, and associated tax prices that they want will find themselves without citizens in the same way that businesses that do not satisfy their customers will find themselves without customers.

With less than perfect mobility, or with locational preferences that extend beyond just the government's activities, the Tiebout model does not work perfectly and residents can end up with governments that do not satisfy them.[26] Note that the Tiebout model may accurately describe locational decisions when people are relocating for other reasons. A person who is moving can have a substantial choice of local options. But once located, moving is costly, and some guarantee of the government's future activities is desirable in the absence of costless mobility.

Constitutions serve this purpose. Constitutional rules are substitutes for mobility, because in a world of costless mobility, governments that want to retain their citizens cannot alter the activities of government in a way that creates a more unfavorable environment than offered by competing governments. But without perfect mobility, constitutional rules constrain the government to try to prevent it from making changes unfavorable to its citizens. It is in this way that constitutional rules substitute for mobility.

Constitutional rules become more important, therefore, the less mobility is present. Constitutional rules for local governments are less important than for national governments because it is easier to move away from an oppressive local government than from an oppressive national government. The continuum discussed earlier makes a difference, but the distinction between clubs and governments also makes a difference. One can quit a country club, but not a local government, without physically moving. Thus, there is a distinction in principle between the constitutional rules of clubs and the constitutional rules of governments.

Conclusion

This chapter has covered much territory, but all within the general subject matter of the role of government in a society. The chapter began by examining the continuum between clubs and governments. There is a difference between clubs and governments, and arguments that obscure the difference are potentially dangerous because they promote the illusion that in some sense a government is a voluntary organization. Governments are fundamentally coercive organizations.

Private organizations have the ability to enforce certain rules of conduct, but not in the same coercive manner as governments. Restaurants can enforce dress codes, colleges can enforce rules of social conduct (which can be severe at some religious institutions), and country clubs can impose social rules on individuals extending even to who one's friends are. How constraining these organizations are depends upon an individual's alternatives. The continuum from clubs to governments might be viewed in this light as a continuum from less constraining to more constraining collective arrangements. But just as some private groups can be very constraining, some governments exert relatively little in the way of constraints. Small city governments where it is very feasible to live outside the city limits are examples of governments that have relatively little power to constrain their citizens.

The lack of constraints results from the fact that it may be easy to escape the government's coercive activity. If coercion is defined as the stated willingness to harm an individual who does not comply with the demands of the coercing party, then if it is easy to move away from a government's jurisdiction, the government will be able to exert relatively little in the way of constraints on its citizens. Following this view of coercion, market activity is never coercive, but government taxation in general is coercive.

It may at first seem that there is a contradiction in having a continuum between clubs and governments and yet still identify a clear dividing line between them. To see that there is no contradiction, consider the set of real numbers as a continuum from negative infinity to infinity. Even though this set makes a continuous number line, zero is a clear dividing line between the positive and negative numbers. The reader might still question the validity of a continuum from clubs to governments or the assertion that there is a clear dividing line between them, but the example of the number line shows that there is no logical contradiction in identifying a continuum between clubs and governments with a clear dividing line to identify when an institution is a government.

In an attempt to draw a line between governments and non-governments, this chapter has proposed the following definition: Government is an organization that has the ability to finance its activities by compulsory contributions from all individuals in a given geographical area. This definition draws the line on the continuum from clubs to governments at about the place where it is typically thought to belong, and identifies the power to tax as the hallmark of government. It also identifies taxation as a coercive activity, which distinguishes taxation from dues.

In a purely positive framework, there is little reason to be concerned about the definitions of government and coercion. The last few chapters of this book turn to normative issues, however, and there it is important to distinguish governments from clubs, and to identify coercive activity. The promotion of individual freedom is a widely held value, and an implication is that social rules should be designed so as to limit coercion and control the activities of government, while allowing voluntary action and allowing individuals to design their own rules within a club setting. As such, there are some rules that clubs should be allowed to have, but governments should not.

Normative applications will be developed later, after extending the exchange model of government in the next several chapters. The next chapter builds upon concepts discussed in this one. While governments cannot be defined as monopolists, they can profit by exerting monopoly power when they are able. Chapter 6 examines the way in which governments try to extract monopoly prices by restricting competition.

6 Government as Monopolist

Neoclassical microeconomics is based on the models of competition and monopoly. In the competitive model, buyers and sellers face many alternatives, so the terms of exchange are set by the market. No actor can exert noticeable influence on the the terms of an exchange since the individual on the other side of the exchange can always trade elsewhere.[1] In the monopoly model, the seller is able to keep competing sellers out of the market, so can influence the terms of the exchange. Beginning economics students tend to believe that monopolists can sell as much as they want for any price they choose, and their teachers try to convince them that monopolists can raise their prices only by selling less, since the law of demand dictates that there is an inverse relationship between price and quantity demanded.

Although the models of competition and monopoly provide the foundation, microeconomics can become very complex when there are varying degrees of monopoly power on each side of the market (the monopsony model of a single seller being the mirror image of the monopoly model), and when actors on each side of the market look for strategies to try to reinforce their monopoly power. But fundamentally, neoclassical microeconomics is based on a competitive model with many alternatives on each side, augmented by individuals acting to restrict alternatives on their side of the market in order to produce more favorable terms of trade.

These same principles apply to the exchange model of government. Often, government is depicted as an all-powerful coercive institution. The impression is that unless the government is constrained, it can do as much of anything it wants. But government is constrained because it does not have the resources to monitor and enforce any arbitrary set of commands. If it tries to coerce the population to do things they do not want to do, the government must use resources to enforce its edicts, and it must get those resources from the people it is trying to coerce. As a result, it will be impossible to make the population do certain things because some mandates would be too costly to enforce; but more to the point, the closer the government's mandates are to the population's desired course of action, the fewer resources the government will need to use to monitor and enforce its mandates. Thus, the same type of trade-off occurs with the government's setting its policies as with the monopolist setting its policies. Neither can do anything it wants, and in both cases, the most profitable course of action is a function of the demands of the population. Compliance through coercion is no more guaranteed through the government than are sales for the monopolist, and in both cases there is an optimal profit-maximizing strategy.[2]

In the Tiebout model of intergovernmental competition,[3] individuals have the opportunity to live under any one of a large number of local governments, and can costlessly move to the government they like best. In such a situation, individual governments acting on their own cannot be coercive at all. Individuals who do not like an action of one government can always move to another. The assumptions that produce competition in the Tiebout model point to the sources of coercion in government in the real world. First, it is costly to move, so governments can impose costs less than the cost of moving on their residents and still retain them. Second, governments can act collusively, so that coercive action by one government is duplicated by others. Moving does no good when all governments agree to be equally coercive.

In democratic governments, elections can serve some of the functions of mobility. People who do not like their governments can elect new ones, and if electoral competition were perfect, once again, governments could not coerce their citizens – at least, not for more than one term – because challengers could offer voters the governmental characteristics they want and replace the incumbents through election. If incumbency by itself conveys an advantage in the electoral process, however, then incumbents will have some monopoly power, so can act in a coercive manner.

This chapter considers the process by which those in government are able to gain monopoly power and use it to charge monopoly prices to its citizens. The monopoly profits then accrue to those in government. The exercise of monopoly power is one way to view the coercive element in government.

Competition, Monopoly, and Coercion

In order to be identified, the coercive activities of government must be viewed in context. Is taxation coercive? If the government threatens to use force to harm those individuals who do not cooperate, then taxation is coercive even if in some sense individuals could be said to agree to it.[4] In small localities, it is feasible to move outside the city limits, so city taxes would not be as coercive as national taxes, since it is less feasible to move outside the nation's borders. And individuals can quit clubs without moving, making club dues less coercive than city taxes in most cases. One could imagine, however, a setting in which for job or social reasons, individuals felt pressured to be members of one particular club, but had the choice of many local governments in which to live. Such a setting would make club dues and rules more coercive than those of local governments. Any organization can be coercive if it can threaten the individual with harm unless the individual complies with the organization's rules. However, one might legitimately question whether one is ever really forced to belong to a certain club, or live in a certain municipality.

When individuals have a choice of governments, either because they can move or because they can select the government they prefer through election, then the competitive setting will push governments to act as their constituents desire. Political leaders in a competitive setting will earn only competitive returns for the services they provide. If there are restrictions on the level of competition, then political leaders will be in a position to charge monopoly prices for their services. In a manner analagous to profit maximizers in the private sector, political entrepreneurs have an incentive to reduce the alternatives available for their services in order to enhance the profits they earn from providing them.

Natural Monopoly in Government

Following the model of government developed earlier in the book, government automatically has a position of natural monopoly. As an organization that exchanges protection for tribute, there will be a tendency for protective organizations not to compete with each other. Nozick develops a model in which the protective state is a natural monopoly,[5] and although in a federal system one does observe several layers of government ruling over a particular area, there is little competition among the protective services of various governments. Government, in its role as an institution of power that protects the productive capacity of its citizens, automatically limits others from entering the market for protective services, so gives government some monopoly power.

As already noted, individuals can move, or in democratic settings can elect new governments to replace existing ones, but even here there is an element of natural monopoly. Individuals can shop at several different stores, but they live under the jurisdiction of only one local government at a time, even if mobility gives an option. Their new location would simply enable them to deal with another monopolist. Likewise, although new governments can be elected in a democratic setting, there is only one government that exists at any one particular time. Thus, political competition is competition for the right to be a monopolist. In a very competitive setting, citizens will be able to choose political leaders who offer their services in exchange for only a competitive rate of return.

In an insightful article, Harold Demsetz asked, "Why Regulate Utilities?"[6] The traditional theory of regulation says that utilities are natural monopolies that must be regulated to charge competitive rates. Demsetz argued that if competing companies bid for the right to be the monopoly supplier, competition among bidders would push the price down to the competitive level. That is, if there is competition for the right to be a monopolist, the result is the same as would be produced by a competitive industry. The same principle applies in electoral politics. If candidates compete for the right to be monopoly suppliers of legislation, they can win the competition only by offering a platform which leaves them with no monopoly returns.

As a result, incumbent legislators have an incentive to erect barriers to entry that restrict competition and enable them to earn monopoly returns. Many of the activities of government can be understood simply as ways of restricting entry to allow some type of monopoly profit. Incumbent legislators can erect barriers to entry into the legislator to increase the monopoly profits they receive, but can also erect barriers to entry into other markets by passing legislation. Legislators profit from erecting barriers to entry into other markets because they can sell the monopoly rights. Tariffs can create barriers to entry for foreign producers, and regulations and licensing requirements can create barriers to entry for potential domestic competitors, for examples. These barriers, created through legislation, are sold by legislators who receive campaign contributions, political support, and perhaps other more direct benefits.

The Government Cartel

These benefits can accrue to legislators only if they can reduce the competitiveness of the electoral process so that all the gains from being monopoly producers of legislation are not competed away. In the absence of a single dictator who collects all of the monopoly profits, this means forming a cartel of legislators who are able to act jointly like a monopoly.

The next chapter considers dictatorship in more detail. In democratic governments, elected officials form the cartel that exercises monopoly power over the production of legislation. As already noted, a competitive electoral process can reduce the monopoly profits of legislators to zero, so legislators have an incentive to form a cartel and create barriers to entry that increase their profits.[7] Considering the payments that dictators must make to their protectors, as well as the potential for being overthrown, it is not clear that the expected payout from attempting to become a dictator is higher than for being elected to office in a democracy.

The point is that any government is a cooperative venture among those who maintain power. Thus, the arrangements by which those in government erect barriers to entry, charge monopoly prices, and agree to share the profits, are of interest in the study of any type of government. The next section discusses the competitive model of democratic politics in more detail in order to set the stage for an analysis of monopoly power.

The Competitive Model of Politics

An important work in the formal development of a theory of competitive politics is *An Economic Theory of Democracy*, by Anthony Downs.[8] Downs develops a model of political competition in which candidates formulate platforms on which they run for election. Downs depicts the most preferred outcomes of voters as existing on a single-dimensioned continuum from political right to left, and argues that voters vote for the candidate closest to their most preferred position. Within Downs's model, the candidate whose platform is closest to the median voter's most preferred platform wins the election.

The Downsian model has been extended to various types of majority rule elections, ranging from referenda to committee type decision processes,[9] and has been analyzed extensively.[10] The general conclusion that the outcome of majority rule politics is the outcome most preferred by the median voter is of interest, but of more direct interest for present purposes is that candidates within the Downsian model must act in a specific way in order to be elected. They have no discretion. If a candidate does not produce the platform the median voter wants, then a competing candidate will, so all candidates are forced to follow the vote-maximizing strategy if they want to be elected.

This model of politics places incumbents and nonincumbents on equal footing in the competitive process. The electoral process polices legislators to produce that legislation most preferred by the voters; otherwise, a competing candidate will offer to produce what the voters want and will be able to unseat the incumbent.[11] In the competitive model, no monopoly profits can accrue to legislators, and candidates have no choice but to pursue the vote-maximizing strategy. Downs outlined in general terms the vote-maximizing strategy, but the competitive theory has been developed further since Downs.

Competition and Special Interests

Downs observed that voters have little incentive to become informed about their options in an election. Because there are many voters, and because elections are very unlikely to be decided by just one vote, all voters realize that their vote will not be decisive. Since no one vote will be likely to influence the outcome of the election, no voter has the incentive to collect information to cast an informed ballot. Voters may be interested in politics, just as sports fans are interested in sports, so may collect information for that reason, but no voter has an incentive to collect any more information, because all voters know that the election outcome will be unaffected by how they cast their one vote. Voters will be rationally ignorant.

Special interests, on the other hand, have an incentive to become informed about issues that directly affect them. A farm subsidy, for example, might cost each voter a small amount, so voters have little incentive to become informed, but the small amount taken from each voter, when transferred, becomes a large addition to each farmer's income. Thus, the special interest has an incentive to become informed about specific programs that can provide them with concentrated benefits. For policy proposals that impose small costs on all voters to transfer concentrated benefits to special interests, the general public has little incentive to become informed, but the special interest will be informed and will lobby legislators to implement the proposals.

Special interests can offer legislators votes and campaign contributions to help them win the next election. Thus, supporting the program can produce votes for the incumbent. The general public will be rationally ignorant of the program, so will not vote differently whether the legislator supports or opposes the special interest program. Therefore, the vote-maximizing legislator, facing an informed special interest and a rationally ignorant general public, has an incentive to support the special interest legislation.[12]

The competitive model of politics can be taken a step further than this. Since there are opportunity costs involved in working for the passage of legislation, legislators must choose which legislation to support. In addition to the time costs, supporting legislation in a logrolling legislature means exchanging votes to build support for legislation, and votes traded for one issue are votes that cannot be used again to support another. When faced with the choice of supporting public interest legislation, about which most voters will be rationally ignorant, or supporting special interest legislation which can produce political benefits from special interests, the vote-maximizing legislator must pursue the special interest legislation.

Otherwise, a challenger will campaign on the vote-maximizing platform in the next election and unseat the incumbent.

The special interest model of government, built on the foundation of the competitive model of elections, implies that the process of competitive politics leaves legislators with no choice but to pass legislation which benefits special interests rather than legislation that is in the general public interest. The result is a distributive government that takes tax revenues from the general public and redistributes those revenues in the form of programs that benefit special interests. Legislators who do not pursue special interest legislation will be displaced by those who do.[13]

Barriers to Entry and Monopoly

There are two reasons why extreme competitive model of special interest politics depicts legislators as more constrained than they are in the real world. The first, and least important reason, is that agency costs prevent perfect monitoring of legislators' activities, and to the extent that there are costs involved in keeping legislators from shirking and behaving in a discretionary manner, they will be able to deviate from the vote-maximizing strategy.[14] The second, and more important reason, is that political institutions contain barriers to entry which prevent challengers from competing on level ground with incumbents.

The advantages of incumbency are well-known, and range from legislatively created advantages such as the franking privilege, a paid staff, and favorable campaign finance laws, to advantages not created by legislation, such as more ready access to the media. These advantages produce a barrier to entry and mean that if an incumbent ran against a nonincumbent with similar characteristics, the incumbent would win every time. Incumbency thus creates a cushion of votes that are political capital to the incumbent. The incumbent does not need to spend this political capital in order to win the next election, so is able to use some discretion and is not forced to follow the strict vote-maximizing course of action.[15]

Even the fundamental organization of representation in the United States lessens the degree of political competition. The legislature acts as a cartel whose members are able to charge monopoly prices for their services. But like any cartel, there are incentives to cheat on the cartel agreement once monopoly prices are established.[16] One way that firms in a market might try to enforce a cartel agreement would be to divide up the market into geographic territories and assign each firm a monopoly over a specific territory. This way, the firm can act as a monopolist with all of the monopoly incentives intact, and can detect cheating by other firms if the products of other cartel members are sold in a member's territory. Such a geographic division can help stabilize a cartel because members never directly compete against each other.

Exactly this type of division occurs in representation in the U.S. Congress. Each state is allotted a certain number of representatives, but rather than having the representatives run against each other in at-large elections, each state is divided into districts, and a representative has a monopoly over the production of legislation for constituents in that district. There is no reason why, for example, in a state with ten representatives, all could not run in a general election to represent the state, with the top ten vote-getters being elected. But this would force cartel members to compete with each other. By dividing the market geographically, incumbents never compete against each other,[17] which helps to hold the legislative cartel together. Even in the U.S, Senate, where two senators do represent each state, the terms are staggered so that once again, incumbents never compete against each other. Just as in a well-organized cartel, members must be concerned about others outside the cartel who want to enter the market, but members do not need to compete directly against each other because of the way the cartel is organized.[18]

These barriers to entry that face challengers create monopoly profits for incumbent legislators, which they can then spend as they desire. Legislators might spend their profits by attempting to gain a national reputation as a statesman, so could pursue public interest legislation rather than special interest legislation as a method of building a national reputation. Ironically, the creation of monopoly in government could lead to legislation in the public interest.[19] But monopoly profits could also be used to add to their personal wealth through speaking fees and book royalties, to shirk on the job, or to take personal benefits such as junkets at taxpayer expense. However they are spent, these monopoly profits are produced through barriers to entry in the political process.

Seniority as a Barrier to Entry

The seniority system in legislative bodies has been analyzed as a method for organizing legislative exchange. The legislature divides its work through the committee system, and senior members act as middlemen in political exchange. As compensation for their actions as middlemen, they take some of the gains from trade. Thus seniority pays a return over and above simple membership in the legislative body, because senior members serve the function of acting as brokers.[20]

While such models explain the function of individuals in senior positions, they do not explain why these positions are allocated on the basis of seniority. Since the currency of legislative exchange is votes, making votes the measure of wealth in legislative exchange, every legislator has the same number of votes and is equally wealthy. Why would junior members agree to a system that transfers some of their power to senior members when a coalition of junior members could form to take the differential power away from senior members? Committee assignments could be made randomly or rotated on a regular basis, to mention two possibilities, yet they are given on the basis of seniority. This is especially curious since the seniority system is a relatively recent innovation. At the end of the 19th century committee assignments were made by party leaders, but early in the 20th century seniority began evolving as a system replacing the power of party leaders. The seniority system obviously is not necessary for the operation of the legislature, since at one time it was not used, yet the power attached to seniority has been growing over time.

While it is true that every legislator who remains in the legislature eventually moves up the seniority ladder, this does not explain the acceptance of the system by junior members. For one thing, some junior members will not become senior members, so they should oppose the system using this justification. And assuming that legislators have a positive rate of time preference, they should prefer to have more power earlier in their careers to having it later. Following this line of reasoning, committee chairmanships and similar positions of power should go to junior members, not senior members. Yet junior members, despite their voting parity, give differential power to senior members by agreeing to the seniority system.

The seniority system can be explained by looking at political competition in a broader context. Legislators do compete among themselves during the legislative session, but they also compete against challengers to try to win reelection. The power attached to seniority gives junior members a disadvantage when they are in the legislature, but even the most junior member will have more seniority than any challenger on election day. Thus, if it is to the advantage of voters to have the most senior legislator possible, voters can always maximize the seniority of their representative by reelecting the incumbent. Therefore, the seniority system works to the benefit of even the most junior member of the legislature on election day, giving all legislators an incentive to abide by the seniority system.[21] The seniority system thus acts as a barrier to entry in political competition, and enhances the monopoly profits that legislators are able to receive for their services.

Political Competition

This discussion on the structure of political markets lends some insight into the nature of political competition. Traditional models of political competition depict competition as occurring between political parties. The purely competitive political model discussed earlier depicts candidates and parties adjusting their platforms so as to try to win a majority of the votes. In elections, a candidate from one party tends to run against a candidate from another party, and this party identification obscures the fact that typically an incumbent also will be running against an incumbent. The most significant dimension of political competition in this case is not between parties, but between incumbents and nonincumbents.

The organization of political representation sets up a system whereby incumbents do not compete directly with each other, and institutional developments over time, including the seniority system as an excellent example, have strengthened the advantages of incumbents. If party competition were more significant than the competition between incumbents and nonincumbents, then members of the minority party should want to lower barriers to entry to enhance the probability that their party could become the majority party. Yet when it comes time to choose between increasing or decreasing competitiveness, existing legislators from all parties invariably choose the option that reduces competitiveness. This provides evidence that competition between incumbents and nonincumbents is more significant than party competition.

This dimension of political competition is consistent with the model of government as a monopoly seller of legislative services as well. An abstract view of government as creator of public policy highlights party differences and pushes ideological concerns to the forefront, but public policies are created through the government production of legislation, and the legislature has an incentive to maximize its return from legislation. Government activity is essentially economic, with the legislature acting as the marketplace for political outcomes. The legislative cartel produces these outcomes, and when viewed in this way it is clear that there is a stronger tie among legislative members of different parties than there is among incumbent and nonincumbent members of the same party.

Needless to say, there is competition among parties, and members of one party would like to have more of their own party in the legislature because this enhances their ability to produce legislation. There is real competition among parties, just as there is competition among employees of the same firm who, for example, might want to have the most sales in order to get the biggest raise. But just as an economic model focusing on competition among employees of a single firm rather than competition among firms would miss the essential elements of the competitive process, so do political models which focus on party competition without looking at competition between incumbents and nonincumbents miss the key element of political competition.[22]

This point is important because models which focus on party competition overestimate the degree of political competition in a political system. When looking at political competition in the U.S. Congress, for example, one would overestimate the degree of competitiveness of one looked only at the degree of representation of various parties. While party membership may be split relatively evenly, since competition is not primarily between parties but between incumbents and nonincumbents, one would need to look at the degree to which nonincumbents are able to successfully compete. Incumbents win over 95 percent of the elections they enter, and the electoral safety of incumbents has been increasing over the decades. Thus, despite party representation, Congress is not a very competitive institution. This lack of competitiveness is what enables legislators to charge monopoly prices for their legislative services.

Government and the Profits from Government

In Chapter 3, the essential activity of government was identified as the exchange of protection for tribute. The government enforces the exchange by forcing individuals to give a share of what they produce to the government, and in exchange the government agrees not to harm them. If individuals do not pay government the tribute it asks for, then the government not only forces them to pay, but harms them in other ways as well, such as taking more tribute through "penalties," taking their assets in excess of the tribute originally demanded, and imprisoning them. Individuals may be able to escape detection and not pay tribute, but the government places additional costs on violators it does catch in order to give people an incentive to "voluntarily" comply. In this way, the government forces people to trade with it, exchanging protection for tribute.

This system has the advantage that, because the government's wealth comes from its citizens, the government has an incentive to protect its citizens in order to protect its source of income. Thus, the exchange of protection for tribute has a natural enforcement mechanism. The government wants to protect its citizens and create institutions under which they can be productive in order to enhance its own income. This does not necessarily imply that the government creates the most productive institutions possible, however, because the government as a monopolist has an incentive to charge monopoly prices for its services, which means restricting output.

One theme in international politics has been the violation of citizens' rights by their governments. The concept of government rights violations might be analyzed under the premise that government have an incentive to extend those rights to people that would allow them to be as productive as possible.[23] But the discussion in this chapter points out the incentives for governments to restrict the rights they extend to their citizens. The government has an incentive to charge monopoly prices for the rights that it grants, and monopoly prices can only be charged by restricting the quantity. Restricting the rights it grants to its citizens is a method by which the government can extract monopoly profits from its citizens.

Federalism and Cartels among Governments

A threat to the monopoly power of government is presented by competing governments. Intergovernmental competition for residents, and more directly, competition for tax base, can prevent governments from collecting monopoly prices for their output. Just as in the market, competition among suppliers takes away the suppliers' ability to charge monopoly prices. This is a prime reason for the desirability of a federal system of government, as well as a reason for producing governmental goods and services at the lowest level of government possible.

Local governments have an incentive to reduce intergovernmental competition in order to enhance their abilities to charge monopoly prices for their services. A cartel arrangement among local governments is a possibility, but as noted earlier, it is difficult to enforce a cartel agreement. One way that such enforcement might be accomplished is for the federal government to act as an enforcing agent. Local government activity through intergovernmental grants provides this possibility.[24]

Intergovernmental grants provide federal tax revenue for local programs, but with strings attached. Programs must be structured in a particular way to comply with federal requirements. Such programs enforce uniformity among local governments, which reduces intergovernmental competition. Since revenues are not raised from the local tax base, taxpayers cannot move to escape the cost of such programs. And since such programs are subsidized, localities have the incentive to participate in any programs for which they are eligible. Intergovernmental grants produce uniformity among local governments and prevent taxpayers from moving to escape the costs, so reduce intergovernmental competition.

Reduction in intergovernmental competition helps cartelize local governments, enabling them to reap monopoly profits from the sale of their services. Because it acts as the agent in the cartelizing process, the federal government can keep a share of the profit for itself. The federal government is paid for creating a cartel, and local governments benefit from being members of the cartel.

Justifications of such programs tend to center around externalities that prevent local governments from undertaking such programs in the absence of federal assistance, but from the point of view of localities, there is little reason to think they would want to participate unless the cartelization argument has some merit. Tax revenues come from people who live in localities whether they are paid in local taxes or federal taxes, and localities give up much control of the programs by having the federal government collect taxes from local residents only to return a portion in the form of intergovernmental grants. If such programs actually enhanced the value of living in the localities, intergovernmental competition would push the governments themselves to pursue the programs cooperatively without federal involvement. The fact that federal involvement is necessary is an indication that the programs lower – not raise – the value of living in the affected localities.

One could understand the externality argument with regard to explicitly redistributive programs, but programs to support schools, roads, wastewater treatment, and so forth, should enhance the value of living in communities. If externalities exist, intergovernmental competition should force communities to form associations among themselves to promote these projects that enhance the value of the communities. Such voluntary associations among communities could still be motivated by the desire to form cartels, but the fact that involvement by the federal government is necessary is strong evidence that the program is motivated by the desire to cartelize and share monopoly profits rather than to improve the quality of life in the affected communities.

Intergovernmental grants provide a method of cartelizing local governments in order to create monopoly profits in the production of government services. The cartel can benefit from monopoly pricing, and the federal government benefits by taking a share; that is, by selling the right to cartelize.

Regulation

Much government regulation can be viewed in the same framework as that just described for intergovernmental competition. Regulation in the marketplace serves as a barrier to entry, enabling those in the regulated industry to receive a degree of monopoly profit. This theory of regulation is well-established in the economics literature, so only needs to be outlined here.

The fundamental premise underlying what Stigler called the theory of economic regulation is that regulation can be used to produce benefits for those being regulated.[25] The benefits can be broadly classified as the creation of barriers to entry. A clear example is utility regulation, where the government grants one firm a monopoly and then regulates its service and price. While in theory such regulation could produce results that approach what would be produced in a competitive market, in practice the general public that is supposed to be served by regulation is rationally ignorant of the government's regulatory activities, while the regulated firms are special interests that have an incentive to become informed.[26] Thus, regulation creates a barrier to entry which allows those in the industry to earn a degree of monopoly profit.

Government licensing serves the same role. Doctors, accountants, realtors, and barbers, to mention a few practitioners, must be licensed by the state in order to practice. While the arguments favoring government control concern the public interest, government restriction into an occupation creates a clear barrier to entry, so must raise the incomes of those in the regulated professions. The public interest argument for regulation can be questioned,[27] but regardless of the benefits, such regulation creates a barrier to entry, so creates a larger return to those in the industry. Because the legislature has monopoly power in the creation of regulatory benefits, it can charge those who are regulated a monopoly price for the regulation. It is worth emphasizing that regardless of the benefits of regulation, the barrier to entry is valuable to those in the regulated industry or profession, so the government is in a position to extract payment for the service of creating the barrier to entry.

Just as regulation can be used to confer benefits to those being regulated, it can also be used as a tax.[28] Firms can be taxed in order to provide resources to carry out some government program, or regulations can require that firms carry out the government's program at the firms' expense. Just as firms are willing to pay for the benefits of barriers to entry, they are also willing to pay to avoid taxation by regulation. The government will balance off the demands of various interests in order to produce the profit-maximizing mix of regulation.[29]

The government can use its regulatory powers to create barriers to entry in markets, and these barriers create monopoly profits. Since the government itself has a monopoly on the creation of regulations, it can receive a monopoly payment in exchange for the creation of barriers to entry through regulation. This type of regulation gives some people the right to do certain things that others do not have the right to do. For example, the licensing of real estate agents means that unless a person passes a state examination, that person is not allowed to sell real estate. This barrier to entry increases the return to those who are allowed to sell real estate.

Note that the creation of barriers to entry is profitable to legislators only if the market for legislators is not perfectly competitive. Competition in the market for legislators would drive the return to the creation of barriers to entry to zero, taking away any incentive to create them. Thus, the greater the barriers to entry into the legislature, the more profitable the creation of barriers to entry into economic markets would be, so larger barriers to entry into the legislature should create more barriers to entry in economic markets.

Corruption

Corruption in government occurs when individuals are able to bribe government officials to allow those individuals to violate the law without punishment. For example, drug dealers might pay police officials to allow them to sell drugs without being arrested. They might even pay police to protect them as they engage in their business. Because dealing in drugs in this example is illegal, the supply of drugs is artificially restricted in the market, allowing the opportunity for monopoly profits for anyone who is able to enter this market with legal barriers to entry. The monopoly profits from selling in the restricted market provide the means by which those selling in the market can afford to pay corrupt officials.[30] Thus, corruption is another way in which government can profit from its legislative monopoly and its position as producer of protection.

What is the difference between corruption and regulation? In both cases, the government allows some individuals access to a restricted market, selling the privilege of access. Consider two concrete examples. In the case of drug dealers, most people are not allowed to sell drugs. Through corruption, the government protects the right of particular dealers to sell in the market, receiving monopoly profits, which are then shared with government officials. In the case of electric utilities, most people are not allowed to sell electricity. Through regulation, the government protects the rights of particular sellers to enter the market, receiving monopoly profits, which are shared with government officials. Corruption is just another form of regulation.

The most important difference between corruption and regulation is that regulation is a matter of public record. This can make a difference for two reasons. First, corrupt officials need not comprise the entire government. For example, individual policemen might be corrupted into protecting a drug dealer without informing the police chief or the legislature. In this case, those higher up in government are prevented from receiving some of the monopoly profits they could otherwise earn. Thus, higher officials have an incentive to prevent corruption in lower officials because corruption among lower officials reduces the potential return to being a higher official. Second, because regulation is a matter of public record, voters can see the monopoly profits and vote out legislators who produce overly burdensome regulation. With corruption, the costs are harder to detect and to attribute.

In a monolithic dictatorship where everyone in government acts as a perfect agent to the dictator, regulation and corruption will be indistinguishable. In both cases, people buy rights not available to the general public. Whether the restriction is the result of a private agreement with the government or is publicly announced is irrelevant. In some countries, bribes are necessary to do business. In democracies, voters try to hold public officials accountable for their actions in order to reduce their monopoly returns, which is why people in democracies prefer regulation to corruption.

In a federal system of government, one method of reducing corruption is to make crimes a violation of the laws of several levels of government. The risk of corruption at one level of law enforcement is thereby increased because of the potential of being caught by other law enforcement agencies. For example, local police might be bribed to protect the business of a drug dealer, but if dealing drugs is also a violation of federal law, the local police run the risk of being discovered by federal agents.[31] In law enforcement, as in other economic ventures, competition lessens the ability to reap monopoly profits.

The Secret Ballot

One way to purchase legislative outcomes that can produce monopoly rents is to purchase the election of legislators. Through the buying of votes, individuals can get their candidates elected. The candidates will be well aware of who paid for their election, so will act in order to further the interests of those who paid for them. The purchase of votes is relatively easy when votes are a matter of public record. The secret ballot puts a major impediment in the way of purchasing election outcomes, because there is no way for the purchaser of the vote to know for sure that those who were paid to vote a certain way actually did so. Even a voter who is willing to sell his vote has no way to prove that he voted as instructed.

Without a secret ballot, a market would develop in payment for legislative outcomes through the buying of votes for public office. A secret ballot suppresses that market, so gives rise to the existence of lobbying, logrolling, and the special interest politics that characterizes contemporary legislatures. Such lobbying would be unnecessary if legislative outcomes could be bid for ahead of time through a market for votes in the general election. Under the secret ballot, it is unclear who owns the right to political outcomes, so through lobbying, the bidding process takes place after legislators have been elected rather than during their election. The special interest model of government is built directly on the institution of the secret ballot.[32]

The secret ballot enhances the monopoly power of legislators because they are not committed to particular courses of action as a result of having their election purchased directly by some interest group. This leaves them open to bidding during the legislative session for the production of legislative outcomes for special interests. Thus, under the current system, legislators can capture the profits in the market for legislation, whereas if votes for public office could be bought and sold, voters would capture the profit through the selling of their votes.

Conclusion

This chapter has covered many diverse topics, but all with a common theme. There are barriers to entry into the government, giving those in government monopoly power over the protection of its citizens and over the production of legislation. Those in government profit by selling the services of government at monopoly prices. This chapter has discussed some of the ways in which the government can create barriers to entry, can restrict its output, and can thereby extract monopoly profits from its activities.

The primary dimension of political competition, following this line of reasoning, is the competition between incumbents and nonincumbents.

Incumbents – those currently in power – have an incentive to form a cartel to keep others from sharing in the power of government. Models of political competition often depict competition as occurring between parties, and indeed, when incumbents face nonincumbents in elections, the election is between individuals of different parties. But to focus on their party differences is to miss the more significant aspect of political competition, between those in power and those trying to gain power. Chapter 7 begins by discussing this competition for political power, and then goes on to examine the political institutions and exchange processes that produce political outcomes.

7 Institutions and Exchange

Government power is profitable to those who have it because they can create barriers to entry and charge monopoly prices for their services. The government's exchange of protection for tribute creates a situation where monopoly will tend to emerge, as does the government's ability to create legislation. One could imagine an ideal setting where, following a model like Tiebout,[1] competitive governments would eliminate any monopoly profit, but the government's exchange of protection for tribute naturally leads toward a concentration of power that gives rise to monopoly profits.[2] The lure of monopoly profits from government power means that people will have an incentive to compete for the right to have that monopoly power.[3]

Chapter 6 touched on this competition by noting the rivalry between incumbents and nonincumbents in democracies. Incumbents attempt to hold on to their share of monopoly power while challengers compete for a share. This chapter picks up where Chapter 6 left off by examining how institutions and exchange are able to produce political outcomes in democratic governments. Institutions and exchange are complementary ways of producing political outcomes. Institutions specify the decision-making process that will be followed to lead to an outcome. For example, in the United States, a president is selected by going though a primary system which leads to a party convention and then a general election. Under different sets of institutions, a different outcome could be produced. Exchange is also an important element in the production of political outcomes. The logrolling and vote trading the occurs in legislatures is exchange just like economic exchange and can be analyzed in the same way. When large numbers of individuals participate in the political decision-making process, institutions tend to have the dominant effect on the outcome, whereas in a small number setting, exchange has more to do with the outcome than institutions.

Before getting into the details of institutions and exchange in democratic governments, the chapter will discuss dictatorships and democracies. While dictatorships could be discussed at great length, this chapter only points in the direction which a discussion of dictatorship would depart from democracy, using the concept of monopoly government as the common point of departure. Then the chapter discusses the factors that produce political agreement, and explains why consensus is more readily produced in the private sector than the public sector. When there is not complete consensus, the chapter then continues to explain the role of institutions and exchange in producing political outcomes where consensus does not initially exist.

Dictatorship and Democracy

Chapter 6 explained how monopoly profits are produced for those who have government power, and how those in power can form a cartel to divide the profits and to stifle competition among cartel members. If monopoly profits are the goal, however, a particular individual can receive far more in the way of monopoly profits by becoming a dictator rather than sharing those profits with everyone else in government. Furthermore, a dictator does not have to worry about other cartel members cheating on the cartel, and does not have to devise methods for sharing the monopoly profits. While a single individual could do better as a dictator than one of a group of legislators, competition for the right to be the dictator lowers the probability that an individual can retain a dictatorship, and also uses resources to protect the dictatorship that otherwise could be used more productively.

Government produces monopoly profits and therefore generates competition for those profits. The most obvious way for an outsider to gain control of government is to overthrow the existing government and form a new government in its place. Revolution is one way to compete for government power. In a dictatorship, revolution is the only way an outsider can claim a share of the government's monopoly. One way for a dictator to preserve monopoly power is to produce a line of succession that receives popular support. For example, if the citizens of a country believe that the dictator is appointed by god and is an agent of god, it will be difficult for a challenger to mount popular support against the dictator. This method of preserving a dictatorship is as old as antiquity and as recent as the Islamic revolution in Iran. A monarchy which provides a hereditary line of succession can help preserve a dictatorship also, although a monarchy of this type is more open to challenge than one that is accepted as divinely ordained.

Even with general acceptance, a dictatorship is naturally more open to challenge than a democracy because the only way a political aspirant can reap the power of government is to overthrow the existing government. This means that resources must be devoted to military and police power to create a disincentive to those that might want to overthrow the government. Resources devoted to this protection might be used for more productive purposes in a democratic government. A wise and benevolent dictator might be able to allocate resources efficiently enough to make up for the expense of protecting the dictatorship, making the benevolent dictatorship more effective overall than a democracy, but this does not overrule the point that in a dictatorship the only way to take over government power is revolution, so dictatorships must devote more resources to the protection of the government.

The dictator needs to be protected, and those who protect the dictatorship are likely to share in the monopoly profits as well. Otherwise, they could do better by installing themselves as dictator and keeping the monopoly profits they were previously protecting for someone else. Military coups are a natural threat to a dictator, but even in the military dictatorships that result, others in the military must be paid for their loyalty or they will have an incentive to install yet another dictator. Even a dictatorship produces a coalition of individuals who share in the monopoly profits rather than giving all of the monopoly profits to one individual. Under many circumstances, the present value of a share of the profits of government could be higher as one of a group of legislators in a democracy than as a dictator.[4]

In democracies, political institutions are substitutes for destructive competition for power. Individuals can devote resources to running election campaigns rather than to mounting revolutions. In the most general setting, one can view individuals outside government devoting resources to the goal of obtaining government power. They can use these resources to arm themselves to violently overthrow the existing government, or if there is the opportunity, they can use these resources to mount political campaigns for elective office. Because of the alternative to revolution that exists in democracies, the government requires fewer resources to protect itself from revolution. In this way, democratic political institutions can be viewed as a way of conserving the government's resources. Challenges will always be mounted against those who hold government power. By creating institutions whereby such challenges can occur nonviolently, political institutions serve as a substitute for revolution.[5]

Looked at in another way, political leaders can attempt to extract all possible monopoly profits from their citizens, but to do so reduces the perceived legitimacy of government and makes the government more vulnerable to being overthrown. By designing institutions to share monopoly profits with the general population, the return to government is lowered, but the risk of being overthrown is also lowered. There is a risk versus return trade-off that allows the profitability of governing to be reduced in exchange for making leadership positions more secure.[6]

Agreement in Politics and in the Marketplace

Democratic political institutions might exist as a method for reducing the threat of violent internal challenges to government, but the nominal purpose of these institutions is to produce political decisions. Political decision-making is easy when there is a consensus, but often in political matters there is disagreement, and political decision-making is the means by which a decision is produced when individuals disagree. In the marketplace, in contrast, decision-making does take place by consensus. Individuals voluntarily agree to buy and sell goods, and nobody is forced to engage in a trade against his or her will. The competition that is often referred to in the marketplace is really cooperation. No trades take place unless everyone agrees.

Conversely, political cooperation is often competition. An issue decided as one individual wants goes against the desires of another. Compromise means that none of the participants get what they really want. Majority rule politics is built to work this way, since once a majority coalition is formed on an issue, they can force the minority to abide by the wishes of the majority.[7] It is worth examining why such agreement can take place in the market when it typically does not take place in politics. The following section deals with this question.

Lindahl Equilibrium and Agreement

This section considers a political decision that plainly is also an economic decision. Three individuals will decide how much of a public good to produce for their consumption. The decision-making process will be explained with the assistance of Figure 7.1. In the figure, three individuals have demands D1, D2, and D3, for a public good, defined as a good for which the consumption by one individual does not reduce the amount that can be consumed by the others.[8] An example might be a radio broadcast signal. If one individual turns on her radio, that will not prevent any other individual from listening to the same signal, so the consumption by one individual does not affect the consumption of the others.

The curve labelled MC is the marginal cost of the good, which for simplicity is assumed to be constant. The curve labelled ΣD is the vertical summation of the individuals' demands, which is the market demand for the good. Thus, at quantity Q^*, the sum of the demands equals the marginal cost of the good, which is the Pareto optimal amount of the

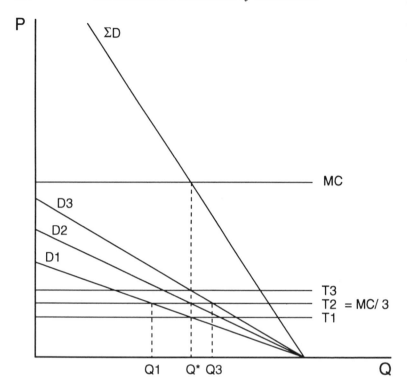

Figure 7.1   Lindahl Equilibrium

good to produce. If economic efficiency is used as the benchmark, then Q* is the amount of the good that should be produced.

Note that MC intersects the P axis above any of the individual demand curves, which means that if left to their own devices, no individual has an incentive to produce the good only for herself. Collectively, though, the three individuals could get together to produce the good and all could be better off. This is an ideal setting for collective action. Assume that this good will be produced by government.

One obvious way in which the costs could be divided for the good would be to have each individual pay an equal share. Thus, each individual's tax price would be T2, which is MC/3. Individuals would prefer the quantity of the good at which their tax price intersects their demand for the good, so individual 1 would prefer Q1, individual 2 would prefer Q*, and individual 3 would prefer Q3. The coincidence that individual 2 prefers the optimal quantity is a result of D1 and D3 being drawn symmetrically around D2, and will not in general occur.[9] With equal tax shares, consider now the political decision-making process that will lead to a determination of how much of the good to produce.

In the simplest case, one could call upon the median voter model, which concludes that the outcome of majority rule politics is the outcome most preferred by the median voter. This would produce Q* of the good, even though D1 would prefer less and D3 would prefer more. Again, note that the median voter's preference is the optimal level of output only by coincidence. It is easy to see that if the median voter's tax share were a little higher or a little lower, the median voter would prefer less or more of the good.

In a political setting more complex than that of the median voter model, it is unclear what the outcome of the political decision-making process will be. Since D1 prefers Q1, D2 prefers Q*, and D3 prefers Q3, there is no consensus, and other possibilities include two of the individuals compromising at some other level of output, or one of the individuals using the political process, through lobbying, legal objections, and other political activity, to stall the process or perhaps produce that individual's most preferred outcome.

Whatever the outcome, however, there will not be a consensus, so even if Q* is produced, individuals 1 and 3 still have an incentive to enter the political process to alter the outcome in the next period. One way to build consensus on the quantity of output is to alter tax shares so that each individual pays a tax share proportional to that individual's share of the total demand for the good. If D1 is charged tax share T1, D2 is charged T2, and D3 is charged T3, then given those tax shares, all individuals will agree that Q* is the output they most prefer. This condition where all individuals have marginal tax prices equal to their marginal valuation of the good is called Lindahl equilibrium.[10]

For a public good, the efficiency condition is that $\Sigma D = MC$, and the way in which the cost is divided among the users of the good is irrelevant as long as they can gain access at no charge, as is the case with goods like national defense, interstate highways, and many other public goods. Lindahl equilibrium is but one of the many possible ways that taxes can be shared if the efficient level of output is produced. Note that since each individual's demand equals the individual's tax price, adding them implies that the sum of the demands must equal the sum of the tax prices, producing efficiency. But while Lindahl equilibrium is sufficient to produce the optimal output, it is not necessary.[11]

On careful examination, there are few economic factors to recommend Lindahl equilibrium over other ways to share the tax burden,[12] but there is an important political factor recommending Lindahl equilibrium. When the tax burden is divided in this way, everyone agrees on the level of output that should be produced. Thus, rather than having conflict in the political process, Lindahl equilibrium produces consensus.

Individuals still have an incentive under Lindahl equilibrium to try to get lower tax shares, but this is always true no matter how taxes are divided. On this ground, Lindahl equilibrium fares no worse than other methods of dividing taxes.[13] Its advantage is that it creates political consensus on the level of output to be produced. With Lindal tax shares, individuals will unanimously agree to the optimal level of output.

This unanimous agreement created in Lindahl equilibrium corresponds closely to the unanimity that is associated with the ideas of Knut Wicksell.[14] In contemporary literature, Wicksell's name is primarily associated with the unanimous political decision-making rule while Lindahl is associated with the assignment of tax shares, but a reading of their original works shows that both were interested in similar problems and proposed similar solutions. Lindahl equilibrium, like Wicksellian unanimity, focuses on how to divide the costs of public sector projects in such a way as to gain consensus for government activity. In summary, if disagreement exists regarding the quantity of public sector output that should be produced, tax prices can be adjusted to produce a Lindahl equilibrium in which everyone agrees on the amount to be produced.

This idea of consensus is very different from the simple democratic view of government. In a democracy, where the guiding principle is majority rule, government follows the will of the majority. In the Lindahl-Wicksell view of government by consensus, proposals for government activity are adjusted until there is a general consensus regarding the course of government action.

Why is Compromise Necessary in Politics?

Many models of democratic decision-making are developed under the premise that people have varied political demands, and that compromise is necessary in order to produce public policy. Descriptive models of the political process have this focus, but it is also very much a part of spatial models of democracy popularized by Downs[15] and used as a foundation for a wide variety of formal models of political decision-making.[16] A simple depiction of such a model appears in Figure 7.2, where X and Y represent two different public goods, and points further from the origin denote greater quantities of the goods.

Three individuals like those from the model in the previous section have

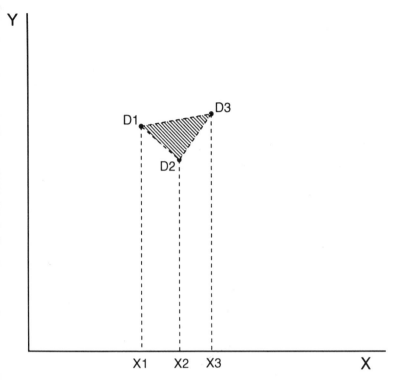

Figure 7.2   A Two-Dimensional Political Issue Space

demands for these two goods such that individual 1 would most prefer the combination of X and Y denoted by point D1, individual 2 would most prefer D2, and individual 3 would most prefer D3. Looking at good X alone, the dashed lines indicate that the individuals' most preferred quantities of the goods are X1, X2, and X3. A simplifying assumption can be made that individuals prefer points closer to their most preferred point to points further away, so individuals will have circular indifference curves around their most preferred points. Looking only at the X axis, individual preferences for X are arrayed in the same manner as they were for the good in Figure 7.1, so figure 7.2 extends the previous model to two dimensions.

With circular indifference curves, straight lines drawn between any two of the points D1, D2, and D3 are contract curves between those two individuals. The shaded area inside the three contract curves has sometimes been referred to as the Pareto optimal region because outside that region, it is possible to move to a point that makes all individuals better off, but inside the region, any move has to make at least one individual worse off.

This type of model has been analyzed extensively. The general line of analysis has been to see under what conditions an equilibrium outcome can be produced under various political institutions. The purpose of this section is not to further analyze political decision-making under this structure of preferences, but rather to question the assumption of an underlying fixed set of most preferred political outcomes.[17]

The general characteristic of the lack of a unique equilibrium under majority rule was known before there was extensive analysis of theoretical voting models.[18] Such an equilibrium exists in the special case where individuals can be paired so that one individual's most preferred point is at the intersection of every contract curve connecting the pairs,[19] but in general, no majority rule equilibrium exists in the absence of additional institutional constraints that can produce one. Institutional constraints and their effect on political outcomes will be discussed later in the chapter, under the assumption that most preferred points like D1, D2, and D3 in Figure 7.2 are given. However, the previous section demonstrated that these points can be changed by altering tax prices.

The reason why D1 prefers X1, D2 prefers X2, and D3 prefers X3 in Figure 7.2 is that those quantities correspond with the points at which their marginal tax prices intersect their demands for the good. There is not consensus since each individual prefers a different amount of the good, but if D1's tax price for X were lowered and D3's were raised, both of their most preferred quantities would move toward X2. Some adjustment of individual 2's taxes might be necessary, but by following the model depicted in Figure 7.1, individuals' tax shares could be adjusted for X and Y so that they all preferred the same amount of both goods, and the Pareto optimal region would shrink to a point. By adjusting tax shares, everyone could agree on how much of all goods should be produced.

The shaded region in Figure 7.2 is Pareto optimal only under a binding constraint that tax shares cannot be altered. From an economic standpoint, the region is not Pareto optimal. Calling it Pareto optimal would be the same as fixing tax shares at T2 in Figure 7.1 and then declaring any level of output between Q1 and Q3 to be in the Pareto optimal region. Clearly, there is an optimal level of output Q* in Figure 7.1, and likewise, there is a single X,Y combination that represents the Pareto optimal level of output for the two goods in Figure 7.2. Thus, as the term is normally used in economics, there is a single Pareto optimal point, not identified in Figure 7.2, rather than a Pareto optimal region.

In short, the situation depicted in Figure 7.2 exists only with fixed tax shares which are not Lindahl tax shares. If everyone was charged Lindahl tax shares for each public good, all individuals would have the same most preferred point. This section is titled with a question: Why is compromise necessary in politics? Compromise is necessary because all dimensions of public sector output are not priced with Lindahl prices. If they were, there would be unanimous agreement regarding the output of the public sector.

While Lindahl pricing is a theoretical possibility, it is a practical impossibility given current political systems.[20] The Lindahl model can nevertheless be used as a guideline for generating politically feasible outcomes. More consensus can be generated by raising the tax prices of big beneficiaries of political proposals and lowering the tax prices of those who receive few benefits. From the standpoint of economic efficiency the distribution of tax shares is not important, but from the political standpoint of building consensus, movement toward Lindahl equilibrium can enhance the political viability of a proposal.

Cycles and Stability

Compromise is necessary in politics because prices of political policies are not Lindahl prices. If they were, there would be no disagreement. But because there is disagreement, political institutions are used to produce an outcome through collective choice. There is a large literature of formal models of the collective decision-making process, and an important issue of analysis in that literature is whether democratic decision-making processes generate stable and deterministic outcomes, and if so, what factors cause those outcomes to be stable and deterministic.

The sophisticated analysis of the theoretical instability in majority rule voting has done much to illustrate the general conditions under which instability can be produced, but the underlying cause of instability is fundamentally the same one Arrow popularized in his 1951 book.[21] To see the mechanism, consider three individuals, 1, 2, and 3, who rank alternatives A, B, and C, such that their rankings are 1(ABC), 2(BCA), and 3(CAB), where the alternatives in parentheses are the preference oaederings of the individuals preceding the parentheses. As in Arrow's illustration, a cyclical majority is produced where by majority rule, A defeats B, C defeats A, and B defeats C.

While the underlying mechanism is well-understood, there is not general agreement on its significance to majority rule decision-making. In a political sense, stability could be observed if cycles took a long time, but there would not be a determinate equilibrium. This indeterminacy

Table 7.1   Cyclical preferences with a possible efficient outcome

		Individual		
		1	2	3
Dollar Value of	A	$1000	$1	$2
Project to Individual	B	$2	$3	$1
	C	$1	$2	$3

in majority rule stands in stark contrast to the uniqueness and stability of competitive market equilibrium.[22] The reason for the indeterminacy is that simple majority voting does not allow individuals to express their intensities of preferences. Just stating the problem does little to solve it, though, because it is not easy to design a voting system that does account for intensities in a consistent way.[23] This problem can be solved, however, if it is possible to take account of intensities outside of the voting system.

Consider again the cyclical majority situation described at the beginning of this section. If all individuals place an equal value on their rankings (e.g., all value their most preferred alternative $3, their second most preferred $2, and their least preferred $1), then the issue is purely distributional. From an economic as well as a political standpoint, the outcome is indeterminate because the social value of all alternatives is the same. A more interesting case arises when the alternatives have different values. Consider the preferences listed in Table 7.1, which retains the same preference orderings as the example above, but associates a dollar value to each individual's preference for each alternative. In this situation, which option will be chosen by majority rule?

If the assumptions in the cyclical majority model hold and all individuals vote for the alternative they most prefer, in pairwise competition, the result is indeterminate. The result depends upon the order in which the alternatives are considered. However, if individuals are able to bargain with one another, alternative A will surely be chosen. Individual 1 can pay one of the other voters to gain a majority in favor of A, or can trade a vote on a future issue. If logrolling is possible, no cycle results; instead, the alternative most highly valued by the group will be the outcome of majority rule.[24]

Formal models of majority voting have done much to identify the conditions under which majority rule does not yield a determinate outcome, but these models examine voting in situations where voters are unable to bargain among themselves as a part of the process. When exchange is possible, voters face the same incentives as do participants in any market. In the absence of transactions costs, the highest valued alternative will be selected by majority rule because that alternative generates the largest surplus that can be divided among the voters.

Large and Small Number Settings

In the preceding section, the same configuration of preferences was used to generate two different majority rule results. When voters simply vote their preferences without exchange, the outcome of majority rule is indeterminate in the absence of more information on the electoral process. When exchange is possible, the most highly valued alternative will be selected by majority rule, even when the configuration of preferences would generate cycles in the absence of exchange. Without transactions costs, exchange among voters produces a unique and stable majority rule equilibrium, and majority rule selects the alternative most highly valued by the trading group.

This conclusion is nothing more than the Coase theorem applied to political exchange. Following Coase,[25] in the absence of transactions costs, the allocation of resources is independent of the assignment of property rights. When applied to majority voting, this implies a great deal about the importance of political institutions. With impediments to exchange among voters, institutions can play a significant role in determining the outcome of a political decision. Even this statement may not go far enough, because if preference rankings imply indeterminacy, the institutional structure of the decision-making process will determine the outcome.[26] However, if there is no impediment to exchange among voters, they will trade until reaching the outcome most valued to the voting group, regardless of what specific institutions govern the decision-making process.

One of the most important factors determining the feasibility of exchange among voters is the size of the voting group. Thus, the two cases above can be named the large number case and the small number case. With large numbers, voters will not be able to bargain among themselves, so election outcomes will be dependent upon the specific political institutions which govern the decision. With small numbers, voters can exchange among themselves to produce the outcome most highly valued by the group, regardless of the specific institutions under which they decide.[27]

Stability in General Elections and in the Legislature

The United States is governed by a representative democracy, so the decision-making process can be divided into two stages. At the first stage, representatives are elected in a general election of all voters, and in the second stage, this representative body makes the actual policy decisions. The general election, in which millions of voters participate by casting secret ballots, corresponds to the large number case described above, because exchange among voters is not feasible. Political decisions made by the legislature correspond to the small number case because there are few individuals involved in the decision-making process, making exchange among voters feasible.

Many public choice models explore the mechanisms that facilitate vote trading,[28] so it is unnecessary to argue that such exchange takes place. Extensive bargaining takes place to determine what issues actually will be voted on, providing every legislator easy entry into the bargaining process. Because there are many issues to be voted on, each representative has a stock of votes that can be traded, which further facilitates exchange. And because votes are a matter of public record, representatives find it easy to monitor the exchange process to make sure they actually received the votes they were promised from other representatives.

The doctrine of continuous dealings enforces the exchange process. Legislators must negotiate in order to produce legislation that is most valuable to themselves, and they must keep their promises if they expect to be able to engage in future exchange. Thus, they have an incentive to bargain, and they have an incentive to honor any agreements they make. Within the legislature, a market exists in which votes are the medium of exchange. Transactions costs are low, so the outcome of majority voting in the legislature is the one that is most valuable to the voters, the voters in this case being the legislators.

This characterization implies that specific political institutions are .of little importance to the outcome of legislative exchange. Some institutions might imply more transactions costs than others, but when exchange is possible, resources should tend to flow to their highest valued uses. The committee system, seniority, and electoral safety are but a few important factors that determine bargaining strength and give some degree of property rights over legislative outcomes. But following the Coase theorem, these institutional factors will have income effects, but not substitution effects. Because bargaining costs are low in the legislature, the legislature will produce outcomes that its members value most highly, independent of specific institutional details.

This does not imply that the outcome will be the most valuable from a social standpoint, because everyone in the society is not a part of the legislative bargaining process. The special interest theory of government, for example, argues that legislators benefit from special interest legislation.[29] The implication is that the legislature will pass more special interest legislation than is socially optimal, even though legislation will be optimal considering only the preferences of the legislators. The outcome is not socially optimal because most voters are not a part of the legislative bargaining process. Other writers have argued that legislators benefit from maintaining a consistent ideological reputation independent of the interests of their constituents.[30] Following this literature, voting may be more ideologically motivated than would be socially optimal.[31] Whatever outcome is most highly valued by legislators will be produced through political exchange, but the outcome most highly valued by legislators is not necessarily socially optimal.

In contrast to legislative decisions, general elections are characterized by voters who do behave much as theoretical voting models posit. They vote for the alternatives they most prefer, and do not have the ability to bargain with other voters to shape the outcome of the election. As a result, voter behavior will more closely correspond to the assumptions of formal voting models in general elections than in legislatures.

Formal voting models have analyzed a wide variety of election systems, but in American politics, elections involving large numbers of voters are limited primarily to the selection of the representatives who make legislative decisions.[32] In such elections, institutional constraints may create the appearance of stability, for example, by having relatively infrequent elections, by creating devices that enhance the probability of incumbents to be reelected, and by enforcing a certain sequence of choice through the primary system. Stability in this sense is not an indication of determinacy, however, and the outcome that emerges from a general election might be the result of a chance interaction of candidates and institutional constraints. After the fact, some result is produced, but the end result is not the equilibrium result of a determinate process.[33]

Formal voting models offer some guidance for understanding general elections. The median voter model may be descriptive because general elections have a limited number of candidates with well-defined positions. If they can be ranked on a continuum from political left to right such that the preferences of voters are single-peaked, then the model seems to apply. While this characterization is not unreasonable, the model has not developed much beyond where Downs left it in 1957. If the issue space is multidimensional, cycles in the manner that McKelvey described would be possible, except that candidates are not likely to be able to change their platforms in a manner that conforms with that model. The purpose of this section is not to develop a model of general elections, however, but to argue that the assumptions of voter behavior in formal voting models apply to general elections with large numbers of voters, so if indeterminacy exists under majority rule, it is most likely to manifest itself there.

This section concludes that majority rule legislative decisions will be characterized by a unique, stable, determinate equilibrium that produces the outcome most highly valued by the legislative body. The result is produced not by majority rule itself, but by the political exchange that precedes voting. Because exchange among voters is not feasible in general elections, general elections are most likely to be characterized by the indeterminacy described in formal voting models.

The American Constitution

Formal voting models have tended to focus narrowly on specific types of elections with specific assumed characteristics. Understanding the operation of specific types of voting procedures is important, but it is also important to step back from specific assumed conditions in elections to look at how these models apply to political institutions in the real world. In the United States, general elections are held to elect representatives, who then – in a small group setting – produce specific legislation. General elections take place in a large group setting while legislative decisions are made by small groups.

If there is indeterminacy in the political process, it is in the large group setting where voters cannot exchange among themselves to produce political decisions. Thus, there may be indeterminacy in the selection of representatives. This is a popular argument in politics. For example, in 1976 Reagan argued that he should be his party's nominee for president because he could beat Carter while Ford could not. When Reagan was not nominated, then as Reagan predicted, Carter beat Ford in 1976. When Ford did not enter the 1980 race, Reagan got the nomination and beat Carter. Many things changed from 1976 to 1980, so this is not proof of a cyclical majority, but it does suggest that a combination of personalities, platforms, and political institutions can shape the outcome of general elections as much as voter preferences. More fundamentally, one could speculate that candidates like Carter, Reagan, and Dukakis, who were nominated under the primary system, would have been unlikely to have been chosen as their party nominees if party leaders selected candidates at the party conventions as they did decades ago. The point is, political institutions can have important effects on political outcomes when bargaining among voters is not possible.

The possibility of indeterminacy in general elections can have beneficial effects. Buchanan has argued that the possibility of cyclical majorities in the election of candidates can help ensure that a permanent majority cannot institute itself through majority rule to exploit a permanent minority.[34] As a counterexample, consider the situation in Ireland where a permanent majority of Protestants has caused substantial political turmoil between them and the minority Catholic population.

In the intent of the American political system, contrary to the Downsian model, general elections do not determine policy, but determine who will be members of the legislature that will determine policy. Indeterminacy in the system that selects policymakers will not necessarily produce indeterminacy in the resulting policies. To the contrary, as Buchanan suggests, such indeterminacy can provide turnover that can be beneficial to the operation of the political system. The possibility of indeterminacy in general elections does suggest, however, that decisions made by direct voter referenda could be a product of political institutions and agenda control rather than being a statement of voter preferences.

These conclusions which apply to majority rule in general elections do not apply to decisions made by legislatures because legislatures are small groups which can bargain to the outcome that is optimal for them. Specific political institutions are less important in legislatures because members can bargain around them. If legislators have motivations that are associated with the office, such as the reelection motive, then the indeterminacy that could characterize general elections will not carry over to public policy. The Coase theorem will apply to the legislature as a policy-making body, and the political process will produce a stable and determinate set of public policies.

Conclusion

This chapter has focused on the similarities and differences between decision-making processes in the market and in politics. The work of Kenneth Arrow has been influential in both areas, and an interesting point of departure is to look at the different conclusions he arrived at regarding market and political processes. Arrow was instrumental in demonstrating the uniqueness and stability of competitive equilibrium in the market, yet opened his book, *Social Choice and Individual Values*, with a demonstration that majority rule cannot be counted on to produce a unique or stable equilibrium outcome. The difference lies in the fact that the market accounts for differences in intensities of preferences, whereas the political decision-making processes that do not generate unique stable outcomes do not account for preference intensities.

If the amount of a public good that is to be produced is voted on, voters will in general have different opinions regarding how much of the good should be produced. This gives rise to the indeterminacies of political decision-making. However, if all voters are charged Lindahl tax prices, they will agree on the amount to be produced. Thus, in theory, tax shares can be adjusted to produce agreement, and if tax shares were adjusted in this way, preferences for public sector output would be structured so that the Pareto optimal allocation of resources would be unanimously agreed upon. The information required to set Lindahl taxes makes this alternative infeasible in practice, but it is possible to see in theory the cause of political instability. It is also possible to see that Lindahl pricing would eliminate any indeterminacy in political outcomes and would allocate resources efficiently.

Public sector decisions can be broken down into two general classes: those made by small groups and those made by large groups. In small groups where logrolling, vote-trading, or side payments are possible, models of economic exchange apply directly to the political decision-making process, and the outcome of political decision-making will tend to be optimal for those in the decision-making group. Because trade can take place, a market will develop in votes – or in other valuable assets used for side payments – and because the group is small, the Coase theorem will apply and the group will allocate the resources over which they have political power in the manner that is most valuable for those in the decision-making group. Creating the most valuable political output means that there will be more surplus for the members of the group to divide.

Some literature on the subject has drawn an analogy between political decision-making and market exchange, but when analyzing decision-making in small groups, simply calling it an analogy is not strong enough. Political decision-making under these circumstances is exchange in the market for legislation, and votes are the currency used in the market.[35] Models of economic exchange apply because political decision-making in small groups is, in fact, economic exchange.

In large groups, exchange is not possible, so political institutions assume more importance in determining the outcome of the political decision-making process. In small groups, the group can bargain around any institutional constraints, whereas in large groups, different institutions can lead the same group of individuals to different outcomes. Institutions are important determinants of the political decisions of large groups, whereas in small groups they act to impede or facilitate exchange.

The next chapter builds upon the distinction between large groups and small groups, as well as the notions of political competition and barriers to entry that were discussed in Chapter 6, to discuss the evolution of political constitutions. Constitutions are the rules by which the government makes its decisions and are a constraint on those in government. Constitutions are subject to change in a predictable way, however, which is the subject of Chapter 8.

8 Constitutional Evolution

The economic foundation of government is the exchange of protection for tribute. Without this exchange, life would be, in the words of Hobbes, nasty, brutish, and short. Even theoretical models of anarchy rely on some organized institutions to provide protection for payment, although anarchists do not call their institutions government.[1] In the real world, there are two extreme possibilities under which government could be formed, as well as a broad middle ground between the extremes. On one extreme, individuals from another society could forcibly take over a society and impose a government on the society they conquered. At the other extreme, the individuals within a society could agree to form a government and write a constitution – a social contract – that is agreed to by everyone, and that provides the rules under which the new government would operate. In the broad middle ground, an internal revolution could replace the existing governmental structure with one favored by the revolutionaries. Revolutions might be relatively broad-based and popularly supported, like the successful American revolution and the unsuccessful Confederate revolution, or they might be as narrowly based as a military coup. In any case, some constitution will be formed that, explicitly or implicitly, provides the rules under which government will operate.

In the case where government is forced upon a society by individuals outside that society, one would expect that the constitution would be written in such a way as to provide the sale of protection at monopoly prices. The government could expand its scope of business, following the analysis from Chapter 6 on monopoly in government, to regulation, the establishment of import and export regulations, and the production of public goods, all of which could be produced at monopoly prices. The primary advantage of conquest is not the immediate plunder that can be undertaken by the conquering country, but rather the production of governmental services over the conquered territory, which can be sold at monopoly prices.

Even in the case where the constitution is forcibly imposed, it will be easier to enforce if it generates the impression of agreement. Rules that people agree to are easier to enforce than those on which there is not agreement. Chapter 10, on the concept of agreement, discusses this idea more thoroughly, and considers ways in which governments generate the impression of agreement with their terms. In cases where individuals within a society form a government and write a constitution, agreement is more explicit and the constitution conforms more closely to the ideal of a social contract. This chapter assumes that a constitution is developed under ideal circumstances, and then examines the way in which the terms of the constitution could be expected to evolve over time.

Constitutions as a Constraint on Monopoly Power

Governments have the potential to reap monopoly profits from their citizens. Individuals can and do compete for a share of the potential monopoly profits generated by government. In the writing of a constitution, one individual might try to impose a constitution on others. But, as argued in Chapter 7, the governmental monopoly is difficult for one individual to maintain, and with many individuals competing, the chance for one particular individual to control government is small. One alternative to to create a constitution before selecting the government. The constitution can then be used to constrain the government, limiting the power of those who eventually gain political power. After the fact, those individuals who control government will be worse off with the constraint, but before the fact when it is uncertain who will gain political power, the constitution can protect all individuals from the tyranny of monopoly government.

The creation of a constitution in an idealized setting can be depicted in Figure 8.1, using the framework developed in Chapter 3. Curve CC′ is a utility possibilities frontier for two individuals in a simplified model of society. Point A shows the level of well-being they would expect under anarchy. With cooperation and an agreed-upon structure of rights, as discussed in Chapter 3, they could reach a point on CC′. The purpose of writing a constitution is to produce the mutual benefits that could be generated in the move from A to CC′.

Before the actual terms of the constitution are agreed upon, there is a range of possible outcomes that might be produced. Both individuals could expect to be better off under the constitution than in a state of anarchy, but it is not clear ahead of time exactly how the mutual benefits of the constitution might be divided among the individuals. If individual X were a good negotiator, the terms of the agreement might locate the outcome near point b, whereas point a would be more likely if individual Y were a better negotiator. As in Chapter 3, points a and b are assumed to be the limits within which individuals expect the outcome of the process to fall. The individuals would accept outcomes in the segment ab, but would revolt against outcomes not in that segment.

In an ideal setting, the constitution would be written behind a veil of

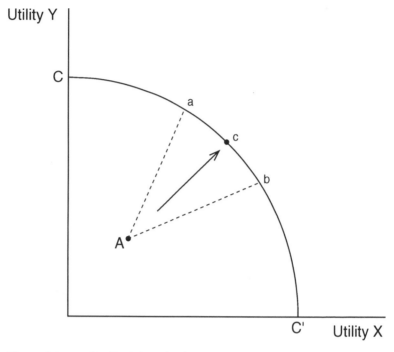

Figure 8.1   An Idealized Constitution

uncertainty where individuals do not know their own particular circumstances at the time that the constitution is created.[2] While individuals will know many of their own specific circumstances in the real world, one that could be kept from them is whether they will share in political power once the constitution is established. For example, the constitution could provide for democratic elections at regular intervals after the adoption of the constitution. Individuals would not know whether they would be elected to office, and especially would not know about their chances of reelection, since that would depend upon voter evaluation of their performances. In one important way, then, a constitution could be created behind a veil of uncertainty. In Figure 8.1, for example, individual X might be an elected legislator and individual Y an individual with no government power. When the constitution is being created, individuals would not know whether they will end up as individual X or individual Y.

There is a range of possible outcomes in the model depicted by the Figure, and good bargaining by X or Y could tilt the outcome to favor the good bargainer. But behind the veil of uncertainty the bargainers do not know which position they will end up occupying. Therefore, the bargaining process will not be biased toward either individual, and will tend toward point c, which splits the gains from trade. This theoretical model suggests the writing of the U.S. Constitution, where the document was drawn up and then elections held to determine who would end up occupying positions of power in the government.[3] But the argument here is not that this process parallels the actual creation of any constitution; rather, this model depicts the creation of a constitution under ideal circumstances from the standpoint of those who eventually will be governed by the constitution.

The assumption that the constitution is written in an ideal setting is made in order to focus on problems that can develop after the constitution is in place. If a constitution were created under less than ideal circumstances, then there would be a ready explanation for the constitution's less than ideal performance. By depicting the constitution as created under ideal circumstances, the constitutional problems that arise in the model cannot be blamed on the setting within which the constitution was constructed. The recent contractarian literature makes unrealistic assumptions about the setting within which constitutional rules are produced, and this chapter shows that even if rules could be produced in such a setting, the constitution as it evolves will not be equivalent to a continually renegotiated social contract.

The Scope of Constitutional Rules

One difference between economic models and the real world is that nothing can be assumed away in the real world. Economic models are able to produce generally applicable rules because unanticipated factors affecting the rule can be assumed away. In the real world, every particular case cannot be anticipated by a general rule.[4] Thus, it would not be possible to write a constitution that anticipated every possible future legal issue. If constitutional rules are written in a rigid manner that is not subject to interpretation, problems are sure to arise when rigid rules are applied to unforeseen events. For constitutions to endure, they must have enough flexibility to evolve to cover new and changing circumstances.

In contrast to written constitutions which must state rules explicitly, the common law is free to evolve in response to changing circumstances.[5] In common law, specific rules are not stated in a specific place so that they can be looked up and applied. Rather, the law is developed as a series of cases, with each ruling applying to the specifics of that case. Decisions in the entire history of particular cases imply the general rule, and legal argument presumes the fiction that there is an underlying general rule consistent with all of the particular decisions. Legal argument would be that this case should be decided in a particular way because the decision would be consistent with all of the past cases.

Most of the time, the applicable law in a case will be clear and there will be no reason to take a dispute to court. Sometimes a case will arise that has enough in the way of new and unusual circumstances that the law is not clear. The dispute then goes to court and its outcome becomes a part of the body of common law. Once several similar cases have been decided, the law in that previously unanticipated area becomes clarified. The use of past cases as precedent for determining current law tends to produce efficient law since precedents can be broadened or narrowed in future cases. A good precedent would be broadened and applied to more cases, whereas a bad precedent would be narrowed until it eventually ceased being current law.

There are a number of models that depict the way the invisible hand of the common law generates a body of law that evolves efficiently.[6] The particulars of those models are of less interest here than the idea that the law must evolve to account for unforeseen circumstances. Circumstances can be unforeseen because they are new, because changes have taken place, or because there are unintended consequences of some legal provision.[7] Therefore, it would not be possible to write a constitution ahead of time that could perfectly account for every future contingency.

The result is that constitutional rules necessarily must be subject to modification. The U.S. Constitution, in addition to being simple and leaving much rule-making to legislation outside the Constitution, has specific provision for amendment, and is subject to broad interpretation by the Supreme Court. While some might object to the loose interpretations the Court accords the Constitution – to the degree that some decisions interpret the document contrary to its literal meaning – the fact that it is interpreted in this way makes it apparent that the Constitutional rules established with the written constitution have evolved considerably since the Constitution was originally written. More generally, any constitution must evolve to adapt to unforeseen circumstances.

Constitutional Evolution

Even when a constitution is written under ideal circumstances, any constitution must evolve to adapt to unforeseen circumstances. This section uses the earlier model to see how the constitution is likely to evolve over time.

When written in an idealized setting behind the veil of uncertainty, the constitution is unbiased in that it does not favor any group of individuals over any other. But once the constitution is in place, it must evolve, and the evolution of the constitution is controlled by those in the government. Assume that once the constitution is written and the veil of uncertainty is lifted, individual X in Figure 8.1 takes a position in government, and individual Y is in the private sector. Those in the government will have a tendency to control the evolution of the constitution to favor themselves. Thus, starting from an unbiased beginning like point c in Figure 8.1, the terms of the constitution will tend to drift toward point b, favoring those who control the evolution of constitutional rules.

This movement is depicted in Figure 8.2. Starting from point c, constitutional evolution will alter the structure of rights to create a society that moves toward point d. As the constitution becomes more biased toward those in power, more monitoring and enforcement of constitutional rules will be necessary. Following the model in Chapter 3, this moves the society from utility possibilities frontier C to frontier S.

The intent of this discussion is not to depict anyone as having sinister motivations. Human nature causes people to see things from their point of view, necessitating the veil of uncertainty to create unbiased rules, necessitating referees in games, and necessitating a court system to settle disputes among individuals. With so many institutions designed to settle disagreements among individuals who tend to see their side more clearly than someone else's, it would be unreasonable to expect that those in government would not tend to be more sympathetic to their own situation than to the situation of those outside of government.

The result is that those who have the power to change the rules will change them in ways that favor themselves. Those in power see things they could do if only they had a little more power. Those things might be for the public good or might be purely self-interested, but gradually the power of government will increase. Increased power paves the way to increased monopoly profits for those in government, as discussed in Chapter 6. Even a constitution created in an ideal setting will tend to erode over time as it evolves.

Those outside of government, like individual Y, have reason to object to the process. One alternative is revolution. Another alternative in a democratic government is to use resources to seek elected office, to then be in a position to change the situation. However, the individual who succeeds in getting elected moves from being like individual Y to being like individual X, and once elected, the institutions are biased in the individual's favor rather than against the individual.

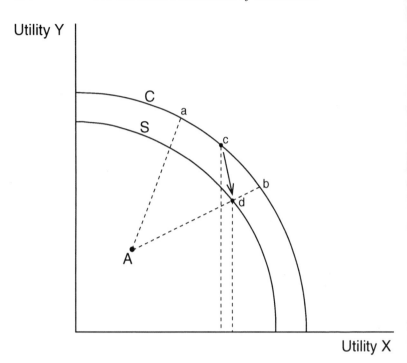

Figure 8.2   Constitutional Evolution

The result is that constitutions will evolve toward favoring those in government over those outside. Constitutional evolution gives the government more control and more monopoly power, and lessens the rights of those governed by the constitution. There may be offsetting factors, such as increasing mobility over time which can increase intergovernmental competition, or factors like increasing productivity and higher monitoring costs that were discussed in Chapter 3. These offsetting factors will be considered further in the next chapter, but without them, constitutional evolution gives the government more power.

Constitutional Evolution and the Division of Labor

Adam Smith's *The Wealth of Nations* begins with the lesson that the division of labor is limited by the extent of the market.[8] If Smith is the father of economics, then the first lesson of economics concerns the division of labor and the enhanced productivity and wealth that is possible with it. But the division of labor also makes people more interdependent. That interdependence implies that while people are better off specializing and working within the coordination of an economy than they would be without this specialization, after having become a part of the division of labor they would also be worse off without the others they have become dependent on. If anarchy replaced existing social institutions, people in less developed economies would probably fare better than those in more developed economies.

This can be illustrated with the aid of Figure 8.3. Economic development will move the utility possibilities frontier out from C to C', potentially increasing everyone's well-being. However, increased interdependence also means that each individual would fare worse without participation in the economy than before. In a less developed economy, people are more self-sufficient, growing their own food, producing their own clothing, shelter, and energy. In a more developed economy, many people would be unable to produce enough of the necessities on their own to survive. Thus, the point of anarchistic equilibrium, A, would move to A' in a more developed economy, indicating that without cooperation, individuals would fare worse.

As Figure 8.3 illustrates, the bargaining range within which the provisions of the constitution might fall will widen from ab to a'b'. If the constitution is biased toward individual X, who is in government, the Figure illustrates how individuals outside government could fare worse in a more advanced economy than in a less advanced economy. At the bottom of the bargaining range on C and C', individual Y has more utility in the less developed economy (UY) than in the more developed economy (UY').

The simple logic behind this illustration is that in more developed economic systems, peoples' alternatives to the existing government are reduced because of their economic interdependence. This gives the government more potential to bias the terms of the constitution in favor of those in the government.

Recall that the angle of the dashed lines from points A and A' represents the expected range of renegotiation. If individuals expected no more than that a constitution would be Pareto superior to anarchy, then the dashed lines would form a 90-degree angle, with point a directly above A, and point b directly to the right of A. Looking at Figure 8.3, the reader can visualize that as the angle from point A increases, the difference between UY and UY' increases. If individuals feel they can expect little of the benefits of social organization in a renegotiation of the social contract, those who are least well-off could find their lot worsened by economic growth.

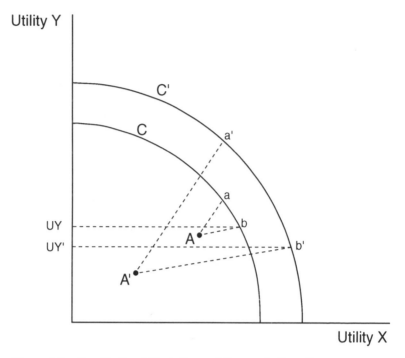

Figure 8.3   Constitutional Evolution and Economic Growth

If, on the other hand, individuals expected to share more equally in the gains from social organization, the bargaining range would narrow, bringing points a and b closer to each other. With a narrow enough range, economic growth must benefit everyone. Looking at Figure 8.3, if the bargaining range is narrow enough, UY′ must be above UY. This may describe the social unrest in inner cities in the United States beginning in the late 1960s. Prior to that time, individuals at the lower end of the economic spectrum may have figured that any social changes would be unlikely to improve their welfare; in the language of the model, they figured that there was a wide bargaining range, and that renegotiation of the social contract would not be likely to improve their condition. Rising expectations narrowed the bargaining range, and if the status quo was close to b′ initially, a narrower bargaining range would place the status quo outside of arc a′b′, meaning that individuals at the lower end of the economic spectrum now felt that renegotiation would be likely to improve their well-being. Social unrest led to new social programs that did alter the social contract to provide more assistance to those at the lower end of the spectrum.[9]

The bargaining range, ab, gives the limits beyond which individuals will not accept the constitution. Although the simple graphical model depicts this as a discontinuity – within ab people accept the constitution, outside ab they do not – in reality the constitution will meet more resistance as it approaches the limits of the bargaining range. Some implications of constitutional evolution leading to more government power will be considered next.

Enforcement, Evolution, and Revolution

Democracy provides an excellent way to diffuse opposition to the government. It gives people an incentive to channel resources into the political process rather than into violent overthrow of the government. If people are successful in entering government through political means, they are accorded a position in the winning coalition and lose their incentive to oppose the institutional arrangements that favor those in government. The possibility of entry by democratic means provides two advantages to the democratic government.

The first advantage, discussed at the beginning of Chapter 7, is that fewer resources need be devoted to protecting the government from violent overthrow. If entry is possible by winning an election, those wanting to take over the government can devote resources toward political campaigning rather than having to resort to violent means. Thus, to protect the government from internal uprisings, the government's defense must only be strong enough to make it cheaper to launch a political campaign than an armed attack.

One implication of this is that stronger defense is needed the more difficult it is to enter government through electoral competition. Defense must also protect against outside invaders, so electoral competition may not be the determining factor for governments that are attempting to protect against outside threats. Casual observation suggests, however, that small dictatorships often have substantial military forces when they neither face substantial outside threats nor are in a position to pose an outside threat to other governments. Their military forces must be substantial enough to prevent violent overthrow when democratic entry is costly.

The second advantage to democratic government is that by allowing outsiders to compete in the electoral process for a position in government, this automatically makes any successful challenger a part of the government, which blunts their incentive to reduce the constitution's bias in favor of government. In the model of this chapter, election of an outsider to government changes the individual from individual Y to individual X, with the corresponding changes in incentives. People will find much less to dislike about the biases of government when those biases change from being against them to favoring them. If people who want to change the biases of government can mount enough support to be elected, democratic government provides a mechanism to change their incentives with regard to making government less biased.

Legitimacy and Enforcement

Governments do not have the power to get people to do anything the government wants. Governments do have the power to use force, but in order to use force to direct peoples' behavior, they must be able to detect behavior they view as undesirable and they must be able to marshall enough force to coerce people to act in the government-prescribed manner. The resources required to do this could be beyond the reach of any government, if the actions the government wanted people to undertake were unpopular enough. Therefore, any government relies to a large degree on the voluntary compliance of its citizens.

Voluntary compliance is facilitated when people view the government's requests as legitimate. The economics literature has focused heavily on the free rider problem of noncompliance. With free riders, the government produces a public good that benefits everyone, and some people try to consume the good without paying. The implied assumption is that the production of the public good is a legitimate activity of government and that free riders are acting opportunistically rather than trying not to participate in something they do not want the government to do.

Typical economic models of government reinforce this view of noncompliance. Samuelson's models of public goods emphasized the problem of revealed preference for public sector output,[10] and Buchanan's theory of clubs draws an analogy between government activity and that of a voluntary organization.[11] Even more emphatically, Hochman and Rodgers have developed a model of income redistribution where upper income individuals are better off if they are forced to redistribute some of their income.[12] Unless they are forced, Hochman and Rodgers reason, they will have an incentive to free ride on the redistributive activities of others, and too little redistribution will occur. A test of this model would be difficult because if asked, individuals would say that they did not want to be forced to part with their income. Are they answering truthfully, or do they claim they do not want to participate because they want to free ride? The government-as-club model obscures the coercive nature of government by making collective arrangements appear to have an element of voluntarism even when they are explicitly coercive.[13]

People might not want to cooperate with government because they want to free ride, but they also might not cooperate because they are not in agreement with the government's activities. Voluntary cooperation will be much easier to elicit when people view the government's demands as legitimate. Douglass North justifiably emphasizes the role of legitimacy, using the term ideology.[14] In North's view, ideology causes people to be loyal to political institutions. They will support candidates, parties, and government activities if they accept the underlying ideology. Thus, if the government generates ideological agreement, people will voluntarily cooperate without having to be forced. The degree to which people will pay taxes, obey laws, and generally cooperate with government will be greater if the government is viewed as making legitimate demands on its citizens. By establishing its legitimacy, the government can reduce its monitoring and enforcement costs.

Factors that Reduce Legitimacy

Factors creating legitimacy are discussed extensively in Chapter 10, which examines the concept of agreement as it applies to government policies. For example, if rulers can convince the population that their positions are desired by the gods, they will be more likely to be accepted as legitimate. In a democracy, legitimacy is created because leaders are chosen by popular vote. Those in power are those the people want in power, and the evidence is the democratic election that gave them power. Elections as a route to legitimacy are used even in dictatorships where no alternatives to the current leaders appear on the ballot.

As the constitution evolves over time, creating barriers to entry and transferring additional power to those in government, legitimacy will be eroded. Elections may still have symbolic value giving a degree of legitimacy to government, but less legitimacy than if the myth that any child could grow up to be president were actually true.[15] Within the model developed earlier, the movement in Figure 8.2 from point c to point d will carry with it a reduction in legitimacy, which implies an increase in the cost of monitoring and enforcement for those in government. Because the government is viewed as less legitimate, people will be less inclined to follow its rules without being forced, leading to an increasing disregard for the government's rules. This causes a shift inward of the utility possibilities frontier, reflecting the fact that additional resources must be devoted to enforcing the government's rules.

Harold Berman argues that Western legal tradition is in crisis, among other reasons, because there is an increasing perception that the law is being used for political purposes. "The view that law transcends politics – the view that at any given moment, or at least in its historical development, law is distinct from the state – seems to have yielded increasingly to the view that law is at all times basically an instrument of the state, that is, a means of effectuating the will of those who exercise political authority."[16] The government's use of law for its own purposes is one way that those with political power can create a bias in their favor, but at the cost of reducing the legitimacy of the law they attempt to use.[17]

Conclusion

Even if a constitution is created under ideal circumstances, it must be flexible enough to change in response to unforeseen developments, and such change will be biased in favor of those who have the power to change the constitution. Since the rules are changed by those in government, this means that over time the terms of a government's constitution will evolve to favor those in government.

Economic development can amplify the process because while economic development enables societies to create more wealth through cooperation, it also makes individuals more dependent upon the cooperative system. The alternatives to the status quo become less favorable with economic development, which gives those with political power more bargaining power in setting the terms of the constitutional rules that govern the society. Again, constitutions evolve to give governments increasing power.

Democratic governments contain an additional element which diffuses opposition to the power of government. Political competition can take place through the electoral process, but if a challenger is successful, the challenger then becomes a part of the established government. The constitutional rules that were biased against the challenger before the election are now biased in favor of the individual who has become a new office holder.

Unless there is a perception of widespread agreement, change in the terms of the constitutional contract reduces the legitimacy of the government in the eyes of its citizens, which therefore requires additional monitoring and enforcement by the government. This implies an expansion of the state's police powers, while at the same time implies an increase in lawlessness. An increase in violations of the law coincident with an increase in government monitoring and enforcement must imply a reduction in voluntary compliance. Voluntary compliance with law declines when the perceived legitimacy of government declines.

This line of reasoning is relatively pessimistic, suggesting an increasing transfer of rights from the general population to the government as a constitution matures. Government becomes more monopolistic and more profitable for those on the inside. From within the model of this chapter, the process can be reversed only by writing a new constitution from behind the veil of uncertainty. There are other factors that can work to reduce the monopoly power of government, however, and those factors are the subject of the next chapter.

9 Competition in Politics

Government, by nature, is coercive. The fundamental transaction of government – the exchange of protection for tribute – makes government coercive because it must be in a position to forcibly deter aggressors in order to protect its citizens. Citizens want their governments to have the power to protect them, but this same power can be used against them too. Much of the analysis in previous chapters has been devoted to seeing how the government can obtain and use coercive power. The government profits from coercion by selling its output at monopoly prices. The government sells protective services, but also can produce and sell other goods and services. Some services have possible market alternatives; for example, governments produce mail services, television and radio broadcasts, health care, education, and more. When producing goods with private sector alternatives, the government typically has a competitive advantage. In some cases, it outlaws private sector competition, but another alternative is to subsidize or even give away its output, making it hard for private sector competitors to compete on the basis of price. Other services are not typically offered in private markets. For example, the government produces and sells barriers to entry into private markets in the form of tariffs and import quotas, regulation, licensing, and the granting of natural monopolies. Much government activity, when analyzed in strictly economic terms, amounts to the creation of barriers to entry which generate monopoly profits.

Competitive forces can offset some of the government's monopoly power and reduce the degree to which governments are able to exploit their citizens. This chapter begins by considering what might be meant by government exploitation of monopoly power, and then considers competitive constraints on government activity. Intergovernmental competition will be considered first, followed by a discussion of electoral competition in democracies. Then, constitutions will be discussed as a substitute for other types of political competition.

Government Exploitation

Most individuals believe that government can provide valuable services to its citizens. In exchange, the government makes certain demands. In this exchange paradigm, how can one say that the demands of government are excessive compared to the services rendered? In other words, how could one ever say that a government exploits its citizens?

The question is not unlike inquiring about what a fair price is in the market. Some individuals might believe that one price is fair while others believe another price is fair.[1] Niskanen's theory of bureaucracy suggests that government bureaucracy produces more output than would be optimal, which implies that a reduction in government could bring social benefits.[2] Niskanen's suggestions for improvement are along the lines of making government bureaus operate more like markets. But many of the functions of government are assigned to government because the market is not a feasible alternative. If the market alternative is not feasible, it may not be possible to have the government behave more like a firm in a market.[3] Government may be inefficient according to some ideal measure, and some government activity that is generally desired may imply a restriction on individual freedoms,[4] but there is not a good absolute yardstick to measure these aspects of government. The government's national defense spending may be inefficient, but compared to what alternative? If the private sector could not produce national defense at all, and if efficiency-enhancing changes cannot be made, then there is no cheaper alternative to providing national defense in the way it is currently provided.

Government's actions cannot be benchmarked against some abstract ideal, but rather against the real alternatives that are available. Governments could be said to exploit their citizens and charge too much for their services to the extent that there are alternative institutional arrangements that could provide the services at lower cost, or less exploitatively. Government exploitation arises from the monopoly power of government, and monopoly power can be reduced through competing governments or political institutions that allow competition. If there is no alternative to monopoly government, then the monopoly price is the cheapest available.

To the extent that competitive forces can be introduced into government, government exploitation of monopoly power can be reduced, which means that government will be unable to charge anything more than a competitive price for its services. The clearest form of competition is actual competition among governments.

Intergovernmental Competition

The economist's model of intergovernmental competition comes from Charles Tiebout,[5] who depicted many local governments as offering a variety of different public goods and services at a variety of different tax rates. People could choose to live in a community of less government services at lower taxes or more government with higher taxes. Different mixes of government services would also be available. Tiebout's model ignored the cost of moving, so people could shop for local governments much as they shop for other goods, choosing the local government that best suited their preferences. Competition among local governments for residents would create governments that are efficient providers of services.

Tiebout's model of perfect competition among local governments differs from reality in a number of important respects. First, peoples' locational choices are often dictated by factors other than the characteristics of the local government. Second, moving is costly, so people cannot shop for local government goods and services the way Tiebout describes. And third, given these other factors, local governments can be inefficient and still retain their residents because the residents find it too costly to relocate, or because other factors besides government keep them in their current locations.[6]

Despite some unrealistic aspects of the model, the Tiebout model is descriptive in important ways. For a person relocating for other reasons, there may be a number of local governments under which the individual could live. Often there are nearby towns, and often it is possible to live outside the city limits altogether. In a mobile society, there may be important aspects to Tiebout competition among governments.

Another important factor in intergovernmental competition is the ability to compare one's own government with other similar governments. Even if the cost of moving prevents individuals from relocating from one community to another, they can still compare the performance of their local government with other similar local governments. If their local government does not measure up, they can replace their local officials at the next election, or in nondemocratic countries, use other means to try to replace their officials.

The ability to compare the performance of one's own government to other governments extends well beyond the sphere of local governments. Even the governments of nations can be compared with one another, and the movements toward democracy and free markets in the former Soviet Union, China, and Eastern Europe in the late 1980s can be attributed, at least in part, to the citizens of those countries comparing their governments to other governments around the world.

As noted in Chapter 6, governments can take steps to make their environments less competitive in order to increase their monopoly profits.

Intergovernmental competition can be lessened if the competing governments can organize to reduce the differences among them. This is often done with the assistance of higher level governments that mandate the lower governments to provide uniformity in services, taxes, and other characteristics.[7] Even without governments actively seeking to limit intergovernmental competition, there will be natural limits because of the costs of moving. If people find it costly to move to new governments, another possibility is to stay put and replace their existing government.

Political Competition through Voting

The democratic election of government officials has some similarities to the Tiebout model of political competition. In the Tiebout model, governments occupy a fixed location and people move to live under the governments they want. With democratic elections, citizens occupy a fixed location and select their governments through elections. In the Tiebout model, people move in and out of political jurisdictions; with voting, voters move politicians in and out of jurisdictions. Thus, democratic government serves as a way for people to select the governments they want to live under without moving.

Formal models of political competition are similar to formal models of spatial competition, further suggesting an analogy between moving and voting. Hotelling's model of competition in economic space was used as the foundation for Downs' model of political competition from which the current formal models of majority rule voting are developed.[8] Models of spatial competition in politics are close to the way that Tiebout discussed mobility and political competition. In the Tiebout model, people move to the jurisdiction that contains the governmental characteristics they desire, and in models of spatial competition, the political issue space is a representation of those characteristics. The efficiency aspects of spatial voting models do not match those of Tiebout models because voters cannot move in order to sort themselves into more homogeneous groups, but the political issue space over which they vote is very much like the locations to which they can move in the Tiebout model.

In a democratic setting, political competition among candidates is a way to limit the monopoly power of governments. Once elected, legislators have a great deal of monopoly power, but if there is competition for elected office, candidates will have to offer a competitive platform in order to be elected.[9] Barriers to entry in politics are directly relevant to this issue, because if there are barriers to entry, incumbents do not have to offer competitive platforms in order to be reelected, so some of the competitive effect of elections is eliminated. If barriers to entry are inevitable over time, as was suggested in the previous chapter, then some other type of mechanism will be required to maintain competition in politics.

Constitutions as Substitutes for Mobility

In a pure Tiebout setting where mobility is costless, there are a large number of political jurisdictions to choose from, and governments compete for residents, constitutional rules would not be necessary. Governments would sell a bundle of services at a price, and citizens, like customers of any business, would decide at which government to shop. Citizens who became dissatisfied with their governments could choose to shop elsewhere. In a Tiebout world of perfect mobility, there is some assurance that governments will have to continue to provide their citizens with the public sector output they desire.

From the standpoint of citizens, constitutional rules can substitute for mobility by providing this assurance. Constitutional rules can define the scope of government to provide some guarantee of continuity in government activity over time. In the terminology of the spatial model of politics, people live under a government that locates at a particular point in the political issue space. If people cannot physically move away from their governments, then constitutional rules can be used as a method for preventing government from moving away from its citizens' political views.

Constitutional rules can help provide a competitive political environment by preventing those in government from erecting barriers to entry. Constitutional rules also can preserve the status quo by limiting the scope of government activity. When relocating to another government would be costly, these services of constitutional rules can partially substitute for mobility and provide some aspects of a competitive environment when actual competition is not possible.

Constitutional Rules and Competition

The idea of constitutional rules substituting for mobility to provide a competitive environment is similar to Harold Demsetz's idea that competition for the right to be a monopolist can lead to competitive results.[10] In the Demsetz framework, a utility is a natural monopoly that, according to conventional wisdom, must be regulated to prevent the undesirable side-effects of monopoly. But Demsetz argues that if many firms compete for the right to be the monopolist, they will be forced to offer the competitive level of output at the competitive price in order to win the competition for the monopoly franchise. Thus, a competitive environment exists despite the existence of a natural monopoly.

Constitutional rules, selected before the monopoly suppliers of government are chosen, can serve the same function. If the rules are written in such a way as to limit the scope of government, to provide competition for political office, and to require competitive behavior of office holders, then despite the monopoly power of government, constitutional constraints can act to produce a competitive environment. The Constitution of the United States was clearly written with this goal in mind.

The question then becomes: what type of constitutional rules create this type of environment? The emerging field of constitutional economics attempts to deal with this question. Optimal rules are difficult to define because they must, on the one hand, constrain the behavior of government, and yet still be flexible enough to adapt to unforeseen future circumstances. The following chapters discuss the issue in more detail.

War: The Health of the State

Randolph Bourne, a prominent journalist early in the 20th century, argued that war is the health of the state.[11] He observed the ratchet effect that occurs when governments go to war and government spending increases to fight the war. After the war is over, government spending remains permanently higher than before the war.[12] By continually going to war, government can continue to aggrandize its power. Not only does government spending rise, constitutional protections of other kinds are weakened because war causes the citizens of warring nations to become more dependent upon their own nation.

Within the framework developed in this chapter, the most obvious reason that war would enhance the monopoly power of government is that it reduces mobility. Since mobility enhances intergovernmental competition, the reduction in mobility reduces competition among governments. War could also enhance the ability of incumbents to be reelected in a democratic setting, if citizens wanted to minimize the risk of electing untested leaders in a time of crisis. And during wartime, citizens seem more willing than usual to sacrifice their constitutional safeguards in order to enhance the power of the government to fight a war. Changes that occur during wars irrevocably enhance the monopoly power of governments.

The changes that occur during wars are examples of changes in the mechanisms discussed in this chapter that produce competitive government. Mobility, democratic elections, and constitutional restraints are all competition-enhancing, and all are eroded during war. This application to wartime is an example, but Chapter 8 showed that constitutional restraints erode over time simply because those that enforce the restraints are also those who benefit from the erosion, and Chapter 6 looked at the way that barriers to entry are erected in politics to reduce the competitiveness of democratic elections. Wars can reduce mobility across international boundaries, but they are but one of many factors that can increase the monopoly power of governments.

Government Growth and Decline

In an insightful analysis, Mancur Olson developed an interest group theory of government to explain the rise and decline of nations.[13] Briefly, Olson argued that when social upheavals, such as those caused by war or revolution, upset the established political order, established special interests are destroyed and individuals are able to be productive in an environment which rewards productivity rather than favoritism for those who have political power. As societies mature, political power bases are established which use the political system to reward those with power rather than those who are productive, which leads established mature societies to stagnate. New societies rise as older established societies decline.

Olson's theory complements the analysis presented here because this analysis describes how governments tend to evolve over time to establish greater degrees of monopoly power. However, the theory remains within national borders and does not consider the possibility of international intergovernmental competition. A more competitive international environment should reduce the monopoly power of government. Intergovernmental competition is normally thought of as a phenomenon related to federalism, where some local governments compete with others, but national governments can also compete with each other if there is sufficient mobility.

Governments have the ability to exercise more monopoly power when their boundaries grow faster than the mobility of their citizens. The ability of government to exert monopoly power declines if the mobility of its citizens increases relative to the government's territorial growth.

This application of factors producing competition in government to the subject of government growth and decline helps explain not only why governments grow, but also why they shrink. There are many theories of government growth, but a complete theory of government growth must also be able to explain those historical periods when government power receded.

The decline of feudalism coincided with the rise of the independent city-state from about 1050 to 1150, which gave citizens alternatives to their feudal government. Intergovernmental competition reduced the monopoly power of government.[14] The 1800s saw a considerable decline in the power of government and a blossoming of individual freedom. The development of classical liberalism during this period coincided with the opening of international markets, and with advances in the technology of transportation. More intergovernmental competition reduced the monopoly power of government.

The growth of government in the 20th century coincides with the reduction in international mobility related to the two World Wars. The aggregation of the Soviet states and Eastern European countries after World War II reduced mobility and enhanced government power in those areas. In the United States, the strengthening of the federal government relative to state and local governments enhances government power.

In the later part of the 20th century, international mobility has been increased partly as a result of advances in transportation and information technology. Even in relatively poor countries, radio and television broadcasts can keep citizens informed about their countries and the rest of the world, and technologies such as telephone and fax make the world even smaller and enhance intergovernmental competition. The movements toward freedom around the world are a result of the decline in the government's monopoly power due to the increase in intergovernmental competition.

Models of the incentive structure of government bureaucracy can explain why governments have the incentive to be large, but not why governments grow. Why have governments not always been large? What factors enable the government to wield more power now than it could a few decades ago? Why did governments decline in the 19th century? These questions can be analyzed by looking at factors that increase the competitiveness of governments and therefore restrain their activities. If competitiveness increases, government power will decline; the growth of government in the 20th century was a result of a reduction in the competitiveness of governments.

The Importance of Constitutional Constraints

This chapter has focused on three factors that restrain the monopoly power of government: intergovernmental competition, democratic electoral competition, and constitutional constraints. Constitutional constraints are important because their effects can substitute for the other two, but also because constitutional constraints can determine the effectiveness of the other two.

Constitutional rules can limit intergovernmental competition in two ways. Most obviously, there can be rules against moving. If citizens are not allowed to move away from their governments, the monopoly power of government is enhanced. In a federal system, governments can also reduce the competitiveness of lower levels of government by enacting rules limiting their ability to compete. In the United States, federal funding of programs and the mandating of the characteristics of government goods and services reduce intergovernmental competition. Typically, the stated intentions of rules which limit intergovernmental competition are to produce more uniformity in the offerings of local governments, but this uniformity reduces alternatives for citizens. Clearly, in the Tiebout model, diversity in local governments is the key to intergovernmental competition. This diversity can be mandated away by higher level governments seeking to impose standards on lower level governments.

The degree of electoral competition can also be affected by constitutional rules. Such rules give the qualifications necessary to run for office and indirectly specify the resources needed to win. The evolution of these types of rules in the United States has led to a large advantage held by incumbents seeking reelection. As discussed in Chapter 6, incumbency conveys a large advantage, and when those in government benefit from rules that keep them in their positions of political power, their monopoly power as governors is enhanced. Rules can be designed to make the electoral process more or less competitive, and the evolution of rules toward making the process less competitive enhances the monopoly power of government.

Constitutional rules can also be used to provide a competitive political environment directly by specifying constraints on government behavior. The United States Constitution was designed to limit the government's monopoly power by explicitly limiting government activity to those items enumerated in the Constitution. Following this rule, the government is prohibited from doing anything not explicitly permitted in the Constitution. The U.S. Constitution also specified three branches of government which are designed to provide checks and balances on each other, again as a constraint against concentrated monopoly power in government. And the

Bill of Rights explicitly limits the government's monopoly power over those items granted as rights. In addition to the direct competitive effect of constitutional rules, the U.S. Constitution also enhances mobility by limiting restraints on the movement of goods and people, and enhances electoral competition by mandating democratic elections. While people can debate how well the U.S. Constitution was designed and how well it has worked, it illustrates the principle of using constitutional rules to limit the monopoly power of government.

Constitutional Design

Within a positive framework, government is an ogranization that exchanges protection for tribute. The government's power also enables it to produce other goods and services, and it can profit from its activities by exercising monopoly power. Comptetitive forces – intergovernmental competition, electoral competition, and constitutional constraints – can act to limit the monopoly power of government. One could stop with an analysis of the environment of government as it actually exists, or could go on to examine how that environment could be designed to enhance the welfare of the government's citizens. By going on, one undertakes the transition from positive to normative analysis.

Constitutional rules are important determinants of the monopoly power of government, and thus of the well-being citizens derive from their governments. But constitutional rules are not given in nature; they are the result of human design. Thus, it seems eminently reasonable to analyze constitutional rules the same way that other results of human design are analyzed, and to suggest modifications accordingly.

There is sometimes resistance among social scientists to recommend changes in social institutions. Alchian and Allen summarize this resistance nicely in their introductory textbook, where they remark, "It is no more proper for the economist than for any other person to sit on Mt. Olympus and decree what is desirable, though everyone may in fact make such pronouncements."[15] Yet while the clear distinction must be recognized between positive and normative analysis, constitutional rules are designed by people and are constantly being modified by people, so it seems reasonable that they could be analyzed for the purpose of recommending desirable changes.

Indeed, if constitutions are the product of human design, then constitutional rules should function better if they are constructed according to the principles of social science. If the way in which constitutional rules work is the subject of inquiry, the results of the study of such rules could be applied to improve the operation of rules in the real world. The economics that Alchian and Allen refer to is the study of individual choice subject to constraints. But the area of inquiry can be broadened to discuss the choice of constraints, where constitutional rules are one factor that constrains individual behavior.[16]

Social Science and Social Engineering

The distinction emphasized by Alchian and Allen has some merit in that no person's value judgments can be held to be superior to another's. But if constitutional design is studied, it is possible to discover principles that could make rules function better from everyone's standpoint. Ideas can have consequences.[17]

The distinction here is between social science and social engineering. The social scientist analyzes the way the world works, while the social engineer tries to design a better one. Social engineering conjures the image of designing policies which allow the government to dictate more about an individual's environment and actions, but arguments that society should be designed with less government involvement also argue for social engineering.[18] There is a danger in arguing for any kind of social engineering; the status quo is one of many possible social systems, and many people will be in favor of changes to the status quo, but far fewer will be in favor of any specific change to replace the status quo. Arguing that there are problems with today's society will attract widespread agreement, but arguing in favor of a specific replacement will attract a much smaller following.[19]

Physical scientists could have been content to study the behavior of electrons or the principles of aerodynamics, but they went farther, engineering more advanced aircraft and more powerful computers. Understanding the laws of physical science, they were able to apply them to design better products. The same potential exists in social science. If the way in which constitutional rules function is better understood, rules can be designed that work better. Admittedly, there is a value judgment involved in arguing that a Boeing 747 is a better aircraft than the Wright Flyer. The Wright Flyer did have the advantages of giving riders a better view of the ground, of being able to land in a smaller area, and of being more inexpensive to build. Arguing that some constitutional rules are better than others also involves a value judgment, but that value judgment must be made by someone, since constitutional rules are the result of human design.

People design constitutional rules, and must use their value judgments to determine what rules they think are best. The only alternative to applying normative principles to constitutional rules is anarchy. If societies are to live under a set of rules, somebody must make some value judgments to design them. Rules for social interaction can evolve as individuals agree among themselves to do things a certain way, but even this involves the judgment of those agreeing that the way they do things is better than the alternative. The better they understand the alternatives, the better position they will be in to select the rules that produce a desirable society.

Governments are the result of human design. Therefore, it makes sense to study them with an eye toward improving their design.

Conclusion

The theory of government developed earlier argued that the essential activity of government is the exchange of protection for tribute. The government allows people to produce in exchange for a share of their production, and once that agreement is made, the government has an incentive to protect its citizens, because they are its source of income. The government enhances its income by exercising monopoly power in the supply of goods and services. Chapter 6 discussed the mechanisms by which the monopoly power of government can manifest itself. This chapter looked at mechanisms that produce competition in politics, and thus limit the monopoly power that government can exert.

Three main factors that can lead to competition in government were discussed: intergovernmental competition, electoral competition, and constitutional rules. In addition to providing their own constraints, constitutional rules also influence the degree to which the other factors can have a competitive effect. In particular, electoral competition is almost entirely determined by the rules within which elections are held.

The previous chapters have analyzed government within a strictly positive framework, describing the way that individual rights are determined, the way that governments interact with their citizens, and the factors that influence how much power a government is able to exert over its citizens. Competition limits the power of government, and this chapter discussed factors producing competition, noting the importance of constitutional rules. Because they are the result of human design, the discussion of constitutional rules provides a natural transition from positive to normative analysis. If people have a better understanding of how constitutions work, they will be in a better position to design constitutional rules that are effective in carrying out their goals.

The next chapter considers an important element of the contractarian theory of the state: the concept of agreement. Then, Chapter 11 goes on to consider various positive and normative theories of government to see how they fit into the framework developed earlier in the book. Chapter 12 extends this discussion to consider ethics and public policy. If constitutional rules are an important constraint on the power of government, then they should figure prominently in a discussion on public policy.

In any political setting agreement is an important element in determining what rules are feasible and desirable. The following chapter considers this issue in detail.

10 The Concept of Agreement

The economic model of government that has been developed throughout the previous nine chapters is built on a foundation of agreement and exchange. The constitutional rules which form the basis of government are a product of an agreement to exchange protection for tribute, and constitutional rules themselves are the agreed-upon principles that define the long-term relationship between a government and its citizens. As developed in the economic model of government, this agreement can be coercive in the sense that citizens might be threatened with harm if they do not go along with the government's offer to exchange protection for tribute. Citizens are better off, nonetheless, agreeing to the constitution rather than being left unprotected in a state of anarchy.

While government coercion could be used to appropriate existing wealth, it could not be used to appropriate a part of a nation's income on a continuing basis unless those individuals who produce the income agree to continue producing even though they know that the government will take a share. Thus, the continuing operation of government requires the consent of the governed, even though that consent may be due solely to the perception that agreeing to abide by the government's rules is preferable to the likely consequences of resisting.

In a hypothetical setting where unanimous approval is required before constitutional rules are instituted, any individual has veto power, so it can be said that there is true agreement about constitutional rules. In the economic model of government developed in the earlier chapters, unanimous approval is not required, so agreement might be reluctantly forthcoming because it is better than suffering the consequences of not agreeing. If someone is coerced into agreeing in this manner, can the person really be said to be in agreement?

Agreement is the natural starting point of an economic theory of government, and this chapter examines the concept of agreement in more detail. The concept of agreement can be examined from both positive and normative perspectives, and this chapter does both. From a positive standpoint, the concept of agreement is relevant for several reasons. First, government, as an institution of collective decision-making, often aggregates diverse viewpoints into a single public policy. How would one evaluate whether those involved in the collective decision-making process are in agreement with the outcome of the process? Second, public policies are more likely to be successfully implemented when people agree with them. Therefore, understanding how agreement is produced goes some way toward understanding what types of public policies are feasible. And from a normative standpoint, policies might be evaluated as desirable if they further the ends of the citizens that approve them. Thus, agreement can be a normative criterion for identifying desirable public policy.

Political systems can be viewed as institutions which produce collective agreement. In this sense, any political outcome is the result of an agreement. There is always the potential of coercion, but people might even agree to be coerced, if others are coerced in the same way. Furthermore, if someone agrees to participate in a political process that produces an outcome, the person might view the outcome as legitimate even while preferring another outcome. Is the person who agrees with the process but dislikes the outcome in agreement? Is the person who abides by government rules while verbally expressing disagreement in agreement? These questions cannot be answered unambiguously without a clearer understanding of what is meant by agreement.

Up to this point, the analysis of government has taken place on strictly positive grounds, and a theory of government has been developed without reference to value judgements. This chapter first examines agreement from a positive standpoint, and then uses that positive analysis as a foundation for a normative evaluation of the concept of agreement. In a positive sense, are people actually in agreement with their governments' policies? What constitutes agreement, and why is it important? Agreement can also be used as a normative criterion for determining desirable public policy. The social contract theory of the state is built on such a foundation. After discussing agreement from a positive standpoint, the chapter then argues that it is an appropriate criterion for evaluating public policy from a normative standpoint. Conceptual agreement such as is in the social contract theory is then discussed at the end of the chapter.

Agreement and the Operation of Government

In the broadest sense, everyone who lives under the jurisdiction of government without trying to overthrow it is in agreement with the government. People indicate by their actions that they are better off living under the government than trying to replace it with something else.[1] Any government must command much more agreement than this in order to function. It is not sufficient for people just not to actively oppose the government; government must also get its citizens to obey its rules, to respect the rights structure it has established, and to contribute toward its operations through some type of taxation. Governments have the ability to use force toward these ends, but no government has the capability to force everyone to do everything it asks. Thus, government must be able to get people to comply without having to actually force compliance.

One way this can be done is to threaten to use force. If the threat is viewed as credible, people will comply without the government actually having to expend the resources to use actual force. If most people comply, and if the government has a method for detecting noncompliance that people perceive as effective, then the threat of force can be effective although very little actual force is being used. While people are being coerced to comply, following the definition of coercion from Chapter 5, the government does not have to use much actual force to maintain compliance. Potentially, a government could use much coercion but little force.

While resources devoted to using force may be low, monitoring costs can be significant if the government must detect those who do not comply in order to convince others to comply. While coercion may underlie all government activity, monitoring and enforcing rules can be costly, and the government can lower its costs if people are willing to voluntarily comply with its rules, without having to rely on force.

Voluntary compliance is the result of people agreeing with the government's actions, and viewing government as legitimate. While economic models of government tend to assume that people comply with government rules because they can be forced to, citizen agreement is an important input into compliance. If people agree with the government's actions and believe that others are complying with the government's rules, then they will often be willing to comply even if it might be possible to behave opportunistically and free-ride. Only a small amount of government monitoring and enforcement might be necessary, partly to give the individual some reason to fear adverse consequences of opportunistic behavior, and partly to assure the individual that others who behave opportunistically run the risk of getting caught.

Legitimacy

Legitimacy is a characteristic of government recognized by political scientists but only peripherally recognized in the economic literature on government. A government viewed as legitimate is able to gain compliance at much lower cost because citizens view that the government has a legitimate right to pursue its activities. Opportunistic behavior may still reduce the amount of compliance, but compliance is easier to enforce when the government's actions are viewed as legitimate.

Consider two reasons for noncompliance. One is that individuals view the government's actions as illegitimate, and the other is that individuals view that they will benefit personally from noncompliance regardless of the legitimacy of the government's rules. Economic models rarely distinguish between the two cases because utility-maximizing individuals are assumed to follow their narrow self-interests. They weigh the narrow costs and benefits of noncompliance and will not comply if it pays to do so. Individuals might behave altruistically in these models and bear some monetary cost to comply. Altruism in this sense means structuring the model in such a way as to give the individual utility from altruistic behavior.[2]

In the real world, however, there will be important differences between the case where government action is viewed as legitimate and the case where it is not. One difference involves what might be viewed as strictly altruistic behavior. People want to act to further the public good, so will be naturally inclined to obey legitimate government rules for the same reason that people give to charity and do volunteer work. Beyond this, however, peoples' interactions with their peers favor compliance with rules they view as legitimate. People comply with the demands of government that are accepted as legitimate because it enhances their reputations. In addition, noncompliance with rules viewed as legitimate could result in others reporting the noncompliance to the government. The likelihood of being reported by fellow citizens for noncompliance if the rule is viewed as illegitimate is less likely.

During World War II, for example, the United States government took extraordinary measures in drafting civilians, raising tax rates, instituting withholding for income taxes, confiscating property, issuing rationing coupons, and so forth. These actions were accepted because people viewed them as legitimate because of the war. There is a ratchet effect in that once an institution is installed and complied with, it tends to persist,[3] but similar efforts in situations that appeared less legitimate have not succeeded. The military draft was abolished after the Vietnam war, and price controls had little effect during the non-war inflationary environment in the early 1970s. The 55 mile per hour speed limit may have garnered compliance when it was instituted shortly after the OPEC oil embargo in the early 1970s, but by the time it was removed as a federal requirement, not only was the law violated, but in many areas almost no traffic on limited access highways was driving as slow as 55 miles per hour. If laws do not appear legitimate, they will be very difficult to enforce.

There is not a general theory linking legitimacy to compliance within a utility-maximizing framework, but such a general theory is not necessary to see the basic connection. If the government's actions are viewed as legitimate, the monitoring and enforcement costs necessary to get people to comply will be much lower. Governments cannot truly force their citizens to do much. Governments do use force to kill political opponents, to relocate people, and to take their wealth. Force can be most effective in taking from people things that they already have, such as their lives and their property. These activities do not require the active participation and cooperation of those being coerced. Force cannot be very effective at getting people to cooperate with government, either by producing wealth for the government, paying taxes, donating labor, or anything else that requires citizen cooperation. Governments always have the threat of coercion, but they are most effective when people cooperate without being forced.

Legitimacy and Agreement

At the beginning of the chapter the question was posed about what it means to agree with the government. One way to view the concept of agreement is that people view their government's actions as legitimate. Legitimacy promotes cooperation and thereby lowers monitoring and enforcement costs, but by the same token, acceptance of the government's legitimacy can also be viewed as agreement with the government.

People do not have to view the entire government as legitimate or illegitimate, but can evaluate various aspects of it. As earlier noted, the federal 55 mile per hour speed limit during the 1970s was widely viewed as illegitimate, and was also widely disobeyed. The federal income tax is often cited as unpopular, and people view individual provisions of the tax code as unfair, but it also has a foundation of legitimacy since it appears necessary to fund the government that is widely viewed as legitimate. If taxpayers disregarded the tax laws to the extent that drivers disregarded the 55 mile per hour speed limit, the government would have to expend much more to monitor and enforce the tax laws than it currently does, and would collect less in revenue. Likewise, people in general respect the property of others and do not injure or kill others even when some opportunistic gain might be available. These rights are viewed as legitimate by most people, so monitoring and enforcement costs are a small fraction of what they would need to be if the government actually had to intervene to prevent all opportunistic behavior. In the context of agreement with government, legitimacy and agreement could be viewed as the same thing.

The Production of Legitimacy

If governments are fundamentally coercive institutions, how can governments convey the impression of legitimacy, which is important to the routine functioning of government? One answer to this question follows along Rawlsian lines. Government actions are legitimate if people agree with them. There may be general agreement on such things as the right to life and property, conveying automatic legitimacy to government rules along these lines, but this line of reasoning poses more questions than it answers. People in government receive little in the way of benefit from protecting the rights of others. If the government is viewed as an institution that exchanges protection for tribute, as argued earlier, then the protection aspect of the exchange does not require legitimacy: this is something the government provides for its citizens. It is the tribute part of the exchange that must be viewed as legitimate for government to be able to operate. People pay taxes, work for the government, and are asked to abide by government regulations. If these institutions are viewed as legitimate, people will pay their taxes, government workers will do their jobs, and citizens will abide by regulations with minimal enforcement efforts.

Government institutions must create the appearance of legitimacy if the government is to be successful. Throughout most of history, the foundation upon which the legitimacy of government rested has been more concrete than in modern times. Sometimes governments have ruled simply because they had the power to keep their subjects under their control, but more often religion was a fundamental element in establishing the government's legitimacy.[4] The ancient Egyptians thought that the Pharaohs were gods. Feudal lords required the approval of the church to be viewed as legitimate rulers. Hereditary monarchies attempt to use the family relationship to establish the legitimacy of the succession of leaders, often with the assistance of the church to approve. When rulers are viewed as gods, or as ordained to be legitimate by gods, it is difficult for mortals to question their legitimacy.

In modern times, legitimacy is a more abstract concept than it has been though most of history. Socialist governments claim to be ruling on behalf of their citizens, making the legitimacy of a socialist government more open to question than one that is ordained by the gods. In democratic governments, legitimacy is conferred through popular election – that is, through agreement. Again, it is reasonable to question whether electoral institutions produce outcomes that legitimately represent the collective will of the voters. The legitimacy of a government's policies often rest on the legitimacy of the individuals who make those policies. Policies are legitimate to the extent that those who determine them have the legitimate right to do so.

The Vietnam war was very unpopular in the United States, yet Presidents Johnson and Nixon were able to send draftees to fight in the war. Their decisions were recognized as legitimate not because the war was generally agreed to be legitimate – it was not – or because Johnson and Nixon were viewed as especially wise people who could be trusted with such important decisions. Rather, both were elected through a process that was viewed as the legitimate way to select the head of the armed services, and the decision to fight the war was viewed as the legitimate decision of the holder of that position. The decision itself was not generally agreed upon, but the decision was viewed as legitimate because the institutional structure through which the decision was made was viewed as legitimate.

Murray Edelman has discussed the symbolic uses of politics extensively.[5] In his discussion of democratic politics, he emphasizes that democratic decision-making has the symbolic function of producing decisions through an institutional structure in which every citizen can participate, thus bestowing legitimacy upon decisions that might not be generally agreed upon were it not for the process used to arrive at the decision. While people in fact may not agree with the decision, they still accept it as legitimate because they recognize the decision-making process as legitimate. Such legitimacy is necessary for the functioning of government; otherwise, government could not monitor and enforce all of its rules. Thus, the institutional structure generates symbolic agreement and produces legitimacy for government actions that in the absence of such institutions might not be viewed as legitimate.

Agreement and Coercion

Could people be coerced into doing something and yet still agree with the policy that forces them to do something they do not want to? To answer this question, both coercion and agreement must be precisely defined. Using the definition from Chapter 5, coercion occurs when a party indicates the willingness to harm another if the other does not do what the coercing party wants. Taxation, for example, is coercive. If the perception of legitimacy is what is meant by agreement, then certainly people can agree to be coerced.

At its most benign, the argument might apply to something with the potential of free riding, such as income redistribution. People with higher incomes would like for those with lower incomes to be better off, but have an incentive to free ride off the charitable activity of others. Therefore, everyone is better off if they agree to allow the government to coerce higher income people into contributing toward the government's redistributive efforts.[6]

Critics of this argument might point out that if high income people really are forced to contribute, with no further evidence there is the possibility that none of them would like for the redistribution to take place; that it is a forced transfer and not a Pareto superior change. If this is true, they would not like that particular policy, so would not be in agreement with it. But if the policy is the product of a democratic political process with which they are in general agreement, then as an outcome of a process they support, they still could view the redistributive process as legitimate even though they would prefer not to have it, and in this sense could be said to be in agreement. The agreement here is with the legitimacy of the activity rather than with the specific policy. People could agree that the collective activity is legitimate even while preferring that it not be undertaken. The point is that agreement and coercion are not necessarily mutually exclusive.

Ideology

Douglass North considers the concepts of agreement and legitimacy to be an integral part of his concept of ideology.[7] Economists have tended to discuss ideology in the context of adhering to a particular political point of view even when it counters one's narrow self-interest.[8] This conception of ideology points toward North's broader discussion which considers the loyalty not inherent in the economist's definition. People believing in a particular ideology are willing to sacrifice in order to try to make it a part of public policy, even when they incur personal costs to do so. One might dismiss apparent ideological behavior as really in the individual's long-run self-interest, but this is hard to do in cases where, for example, a soldier engages in a life-threatening activity when it would be possible for the individual to retreat to safety. Through ideology, the individual has been convinced of the merit of making a sacrifice for his country. Ideology, in this same sense, can be the motivating factor for an individual who volunteers to work for a presidential candidate's campaign, or for a legislator who votes in the public interest rather than abiding by narrow constituent interests.

If individuals can be motivated to work for their government in this way, the government's monitoring and enforcement costs can be drastically lowered. Thus, political institutions are designed, or perhaps evolve, in a manner that generates ideological support for government action.[9] The majority of voters who back winning candidates and who incur private costs such as voting to do so then have an ideological reason to support those candidates once they are in office. Even supporters of opponents who hope to return at the next election have reason to support the legitimacy of the incumbent's actions so that, if victorious, those individuals will have support for their candidates. Ideology produces legitimacy, which lowers the cost of governing. Agreement with political institutions makes outcomes politically feasible even when the outcomes are not generally agreed upon.

Competitive elections are important to a democratic government, then. Opponents will not support the incumbent's policies if those opponents do not view that there is a legitimate chance for their policies to be taken into account through the political process. Furthermore, the act of voting bestows legitimacy for several reasons. First, it shows support for the government through the majority that voted for it, and second, it shows a degree of ideological commitment to the platform of the government. Declining voter turnout is – and should be – alarming to those in government, because it reduces the perception of legitimacy of the election's outcome, and thereby reduces the power of the government to act without expending resources on coercion. This explains why in democratic countries people would be urged to vote in general, without reference to a particular candidate, and why in dictatorships elections are held in which people are forced to vote even though voters have no choice among candidates. The symbolic act of voting bestows legitimacy upon the government.

Positive and Normative Agreement

Up to this point, agreement has been evaluated in purely positive terms. Agreement is important because it enables the government to do more with fewer resources, so the government has an incentive to create institutions which produce the image of legitimacy and agreement. Governments can terrorize people, steal from them, and kill them, but without agreement, they can not hope to get much in the way of productive activity from them.

In this sense, the perception of the legitimacy of government institutions is the mark of agreement.

In a normative sense, agreement can be used as the benchmark for which public policy proposals can be justified as in the public interest. From a positive standpoint the way in which governments use agreement to achieve their ends can be analyzed, but normatively agreement can be used as a measure of the public interest. There are alternative ways to view the public interest, which will be discussed in Chapter 11. At this point, the positive analysis of agreement will be extended to provide a foundation for using agreement as a normative criterion to evaluate the desirability of government actions.

An individualistic view of society implies that a group is nothing more than a collection of individuals, so the welfare of a group is nothing more than the aggregate welfare of the individuals in the group. Many criteria might be used within this individualistic framework to evaluate group welfare, but they all would share acceptance of the Pareto principle of welfare improvement.[10] This principle states that if at least one person in a group is better off as a result of some change, and nobody is worse off, then the welfare of the group is enhanced. Furthermore, the principle uses the individual's own evaluation of his or her welfare as a measure of whether an individual is better off. The Pareto principle in abstract welfare theory naturally extrapolates to the concept of agreement in politics.

If in a group of individuals at least one person will benefit from a change and nobody will be harmed, then if individuals agree to group action based on how it affects their welfare, all would agree to the change. Thus, agreement in a political setting implies the desirability of what is being agreed upon. In this way, agreement can be extended from a purely positive concept to one with normative implications. The social contract theory of the state is based upon the premise that the terms of government that people agree to are desirable.

The social contract theory of the state envisions government as an institution which acts for the collective benefit of its citizens. Individuals agree to abide by the rules of the state in exchange for the benefits the state provides. A fundamental premise underlying the social contract theory of the state is that without governmentally imposed order, a society would degenerate into a Hobbesian anarchy where life is nasty, brutish, and short.[11] Order cannot be maintained if people selectively decide which rules to obey, so for the good of all, individuals are bound by a social contract to abide by the government's rules.

As the previous analysis suggests, agreement in some sense will be necessary for the government to undertake activities such as taxation and public works. However, one can easily envision an oppressive government forcibly subjecting its citizens to rules that none of them views as legitimate, even if they agree to obey the government's rules because they do not view it as worthwhile to try to overthrow the government. The purpose of the social contract theory is to try to identify those rules which would be agreed to by those who are subject to them. The social contract consists of those social institutions and rules that individuals would voluntarily agree to as a basis for organizing their society.

The weak link in the social contract theory is the concept of agreement with the social contract. The fact is that few people ever actually agree to the terms of government. Therefore, the agreement that contractarians refer to is not an actual agreement with the social contract, but a conceptual agreement. If people can be said to agree, in some sense, with a social contract, then the social contract theory of the state can proceed, but without agreement there can be no contract. Is there any way that, in the absence of actually agreeing, the citizens of a government could be said to be in conceptual agreement with a social contract?

Problems with the Concept of Agreement

In the absence of actual agreement with the contract, the contractarian reliance on some type of implied or conceptual agreement is viewed by some as a fatal flaw for the entire theory. Yeager clearly articulates reasons why the reliance on conceptual agreement is sufficient reason for objecting to the entire contractarian framework.

> The writings of Buchanan and other contractarians (including Holcombe 1983, especially chapter 8) bristle with works like "conceptual" and "conceptually" – "conceptually agree," "conceptual agreement," "conceptual social contract," "conceptual unanimous approval," and the like. The very use of the words indicates that a "conceptual" agreement is not an actual one, that a "conceptually" true proposition is not actually true. It is no mere joke to say that "conceptually" is an adverb stuck into contractarians' sentences to immunize them from challenge on the grounds of their not being true.
>
> Buchanan (1975, pp. 123, 125) distinguishes between constitutional and postconstitutional decisionmaking and envisages agreement or "conceptual" agreement at the constitutional stage as authorizing "apparent coercion" and "apparent redistribution" at the postconstitutional stage. By such fictions, realities like actual coercion and actual redistribution

are interpreted away. They vanish into the realm of the merely "apparent" by being deemed in accordance with some agreement that may itself be merely "conceptual."[12]

Yeager's objection is not to the use of metaphor or analogy in explaining the theory, he makes clear, but in the fact that there is no real world counterpart to the analogy. The conceptual agreement in the theory is not analogous to any real world agreement. Yeager continues:

> No one need object to fictions if they are heuristically useful – if they stimulate the flow of ideas. Nor is it necessarily objectionable to employ fictions and figures of speech for expository and stylistic purposes. But a doctrine should not *depend* on them. Ideas that defy expression in straightforward, nonmetaphorical language incur deserved doubt by that very fact.[13]

Yeager's criticisms deserve the serious consideration of contractarians. Yeager argues that if one determines that a government is based on a social contract, any activities of the government can be justified based upon the implied agreement of the government's citizens. If the government drafts a person into the army, makes people of African descent sit in the back of the bus, or sets up "sting" operations to try to entice citizens to violate the government's rules, one cannot object because the actions are based upon agreement with the social contract. Yeager's fear is that under the guise of the social contract theory of the state, any government activity, no matter how coercive, can be justified as "conceptually" agreed to even though the activity itself is clearly coercive.

The main reason that the social contract theory has this potential is the distinction within the theory, made clear by Buchanan and Tullock in *The Calculus of Consent*, between constitutional and postconstitutional decisions. People might agree to rules at the constitutional level knowing that at the postconstitutional level some decisions will go against them. They agree to the constitutional rule because, overall, they expect to be better off avoiding the decision-making costs that can be incurred if no constitutional framework is available within which postconstitutional decisions can be made. For example, at the constitutional level, a group of friends might unanimously agree that if a majority of them can agree on where to eat lunch, the rest will go along with the majority. Some people in the minority might find themselves worse off on a particular day when the lunch crowd makes a postconstitutional decision to eat somewhere they do not like, but overall the individuals in the group are better off avoiding the decision-making costs of securing unanimous agreement by agreeing at the constitutional level to a simple majority rule decision.

This distinction between constitutional and postconstitutional decisions leaves the door wide open for the social contract theory to be abused in the manner suggested by Yeager. Once someone agrees to the constitution, any postconstitutional decision made under the constitution is also agreed to, conceptually. Yeager objects to the fact that there is no actual agreement with the constitution, but the same type of coercion he is concerned about could arise even if someone explicitly states agreement with the constitution. Any constitution is subject to interpretation. In the United States the Supreme Court interprets the actual Constitution. Whether or not one considers the U.S. Constitution a part of a social contract, the fact that the Supreme Court often finds itself split on Constitutional issues suggests that it would be very difficult in any real world setting to develop a social contract that every person agreed to, and that every person interpreted the same way.

It is very possible in the real world to imagine a situation in which a person claims agreement with a social contract, either conceptually or actually, but finds at the moment that a postconstitutional decision goes against him that he would not have agreed with the social contract if he had anticipated that particular postconstitutional decision. For example, a person opposed to abortion in the 1960s might have stated agreement with the Constitution and the role of the Supreme Court in interpreting it, but when the Court's decision in Roe vs. Wade in 1973 legalized abortion, the person could view this legalization as a violation of the social contract, or at least the social contract as she thought she understood it. It would be hard to argue self interest in such a case; after all, everyone who vocalizes opposition to abortion is already born and, if pregnant, has the choice to have an abortion or not. The argument that people have an obligation to an unborn child is probably as close as one can get in the real world to an argument made behind a Rawlsian veil of ignorance, because there is little in the way of directly personal self interest involved.

Yeager argues that because there is no actual agreement with a social contract, the social contract theory of the state cannot be applicable to the real world. The problem is compounded when one realizes that no constitution in the real world can specify every contingency, so people might agree to a decision-making rule which produces postconstitutional decisions so offensive to some that they never would have approved the constitution in the first place if they had been able to foresee the postconstitutional decisions it would produce. Even if these people initially agreed, could they still be said to be in agreement with the constitution? If the answer to this question is no, which seems reasonable, then even actual agreement to a less-than-unanimous decision rule at one point in time does not constitute agreement with every decision that is made under that rule.

The very real danger of the social contract theory is that it can be used to justify government coercion by arguing that those being coerced conceptually agreed to a social contract and now must abide by the government's rules, whatever they are. Any government is, at its foundation, an institution built on the power to coerce, and a theory which portrays the government as an institution of agreement rather than coercion has the power to be misused.

If this is so, can there be anything to a theory that relies on conceptual agreement so crucially? Most of the remainder of this chapter looks at this question by developing a theory of conceptual or implied agreement.

Implied Agreement

This section sets aside questions about the social contract in order to look at the issue of implied agreement in general. The real world is complex enough that it is impractical to state every implication of every agreement made. For example, one person might invite another to his house for dinner. Before dinner, the guest tries to use the bathroom, but the host argues that the guest was invited over specifically for dinner. Nothing was said about using the bathroom. The behavior of the host seems odd because one assumes that along with a dinner invitation is the implied agreement to use the bathroom facilities at the host's home.[14]

More extreme examples could be concocted. The host might invite the guest to spend the day on his sailboat. After hours of exposure to the hot sun the guest might want something to drink, but the host argues that the invitation was simply to spend the day on the boat; nothing was said about food or drink. A this point, the host might offer to sell a drink to the guest for, say $1000. Could there be any objection to this voluntary agreement? Or the host might invite the guest to spend a week at his secluded mountain cabin in the middle of Winter. By now, the reader can see the possibilities.

In all of these cases, there are implied conditions attached to the stated invitations. The point of this section is to illustrate that even in the simplest of social interactions, there are implied conditions present – conditions that go well beyond any stated agreement. In the cases stated above, many readers will agree that the person extending the invitation made an implied agreement to in addition to the simple stated conditions. Thus, a conceptual or implied agreement does not seem unreasonable in and of itself, although the argument is still a long way from defending the social contract theory of the state.

Implied Agreement in Law

The law also recognizes implied agreement in a number of instances, typically falling under the broad heading of reasonableness. For example, two parties may sign an actual contract, entering into an actual agreement, but later the courts may declare the contract (or some specific provisions) invalid because the provisions are not reasonable. Therefore, an actual agreement in the form of a signed contract can be overturned because of a conceptual agreement implied in the law that contract terms must be reasonable.

A common example involves the use of penalty clauses. Courts are willing to assess damages when the terms of a contract are unfulfilled, but are reluctant to enforce the payment of penalties, even when the penalties are clearly stated in a contract. Many things might interfere with the fulfilment of a contract, and some of them might make it reasonable to expect that the contract terms could not be fulfilled. Courts seem to recognize this in their reluctance to enforce penalty clauses. As a result, it is rare to see anything called a penalty. The penalty that businesses assess their customers for bouncing checks or backing out of leases is always called a service charge in order to make legal collection easier.

The use of reasonableness in the law is not limited to contracts. In general, the law views that people are obligated to act in a reasonable manner, but the precise definition of reasonable behavior is left surprisingly vague considering the importance that reasonable behavior plays in the law. Apparently, reasonable behavior is behavior that most people would view as reasonable under the circumstances. "Most people" is a large group, few of whom could ever be present in a courtroom at any one time. It appears, then, that the judge or jury must decide what most people would consider reasonable.

A closely related concept is intent. If parties to a contract intend for a contract to have certain effects, the actual contract could be struck down because its effects differed from their intentions. Examples might be long-term contracts for continual purchases signed during a period of relative price stability. If unanticipated inflation significantly affected prices, the contract could be declared invalid because its stated terms differed from the intent of the contract.

In all cases, a contract can never be written in such a comprehensive manner that it takes account of every imaginable contingency. The law recognizes a conceptual agreement between parties that the provisions be reasonable, and this conceptual agreement is recognized in the law to override even actual agreements in signed contracts. This does not prove that the law is a social contract, but it does illustrate that even when actual formal signed agreements have been made, the law recognizes a conceptual agreement between the parties going beyond the actual stated agreement, and sometimes that even contradicts the stated terms of the signed agreement. In the real world, implied conditions are a part of every agreement, whether or not the parties to the agreement have actually agreed to these implied conditions, and sometimes even when they explicitly agree not to abide by them.

Fictions

Fictions are views that are generally believed or acted on as if they are true, but that are not true or are only partially true. The dictionary says that a fiction is something accepted as fact for convenience, although it is not necessarily true. The law provides a good example, because of the fiction that current legal decisions are based on an objective law that judges only interpret. In fact, when new cases arise, judges make decisions that serve as precedent for future cases: they make new law.

This fiction has a long history. In ancient Greece, the laws of Solon were believed to be the origin of law. In ancient Rome, the Twelve Tablets served the same purpose, and the fiction continues today, both through the common law and through the fiction that the Supreme Court merely interprets the constitution. Clearly, the Court makes law, although the fiction states otherwise.[15]

In the United States it is often said that any person can grow up to be president, although this is clearly not true. Likewise, there is a myth that through popular voting, every citizen has a say in the actions of government. This fiction has been discussed extensively by students of public choice who argue that voters are rationally ignorant because their votes do not count.[16] Yet the fiction continues because it is useful. It provides legitimacy to the actions of government officials because they are acting in the will of the majority.[17] The concept of legitimacy that was important to the operation of government as discussed earlier is also important to the conceptual agreement with government in a normative sense.

Fictions are related to the conceptual agreement with the social contract because fictions are one of the mechanisms that enable people to agree with the actions of the state. One does not always agree with the decisions made by elected officials, but since one agrees with the process, a person can agree that the decision is legitimate even while disagreeing with the decision itself. Fictions facilitate this implied agreement with the institutional structure.

Conceptual agreement in a social setting is common. Because every contingency cannot be specified or even imagined in advance, social interactions as varied as informal invitations and formal contracts are governed by implied conditions that may cause the actual terms of the agreement to differ from the literal agreement actually made. These implied conditions are not a social contract, although the use of fictions often eases their general acceptance and makes them meet the conditions of terms of a social contract.

In a larger sense, the social contract itself, if accepted as an agreed-upon set of rules, is a fiction, following the dictionary definition. It is accepted as fact for convenience, even though it is not actually true.

Conceptual and Implied Agreement

This section steps from the idea of conceptual agreement in general, which, as noted earlier, is common, to the idea of conceptual agreement with a social contract. Two recent innovators in this area are Rawls and Buchanan. Their development of the ideas of conceptual agreement with the social contract are often linked together, but this section makes a distinction. Thus far, the chapter has used the terms conceptual agreement and implied agreement without differentiating between them, but Rawls' theory is a theory of conceptual agreement while Buchanan's is one of implied agreement. The differences are relevant when one considers what it means to agree with the social contract.

Rawls uses the abstraction of the veil of ignorance to determine whether there is agreement. Individuals behind the veil do not know what place in society they will occupy, and decide behind the veil what social institutions are just. Since people do not actually step behind the veil, the contractarian must determine whether a certain social institution would be agreed to behind the veil. Conceptual agreement for Rawls means that people would agree, if they were behind the veil and had no knowledge of their particular status in society, to the provision in question. In essence, Rawls says that if people would agree to a provision if they did not take into account their own particular circumstances, but instead thought of the welfare of everyone, then there is conceptual agreement. This appears to be a reasonable normative criterion for determining if some provision is in the public interest.

Buchanan takes a different approach when analyzing agreement. He develops a model of Hobbesian anarchy and imagines a renegotiation of the social contract from this state of anarchy. A range of possible social contracts might emerge from renegotiation starting at the anarchistic equilibrium, and if an individual expects that the status quo would be included within the expected range of renegotiated contracts, then the individual, by acknowledging that what presently exists would be within the range of expected renegotiation outcomes, implies agreement with the provision.

There are several differences between the approaches of Buchanan and Rawls on the issue of agreement. In the Rawlsian model, individuals behind the veil have no specific knowledge of their individual circumstances, so the individuals should have identical preferences. There is no issue of agreement, per se, because all of the identical individuals behind the veil should have the same preferences for social institutions. Individuals would only agree to provisions that they believe are beneficial. In Buchanan's model, individuals are not stripped of their individuality, but instead imagine how they might fare if the social contract were renegotiated. In this case, each person might well imagine that the social contract would contain some provisions that, taken individually, the person would not like. In the negotiating process, people would accept some proposals by others that they disliked slightly in exchange for proposals they strongly favored. If a person views the provision in question as a likely candidate for inclusion in the renegotiated contract, then the person implies agreement in Buchanan's model, even though if asked, the person might disagree with the provision.

Thus, the Rawlsian model contains a conceptual agreement where everyone would agree to a provision behind the veil of ignorance, whereas Buchanan's model contains an implied agreement where agreement is implied if the individual would expect that the provision would be likely to appear in a renegotiated contract. A provision that an individual does not favor would be a part of the social contract in Buchanan's model if the individual could envision bargaining away that provision in order to include provisions about which the individual feels more intense. In the Rawlsian model, a provision that an individual does not favor would be a part of the social contract if the individual could envision favoring it having no knowledge of his own personal circumstances in life. As would be expected from an economist, there is more of a bargaining element in Buchanan's model of agreement.

The key distinction between the two approaches, though, is that in Rawls' model people would unanimously agree with every provision of the social contract if only they could ignore their own particular circumstances. This is a conceptual agreement, which must remain a hypothetical construct. In Buchanan's model, people imply their agreement if they envision that under a renegotiation, a social institution would be likely to emerge much as it is today. This construction is closer to the real world since it would be possible to ask people to imagine a renegotiation of a social contract from a situation of anarchy, and then inquire as to whether the present social institutions would fall within the bounds of what one would expect out of the renegotiation. If a person answers yes, then in Buchanan's model, the person implies agreement with the social contract. Perhaps the same provisions would emerge in either case, but there still is a difference in the mechanism of the Rawlsian conceptual agreement and Buchanan's implied agreement.

As a more concrete example, consider a group of people moving into a condominium governed by a set of rules, and where all members own some property in common. By moving into the condominium, the residents would be in implied agreement with the rules, since by their actions they reveal that the cost of the rules that particular individuals dislike are outweighed by the benefits of the rules the other rules they like. Different people, of course, might like different rules. This is agreement in Buchanan's sense. There would be conceptual agreement in Rawls' sense if all individuals would unanimously agree to the rules if they had no knowledge of their own particular circumstances.

The ideas of conceptual agreement and implied agreement are close enough operationally that it is likely that similar social contracts would emerge from both models. They are not identical, though, because Buchanan's implied agreement leaves room for a range of outcomes. For someone concerned about the abstract and hypothetical nature of the argument, Buchanan's model comes closer to having a counterpart in reality. It is similar to the concept of legitimacy. People could be asked if they might expect current social institutions to emerge from a renegotiation from anarchy, but the critic could still claim that the whole idea of renegotiation from anarchy is sufficiently abstract to make it inapplicable to the real world.

A Positive Application of Implied Agreement

One objection noted to the social contract theory is that nobody has actually agreed to the terms of the social contract. However, implied agreement does take place in a very real sense for local governments. To the extent that the Tiebout model is descriptive,[18] people can choose the local government under which they will live, presumably accepting the terms and conditions of the government as a group. Few residents will find absolutely everything about a local government to be completely to their liking, but if the hypothetical bargaining behind the veil of ignorance were to take place, the Rawlsian outcome would not be completely to the liking of every individual in the society either. Rather, the interests of some people are compromised on some issues so that they can get what they really prefer on other issues. The bargaining process produces an outcome where the individual accepts less-preferred results on some things in exchange for getting more-preferred results on other things that the individual values more highly.

When moving into a local community, the bargaining has already taken place, and the individual chooses the community that offers the most preferred bundle of goods. Intergovernmental competition is the factor that pushes the bargain toward one that would be agreed to behind a veil of ignorance, and individuals making locational decisions are choosing a set of constitutional rules after the veil has been lifted.

This example points toward a possible set of institutions which can be studied to see how optimal constitutional rules are formed. Many residential developments place restrictive covenants on property in the development which require property owners to pay taxes and abide by certain rules in exchange for receiving public goods and having others in the development be subject to the same rules. In some areas, public goods include roads, utilities, and recreational facilities that parallel what local governments provide in other areas. The constitutions for these subdivisions are drawn up by entrepreneurs who want to maximize the value of the property governed by the covenants, so there is an incentive for them to create constitutions which maximize the value of the governed property.

The institutions make good candidates for the study of optimal constitutional rules. The entrepreneur can be looked at as the designer of rules behind the veil of ignorance, since the entrepreneur will not know which specific people will buy the property, and the future property owners signify their unanimous consent to the rules because each agrees to move there rather than to another area without that constitution.[19]

One might question to what extent moving to a location signifies agreement with its rules. The stereotypical company town, for example, had a reputation for taking advantage of its residents even though they voluntarily moved there to get the company job.[20] However, there is clearly an element of agreement when people move into one local government – or residential subdivision – when there is a choice of many others, and therefore, there is the possibility to study the different rules as an application of the social contract theory.

It is interesting to note that there have been instances in which citizens of a community affirm their agreement to the rules under which they are governed. Harold Berman describes the approval of the city charter of London in 1200, where all the townsmen stretched their hands toward the Gospels and "with one voice solemnly swore" to safeguard the borough and the charter.[21] Summarizing the characteristics of urban law as it emerged from 1050–1150, Berman goes on to note, "Many cities and towns were founded by a solemn collective oath, or series of oaths, made by the entire citizenry to adhere to a charter that had been publicly read aloud to them. The charter was, in one sense, a social contract; it must, indeed, have been one of the principal historical sources from which the modern contract theory of government emerged . . . . Acceptance of the urban charter was . . . an avowal of consent to a permanent relationship."[22] Berman compares the social contract in this setting to a marriage contract.

In a contemporary setting, most likely the closest one can get to actual agreement is movement into the jurisdiction of a local government when there are alternatives – especially if one of the alternatives is to live outside the bounds of any municipality. In a positive sense, surely this would constitute agreement in that people would not move into the jurisdiction of a municipal government when there was an alternative to live outside it. From a normative standpoint, however, something akin the the Rawlsian veil of ignorance might be a better criterion.

Normative Application

The observation of an actual agreement is a good indication that people agree with the issue at hand. With unanimous agreement, a Pareto superior move will be made, which is unobjectionable from an individualistic standpoint. From a normative standpoint, for purposes of policy recommendation, there are some possible drawbacks to the use of actual agreement as the sole indicator of a potential improvement. First, such an observation can only take place after the fact, so cannot serve as a guide to proposing policies. Second, there may be elements of coercion that cause people to go along with a group decision. Third, restricting change to actual Pareto superior moves gives undue weight to the status quo. Each of these drawbacks will be considered in turn.

One can evaluate existing rules and policies from the standpoint of whether people actually agree with them, but for purposes of formulating new policy or proposing changes in the rules, one cannot observe actual agreement. The concept of agreement is still useful at the planning stage, though, because one can attempt to construct policies that would secure agreement among those governed by the new policies or rules. From a normative standpoint, the policy maker at the planning stage would ask, "Is this change something that those affected by it would view as beneficial?" An affirmative answer suggests a proposal that is in the public interest. Thus, the concept of agreement can serve as a guide to the formulation of policies and rules before proposals enter the political forum.

Similarly, the concept of agreement can be used as a persuasive device once a proposal has been made and has entered the arena of public debate. One can argue that people should support a proposal because it benefits them. Even if some particular interests are harmed, one can take a more Rawlsian stance and argue that if people abstract from their own particular interests, they would see that the proposal is in the general public interest. Thus, the concept of agreement is used as a normative criterion for trying to persuade people that something is in the public interest and that they should support it.

If a proposal is voted on, that will reveal whether there is actual agreement, but before this stage, the concept of agreement can guide policy-making by directing policy proposals toward those with which people would agree. The underlying criterion is individualism. Individuals are the best judge of what is good for them. If they agree to a proposal, then the proposal is in the public interest. Thus, agreement serves as the normative criterion for evaluating public policy and changes in rules.

The second problem noted above is that actual agreement in the real world has the drawback that it may be forthcoming only because those expressing their agreement see no real alternative. People might go along with one totalitarian regime because they perceive that the only real alternative is for it to be replaced with another one. The Eastern European governments after World War II might be an example of this. Before 1989, residents of those Eastern bloc countries had good reason to believe that if they attempted to replace their existing governments, the Soviet Union would intervene to prevent the establishment of democracy. When the Sovet Union announced in 1989 that it would not intervene in the internal affairs of those countries, their totalitarian governments fell with startling swiftness. Agreement with an existing regime when there does not appear to be good viable alternatives might constitute agreement in a positive sense, but has potential shortcomings from a normative standpoint.

Again, the Rawlsian criterion seems preferable as a normative criterion. If one did not know what position in society one would occupy after a veil of ignorance was lifted, would people agree to have this type of society? Would they agree to this set of rules and policies? The individualistic perspective is used as a foundation for discussion, and one can argue in favor of social changes using the argument that the people affected by the proposed changes would be in favor of them.

The final problem noted above is that the status quo is accorded a special status under the criterion of actual agreement. For example, the rulers in totalitarian regimes have much to lose if their governments are replaced. While it is possible that they could be compensated for the loss, people could object that they do not deserve compensation. The Rawlsian criterion overcomes this objection because behind the veil of ignorance, nobody knows who would be the rulers and who would be the ruled.

The criterion of agreement provides an apparatus by which an individual can undertake a thought experiment to determine whether some public policy or government action is in the public interest. There are many ways to evaluate the public interest, but the contractarian method begins by asking whether people would agree with the particular policy or action which is being considered. The agreement that contractarians refer to is one that tries to abstract from the specific self-interests of individuals by asking if they would agree that the provision in question furthers the general public interest.

In Rawls' model, this means that if individuals were ignorant of their own particular circumstances in life, would they favor the provision.[23] In Buchanan's model, it means that individuals could agree that the provision would be likely to be produced from a renegotiation of the social contract. The emphasis here is on what would be likely to emerge from a bargaining process – the terms on which people would be likely to agree.[24]

There is clearly a value judgment taking place, but one that appears reasonable. The contractarian favors a policy if it is one that seems likely to command agreement from people who do not consider their own personal circumstances, or that seems likely to emerge from a bargaining process in which people negotiate the terms of the social contract. An individual advocating a policy from a contractarian perspective argues that it is desirable because the people who are affected by the policy would find it desirable. Seen in this way, the contractarian model is the normative extension of the exchange model of government, and desirable outcomes are those that would be likely to emerge from a bargaining process – that is, those on which people would be likely to agree.[25]

Conceptual Agreement

When considered within the general framework of social interaction, the conceptual agreement embodied in the social contract theory of the state is not by itself unreasonable or unusual. Social interactions in general contain implied conditions which are agreed to in concept without explicit statement, and contracts are often interpreted in a manner different from their literal meanings because of an implied agreement to reasonableness or to the intent of the contract, regardless of what it literally says. The conceptual agreement embodied in the social contract theory of the state is the same as the conceptual agreement in these other social interactions.

By itself, the notion of conceptual agreement has a firm foundation. In addition to there being implied conditions in every explicit agreement, individuals expect a certain type of behavior from others in society with whom they do not explicitly negotiate, and are offended when others do not conform to social norms. An implied agreement on acceptable social behavior has been violated. This must be true if people hold any expectations about the behavior of strangers. The question then comes down, not to the issue of conceptual agreement itself, but whether the concept can legitimately be extended to produce a social contract theory of the state. When used as a basis for policy prescription, the social contract theory is clearly normative, and normative theories cannot be proven in the same way as positive theories. However, the preceding sections are intended to persuade the reader that the contractarian method which uses the concept of agreement as its normative principle is a reasonable method for evaluating the desirability of social rules and public policy decisions.

Conclusion

The concept of agreement provides a transition from positive to normative analysis of government. In a positive analysis, the concept of agreement is important for several reasons. First, if citizens are in agreement with the actions of their governments, then those in government will be more likely to be able to achieve their ends, and achieve them at lower cost. The evidence of agreement is the perception of legitimacy, and many public sector institutions are designed to make the government's actions appear more legitimate. Second, agreement is important because agreement makes outcomes politically feasible. Changes in rules and implementation of public policy are more easily carried out if people agree. Thus, from a positive standpoint, generating agreement is one of the steps that must be taken to implement social changes.

The analysis could have ended at this point rather than continuing on to the examination of agreement as a normative criterion, and without the material in the following chapters which analyzes public sector decisions from a normative standpoint. However, normative analysis is important in an examination of government because the institutions of government are the results of the choices of individuals. Whether one is analyzing democracies, where citizens choose their institutions, or dictatorships, where an individual or small group chooses them, political institutions are the result of individual choices, and individuals can choose to change them. This being the case, it seems desirable to extend what was developed as a purely positive theory of government to examine normative questions.

What makes a desirable government? How could one judge whether a constitutional rule is in the public interest? How would one determine whether a particular public policy is beneficial? The concept of agreement emerges naturally out of an exchange model of government as a normative criterion for evaluating the desirability of rules, policies, and governments. Desirable outcomes are outcomes that individuals agree with.

Normative analyses are built on value judgments, and it is not possible to prove that one person's values are any better than another's. This does not rule out an examination and comparison of other normative criteria to see when they are consistent with each other, and even to persuade others of the merits of a particular set of values. The next chapter uses the concept of agreement as the departure point for analyzing several theories of government.

11 Positive and Normative Theories of Government

Any discussion of government naturally points toward normative issues because government is the product of collective choice. In the preceding chapters, theories of governments, rights, and individuals' relationships with each other and their governments were all discussed, but primarily in a positive setting that did not evaluate the desirability of these institutions. Factors that give the government an image of legitimacy were examined also, but from the standpoint of determining whether governments actually would be viewed as legitimate, rather than whether they should be viewed as legitimate. If the exchange model of government that has served as the foundation for the preceding discussion is valid, then at least to some degree the resulting government is a product of the collective choice of the governed. Constitutional rules are produced through some type of collective choice process, so normative issues are always present in the form of examining whether better constitutional rules could be developed. This chapter looks at the link between positive and normative theories of government.[1]

Government is a human creation, and people can modify government, either within governmentally approved channels such as democratic decision-making, or outside of such channels by means such as revolution. In any case, proposals for change must be supported by others in order to be enacted. At this point, normative principles become important, because policy proposals will be supported to the degree that they are viewed as an improvement, and whether a change is desirable is a normative issue. Because people can change the characteristics of their governments, normative principles are important both to understand the government of the past and present and to formulate proposals for improving government in the future.

Why Normative Theories Require Positive Theories

A normative theory of government is a value judgment that describes what government should be. In making value judgments about the ideal state of affairs, people are free to speculate on desirable arrangements without being constrained. But if they are advocating institutional changes that should be implemented in place of existing institutions, then their suggestions can succeed only if they are consistent with an accurate positive model of social interaction. Idealistic models of political processes can work only if the actions of individuals in those idealistic models are consistent with real-world individual behavior.

The constraints imposed by physical laws are easier to comprehend than those imposed by social laws. For example, the internal combustion engine creates air pollution, and one ideal solution to the pollution problem would be to pass a law requiring that automobiles continue to take people where they want to go, but without emitting any pollutants. People recognize that this is not feasible using currently available technology, though, so seek other solutions (including the passage of laws requiring less pollution). The ideal pollution-free world cannot be produced simply by mandate that the world be that way, so realistic solutions take account of the constraints of physical laws to try to develop ways to reduce pollution.

Social laws imply the same types of constraints on the operation of the ideal society. For example, in response to the concern that some workers earn an inadequately low wage, a minimum wage law might be enacted. But as is well-known, a minimum wage law that raises the wages of some workers will reduce the demand for low-skilled labor and will cause others to be unemployed. Because unemployed people earn no wages, a minimum wage law cannot guarantee that some workers will not earn an inadequately low wage.[2] While sometimes more difficult to recognize, the laws of social science are just as binding on the operation of a society as the laws of physics.

This same line of reasoning applies to any proposed change in a society's constitutional rules. Ideally, one might argue that people should have certain rights and that government should have certain obligations to its citizens. However, in order to have the potential for successful implementation, those rights and obligations must be consistent with the underlying laws of social science.[3] Any normative recommendation for social change must be consistent with the social laws which dictate the way the world works in order for the changes to work as intended.

Thus, a complete normative recommendation for change must include a positive analysis which demonstrates that the proposed change is consistent with the laws that govern social behavior. Simply arguing that the intended consequences of the recommendation are desirable is insufficient. There must be a positive theory showing how the recommended change will cause the proposed consequences to actually occur. To be judged completely, the normative recommendation must be subject to both a positive and a normative review. The normative review evaluates whether the proposed means and the proposed ends are desirable, while the positive review evaluates whether the proposed means can actually be expected to produce the proposed ends. Any normative theory requires a positive theory as a foundation.

The preceding chapters stand as a positive theory of government. If government is the result of human design, one can hope to constantly refine and improve the design, which opens the door for a normative analysis. Much of the discussion in this chapter will be about various normative principles that can be used to guide the design of government. The previous chapter argued the merits of using agreement as a normative criterion, and this chapter will consider agreement in more detail through an examination of contractarian models, and will use agreement as a point of departure for discussing other normative criteria.

Contractarianism

The social contract theory of the state is a normative application of the concept of agreement as an indicator of social desirability. The public interest is furthered by changes that are agreed to by those who are affected. The logic of this position is that the welfare of the group means nothing other than the welfare of the individuals who are in the group; thus, group welfare is increased when the people who compose the group are better off. If individuals are best able to judge what makes them better off, then if individuals agree to a change, they must feel that they are made better off, which in turn enhances the welfare of the group.

This argument does not imply that individuals always know what is best for them, but rather that they are in a better position to judge than anyone else. An omniscient observer would be in a position to judge that what an individual thinks would be beneficial would actually be detrimental, but other individuals would not be in a better position to judge the individual's best interests than that individual. It goes without saying that individuals could be mistaken about what is in their self-interest, but it is also true that people who judge what is in the best interest of others could be mistaken. To be less abstract, the policy-maker who argues that something to which people do not agree is really in their best interest could be wrong. The contractarian criterion of agreement would side with the affected individuals rather than the policy maker.

The key feature of contractarianism as a method of public policy formation is agreement among those covered by the policies in question. In the case where a public policy change would make everyone better off, agreement should be easy to come by, at least if individuals correctly evaluate their self interests. But contractarians invoke more abstract concepts of agreement for policies that make a better society, even though their daily application may make some individuals worse off. The classic example is the discussion by Buchanan and Tullock in *The Calculus of Consent* regarding the possibility that a group would unanimously agree to a less than unanimous group decision-making rule, knowing that sometimes individuals would find themselves in the minority on particular issues.[4]

Agreement behind a Rawlsian veil of ignorance is one way in which contractarian models depict agreement. There, individuals are ignorant about who they will be in society; they have an equal probability of being anyone after the veil is lifted. In such a setting, individuals have an incentive to choose rules which produce general benefits to a society and have no way to consider their own narrow self interests. The government agreed upon behind the Rawlsian veil of ignorance receives the normative recommendation of the Rawlsian contractarian. From a normative standpoint, the contractarian recommends institutions that people would agree upon if they consider the general public interest rather than their own narrow self interests. The veil of ignorance is simply a device that forces people to abstract from their own narrow self interests.

Because the Rawlsian model depicts a conceptual agreement, but there is no actual agreement, the contractarian model could be used to justify, based on agreement, institutions to which nobody would actually agree. The argument would be that people would agree behind a veil of ignorance. But this argument is subject to the counter argument, "No, they would not!" The same criticism could be made of the utilitarian framework, where a utilitarian could say that a certain proposal would enhance social welfare. The burden of proof is on the individual who proposes the change to illustrate that people actually would agree to it, or that it actually is utility-enhancing.

The contractarian model will be considered in more detail as a framework for policy proposals in the next chapter. Consider now some alternative models.

Utilitarianism

For more than a century, economists have used variants of utilitarianism to recommend changes in the design of government. Utilitarianism is based upon the principle that it is possible to compare utilities among individuals and to evaluate the benefits of the gainers in any proposed change relative to the losses to the losers. If the gains to the gainers outweigh the losses to the losers, then the policy change is desirable in the utilitarian framework. Government is then structured in such a way as to maximize social utility.

Early utilitarians argued that the utility levels of individuals were cardinally measurable and interpersonally comparable. In theory, it would be straightforward to compare the utility gains of the gainers against the utility losses of the losers in order to choose the utility-maximizing option. The practical challenge was trying to estimate actual utility levels. Contemporary utilitarian analysis makes use of a social welfare function that ranks all combinations of utilities possible for individuals in a society. From a mathematical standpoint, a social welfare function is more sophisticated than simple addition of utilities, but it still allows for utilitarian comparisons. The social welfare function enables its user to evaluate whether a gain in utility for some people more than offsets a loss to others to produce a net gain in social welfare.[5]

In trying to design desirable governmental institutions, one method would be the utilitarian method of designing institutions that maximize social utility. One criticism of utilitarianism is that it requires interpersonal utility comparisons, and in reality, there is no way to evaluate whether the gain in utility for some offsets the loss to others. But in reality, such trade-offs are always faced, and policy-makers must in fact choose among policies none of which Pareto-dominates the others. Any choice will make some better off and some worse off, so real-world policy-making requires making the judgment of whether the gains to the gainers offset the losses to the losers.

A more substantial critique of utilitarianism as a normative criterion for choosing among governmental policies is that because there is no objective basis in reality for the interpersonal utility comparisons that must be made to judge one option superior to another, differences among utilitarians regarding which is a better policy reduce to differences of opinion. If, in considering replacing policy A with policy B, one person thinks that the gains to the gainers would outweigh the losses to the losers while another does not, there is no way to objectively identify who is right.

Cost-benefit analysis might be viewed as an attempt to implement utilitarianism in an objective manner. If the total costs and benefits are estimated and utilities are compared using the common denominator of dollars, then there is at least some objective measure. But individuals clearly reveal in their behavior that money income provides more utility to some individuals than others, so this is not entirely satisfactory either.

Act versus Rule Utilitarianism

A significant distinction when discussing utilitarianism is the difference between act utilitarianism and rule utilitarianism. Act utilitarianism advocates performing those acts which maximize social utility, while rule utilitarianism considers only the choice of social rules as subject to the utilitarian calculus. While it is clear that much contemporary economics is act utilitarian,[6] rule utilitarianism has more in common with the constitutional paradigm of contractarianism. The issue with rule utilitarianism is choosing the constitutional rules which maximize social utility.

For example, an act utilitarian might ask whether taking a dollar from a rich person and giving it to a poor one would increase the utility of the poor person more than it decreased the utility of the rich. If so, the transfer would be made. Rule utilitarians would not consider such individual acts, but would instead consider whether a rule that required higher-income people to transfer some of their income to lower-income people would increase total utility. If so, they would advocate instituting the rule. But the problem remains as to how the losses to the losers are to be measured against the gains to the gainers. If one utilitarian argued that the gain would be utility-enhancing while another argued it would not, how could the dispute be settled?

While there is no objective evidence that can be presented about the relative utilities, the utilitarian presumably is abstracting from his or her own actual position in life to make a judgment about the magnitude of the gains to the gainers and losses to the losers. This thought experiment is much like retreating behind a Rawlsian veil of ignorance, where the utilitarian imagines that, if a person did not know what position he or she would occupy in life, would the objective observer view that the policy in question produced gains to the gainers that outweighed the losses to the losers. In other words, would the person be willing to risk the chance that he or she would end up being among the losers in order to gain the chance that he or she would be among the gainers? If so, then both the utilitarian and the contractarian would view the policy change as desirable. When reduced to their ultimate methods of evaluation, there may be a close affinity between rule utilitarians and contractarians.

Distinctions Between Utilitarians and Contractarians

In an insightful paper, Leland Yeager discusses the differences between utilitarians and contractarians.[7] Yeager approaches the issue as a utilitarian, but after some of the semantic issues are cleared away, there seems to be little difference between the logic of policy recommendation following rule utilitarianism and contractarianism.

The utilitarian must in the abstract decide whether a policy on net produces utility gains; that is, whether the gains to the gainers are sufficient to offset the losses to the losers. The contractarian decides, behind a veil of ignorance or some other device to abstract from peoples' narrow self interests, whether people would agree that the policy is in the best interest of the group. For the contractarian, what could this mean besides saying that the gains to the gainers outweigh the losses to the losers? For the utilitarian, what could this mean besides saying that if people abstract from their own narrow self interests, they would agree with the proposal? From a practical standpoint, it appears that the recommendations of the rule utilitarian would be the same as for the contractarian.

At a more conceptual level, there may be differences. The two methods of evaluating the public interest would be identical if everyone perceived the same costs and benefits for all potential changes. However, what if people were not able to correctly understand the true effects of proposed changes? For example, everyone might agree out of ignorance to a proposal that in fact would make them all worse off. In this case, the contractarian would say that since everyone agrees, the change should be implemented, whereas the utilitarian would argue that despite their ignorance, implementation would lower everyone's utility and should not be undertaken.

This example overstates the power of the utilitarian position for two reasons. First, it assumes that the utilitarian knows more about the actual results of a change than anyone else. In the above example, everyone else is wrong, but in the real world there is the possibility that the utilitarian is wrong and everyone else, in agreement, is right. Without omniscience, there is no way to be sure that the utilitarian is right in evaluating the social costs and benefits of a proposed change.

Unless the utilitarian is a dictator, he or she will not be able to implement change unless others go along, so the utilitarian is left in the position of having to convince others that the change actually would enhance the social welfare – that the gains to the gainers actually do outweigh the losses to the losers – if the proposed change is to have a hope of being implemented.

Under such circumstances, it might be particularly challenging to convince the losers that their losses are more than compensated for by someone else's gains.

The contractarian making a policy recommendation is unlikely to favor a proposal that commands agreement if the contractarian believes the recommendation is against the public interest. Rather, the contractarian would argue that if people abstracted from their own personal circumstances and truly understood the effects of the recommendation, they would agree. The contractarian, like the utilitarian, would argue that if people abstracted from their own self-interests, they would agree that the recommendation is in the general public interest.

The conflict in principle seems to be that the utilitarian assumes his or her position to be correct and argues that it should be implemented despite people who do not agree because they do not understand it, and despite people who do not agree because the proposal in the public interest hurts their narrow self-interests. The contractarian argues that if people abstracted from their own self-interests and understood the issue, they would agree on the correct decision. The utilitarian would push on without agreement, but might be wrong, whereas the contractarian would not want to proceed without agreement, even though those dissenting might be wrong.

In practice, the positions are even more similar, because anyone making a policy proposal will think the proposal merits adoption, whether the person is a contractarian or a utilitarian. Furthermore, the twentieth century contractarian paradigm builds in conceptual agreement, such as agreement behind a Rawlsian veil of ignorance, or agreement in renegotiation from anarchy, which can never be observed. Thus, a twentieth century contractarian is armed with an intellectual arsenal that allows him or her to argue that there is conceptual agreement, such as behind a veil of ignorance, whether or not there is actual agreement.

In practice, the governmental institutions favored by a rule utilitarian are likely to be the same as those favored by a contractarian. As discussed in the following chapter, the contractarian paradigm may have something to recommend it in formulating policy, but this need not be considered now. In considering theories of social welfare, the outcomes of rule utilitarianism and contractarianism are consistent. The preceding chapter examined the contractarian criterion of agreement as a normative criterion for evaluating policy change, and despite possible philosophical differences, the point here is that rule utilitarianism will be consistent with the same positive theories as contractarianism.[8]

Disagreement about Facts and Values

There would be no reason to discuss different theories of government if everyone agreed about what constitutes desirable government institutions. People do disagree, but it is useful to consider the origins of disagreement. Different normative conclusions might be reached because people have different values, but in public policy debate, different normative conclusions can also arise as a result of different perceptions about facts and causal relationships.

For example, some people might argue that a prosperous nation should have an extensive welfare system to help those less fortunate members of society. Others argue the opposite. The disagreement between any two individuals might be entirely normative. The individuals agree about the results of a welfare system, but disagree about whether the results are desirable. However, the disagreement might have a substantial positive component. Charles Murray, in his book, *Losing Ground*,[9] argues that the welfare system in the United States creates welfare dependency and has made many people who have used welfare programs worse off than if the programs had not been available. If one person argues that the effects of the welfare system have been beneficial to the recipients while another argues that they have been harmful, then what at first appears to be a normative disagreement may actually be a positive disagreement. If the individuals agreed on the facts, they would also agree on the appropriate policy.

Many defenders of market systems have seen the debate between capitalism and socialism in this light. For example, Friedrich Hayek[10] and Milton Friedman[11] have argued that the consequences of interference with markets and, in the extreme, socialist economies, make everyone worse off, and that their proponents do not understand the true effects of what they are advocating. If the true effects of different economic systems were recognized, everybody would favor a market system. Whether this argument is right or wrong, it moves what appears to be a normative debate into the arena of a positive analysis of alternative social systems. At one level, people have normative disagreements because they disagree on the underlying facts rather than values.

If people agree on the facts, they still may disagree about the appropriate activities of government for two reasons. First, they may find particular policies against their own narrow self-interests, and second, they may disagree on the public interest. For example, domestic manufacturers might favor a tariff on competing imported goods not because tariffs are in the public interest, but because the tariffs make them better off. A hypothetical construction such as the veil of ignorance is designed to abstract from this type of narrow self-interest, but in the real world, people advocate policies for their own interests.

People also have differences about what is in the public interest, but once differences stemming from different understanding of the facts and differences resulting from narrow self-interests are eliminated, there will be much greater general agreement about public policy and the role of government.[12] There is then greater possibility to frame public policy decisions in such a way as to make everyone better off. For example, eliminating a tariff might make the people in the tariff-protected industry worse off, but if all tariffs and other trade restraints were simultaneously eliminated, the general benefits from the elimination of restraints of trade could outweigh the costs to each individual from the elimination of some specific protection.[13] The point is, after accounting for disagreements over facts and peoples' consideration of their own narrow self-interests, there may be a more general conception of the general public interest than is commonly perceived.

Natural Rights

Theories of natural rights argue that individuals are entitled to certain rights as a fact of nature. Just as there are physical laws that dictate the interaction of physical objects, so there are ethical laws, given in nature, that dictate the natural rights to which people are entitled.[14] The concept of natural rights is normative. To illustrate by example, most natural rights theories maintain that all individuals are entitled to the same rights. Despite the equality of rights contained in these theories, slavery has existed for most of human history. Political opponents of modern governments are sometimes jailed or even executed. Some theories of natural rights argue for the right to private property, which is violated in socialist countries. Regardless of one's views on the specific rights that are included in peoples' natural rights, the above examples illustrate that people are not always able to exercise these natural rights. Natural rights can be violated even to the extent that some people might never have their natural rights. In the pre-Civil War American South, a person could be born into slavery and die a slave, never having the rights to which a natural rights theorist would say the person was entitled.

Natural rights theory is a theory of the rights that people should have, not a theory of the rights that people actually are able to exercise. Recognizing that one's natural rights could be violated, a natural rights theory can be developed by asking what rights people would be expected to have in nature, if no rights violations occurred. Following this line of reasoning, a parallel appears between natural rights theory and the hypothetical formation of a social contract through agreement. In isolation in a state of nature, an individual would have the right to use resources in a productive manner, and the individual's production would belong to that individual. The right is natural because in isolation nobody else would be in a position to deny the individual the right to his or her own production. Thus, private property and the right to ownership of one's own production can be justified as a natural right.[15]

People could voluntarily agree to exchange their production for the production of others, but in a social setting, natural rights could be violated by force. Slavery would violate the slave's natural rights because the owner would have the right to the production of the slave. A right to be free from hunger or to have a public education are not natural rights because if individuals cannot produce those things themselves, they require that some people must produce for others in order to give them those rights. Giving some people command over the production of others violates the rights of those others.

Rights are incomplete unless they are alienable.[16] The right to exchange implies that individuals could get together, and by agreement, develop a set of rights within a social setting. Thus, natural rights in a social setting would be rights that people would agree to voluntarily. This suggests a similarity between natural rights theories and the contractarian theories such as those developed by Buchanan and Rawls.

In a contractarian setting, people agree to the rights that they will have. If the contractarian model protects individuals through a unanimity requirement, such as requiring agreement behind a Rawlsian veil, then individuals begin with equal bargaining power, and would trade away rights only when similar concessions from others made everyone better off. The veto power of every individual which is inherent in unanimity rule would give all individuals the right to their life and property unless they chose to override these rights for the common good. Thus, it is possible to develop a theory of natural rights that is consistent with the criterion of agreement that has been used as a benchmark for discussion.

Natural rights theories along these lines that begin by giving individuals ownership over their persons and over their production have been developed in detail by other authors.[17] The purpose of this discussion is not to argue that natural rights theories are really just variants of a contractarian theory of rights. They are not, because natural rights theorists argue that rights emanate from nature, whereas contractarians argue that rights are the product of agreement in a social setting. Rather, the purpose of this section is to illustrate that the conclusions of natural rights theories are not necessarily inconsistent with either contractarian theories of rights nor with the purely positive economic theory of rights developed earlier. Natural rights, seen in the light discussed above, can be consistent with the pure economic theory of rights.

If people do have natural rights, and if they hope to be able to exercise them, then those natural rights must be consistent with the rights that would be produced by the pure economic theory of rights developed in Chapter 2. In the real world, people do try to take away the rights of others, and for rights to be exercised in a real-world positive setting, as opposed to being just an unobtainable normative ideal, natural rights would have to be consistent with the economic theory of rights. The preceding discussion shows that this is possible, so it is possible for a natural rights paradigm to be used to generate the same policy conclusions as the contractarian paradigm based on the criterion of agreement.

Natural Law

Within the framework of government, law can be developed in two ways. Legislatures can pass statutes which then become a part of the law, or courts can make decisions in particular cases which will be used as a precedent in determining similar future cases. Law of the first type is statute law, while law of the second type is common law. In the common law, decisions in specific cases are made based upon the precedent of decisions in earlier similar cases. There is a fiction involved that the underlying law does not change, but that the same law is merely being applied to new cases as they arise. This process in fact allows for the law to evolve gradually over time as small changes in legal decisions alter the legal structure. The common law is not static, then, despite the fiction to the contrary, and there is a substantial literature that explains how the common law evolves in such a way as to provide efficient legal rules.[18]

Natural law is closely related to the concept of legitimacy. As it evolves over time, natural law is legitimate, so governments that act in accordance with natural law are viewed as legitimate by their citizens. Departures from natural law remove some of the aura of legitimacy, requiring the government to use more force in order to maintain power. Departures could be so great that the government would not be able to marshall sufficient force to retain its power. Thus, natural law, viewed in this way, is a concept consistent with the exchange model of government.

Natural law evolves, but not in a random manner. Paul Rubin discusses the mechanisms in common law that lead toward efficient legal rules, and there are likely to be the same types of tendencies whether the rules are a part of the government's accepted common law or whether they are a part of the common practice of individuals.[19] People have a natural tendency to arrange their affairs in such a way as to maximize the value of social interaction.[20] If the government's legal rules are consistent with efficiency, then they will be easier to enforce because people benefit from their existence. If government's legal rules are inefficient, then people have an incentive to break them.

Bruce Benson explains the corruption of government officials in this framework.[21] If laws are socially efficient, such as laws against theft, then individuals have an incentive to cooperate with law enforcement efforts and to oppose corruption that reduces the effectiveness of the laws. Inefficient laws, such as those against victimless crimes, encourage corruption because there are no victims who have a direct interest against it, while those participating in the illegal markets have an incentive to pay officials not to prohibit the transactions.

Viewed in this way, natural law is law that protects private property and freedom of exchange. The invisible hand of the market will lead social activity in this direction whether the activity is officially legal or illegal. Government opposition will drive the activity underground, creating corruption and lessening the legitimacy of government law. Thus, there is a theory of natural law that is consistent with the exchange model of government, and out of which public policy recommendations can be developed. Natural law consists of those rules that would be agreed to because they maximize the value of social interaction.

The Role of Fictions

In ancient societies, the fictions of common ancestry and natural law were employed as a device to provide order in society and lend legitimacy to the actions of decision makers. The fiction of natural law also placed bounds on the permissible actions of political leaders. Common law in the English tradition employs the fiction that the law remains unchanged, with rulings in particular cases to be determined by the already existing laws embodied in past decisions, and democratic nations like the United States rely on a fiction that the majority rules in order to give legitimacy to state action. In fact, a small group of individuals determines American political policies, and the vast majority have no say at all.[22]

Individuals may choose to engage in the symbolic act of voting, but each individual knows that the same political leaders will be elected no matter how (or whether) he chooses to vote.[23] This is not to say that the political elite have unlimited political power. They are limited by the fiction of majority rule and representative government in the same way that ancient rulers were limited by the fiction of natural law. It appears, for instance, that Richard Nixon was forced from office for ignoring those fictions, since his actual acts appear no worse than those of his predecessors. The point is that fictions have been employed in societies from antiquity to the present, and the use of fictions requires an explanation.

Individuals are always in pursuit of their own self-interest, at least when self-interest is broadly defined.[24] If this pursuit is to be undertaken by peaceful and orderly means, individuals must be able to bargain and exchange with one another. But for these transactions to occur among individuals, there must be some agreement regarding what an individual legitimately owns, and therefore what he can legitimately offer in exchange. The status quo offers itself as a strong candidate for the legitimate definition of property rights, simply because it is already in existence, and any non-voluntary alteration would imply the use of force rather than voluntary exchange. Individuals can readily perceive that if the use of force is viewed as legitimate against some people now, it could be applied against almost anybody later. After a lengthy period over which transactions occur in a legitimate manner, the status quo naturally presents itself as implying a fair distribution of rights.[25]

The status quo is the Schelling point – the only point of natural agreement on the distribution of legitimate rights.[26] Voluntary agreement is the only mechanism that guarantees that changes in the status quo will benefit all members of society. In other words, only with voluntary agreement will changes be in the spirit of cooperation, where everyone is made better off, rather than in the spirit of conflict, where some benefit at the expense of others.[27] The general purpose of fictions is to lubricate the mechanism for social change, either by asserting that the status quo has not changed, or by asserting that changes occur with the voluntary consent of society's members. At the same time, these fictions place bounds on the acceptable behavior of political decision makers. Thus, fictions are a way of implementing in the real world a type of approximate unanimity, to use the terms of Wicksell.

The social contract theory of the state is a fiction that serves the purpose of offering an explanation of why the power of the state is legitimate, and therefore why political leaders are justified in their actions. This fiction differs somewhat from other fictions because it seems to have been invented by philosophers rather than having evolved as a part of the society's beliefs. Does the typical member of society believe that he has conceptually agreed with all other members of the society to abide by a social contract? This abstract fiction probably would be accepted more readily by the more intellectual members of society, whereas the opposite would be true of most other fictions, such as that judges merely interpret and apply existing law, or that democracies carry out the will of the majority. The fact that the social contract theory is different in this respect may explain its existence, though. As the world became more intellectually sophisticated, the existing fictions became more transparent. The social contract theory suggests that even if the common fictions are obviously false, members of society are still in principle bound by a social contract to act within the rules of the state. The social contract theory says, in effect, that at a higher level there is a conceptual reason why members of society are bound to abide by the social contract.

The role of fictions, then, is to facilitate social change, either by asserting that the status quo has not changed, or that it has changed only with the voluntary consent of the society's members. At the same time, fictions constrain the range of permissible actions of those in power. In this way, fictions act as a bridge between positive and normative theories of the state. While fictions are in fact not true, people accept them as true and act as if they are true. They are accepted because they are generally agreed upon normative principles which enable people to interact in societies more successfully.

Conclusion

The characteristics of social institutions, including government, are a result of the choices of individuals, but individuals cannot simply choose any kind of social institutions they want. Rather, the interaction of individuals, each pursuing their own self-interest, ends up producing the rules of social interaction and government. Much of the preceding material in this book has been devoted to developing a theory of governmental institutions based on the principles of individual exchange. In the real world, governmental institutions must be consistent with these laws of social science.

Institutions can evolve as a result of human action but not of human design, but individuals can also choose to change their institutions. Poorly designed changes might not produce their intended results, but institutional changes that are designed well can benefit everyone. The Constitution of the United States is often cited as an example. From a normative standpoint, the challenge is to recommend institutional changes that are feasible to implement, and that will be beneficial if implemented.

This chapter has examined several theories of government using the exchange model of government as a basis for the examination. In all cases, these theories could be reconciled with the exchange model that was developed earlier in the book. Such reconciliation may have been unfair to those theories in a sense, since the reconciliation argues that if the exchange model of government is correct, this is what natural rights, utilitarianism, and so forth, must mean to be consistent with the exchange model. The benefit of such an exercise is that it opens the way for dialogue about the use of various theories for public policy recommendation. Individuals might disagree about criteria for judging the desirability of potential public policy changes, but the use of different criteria still might result in the same public policy recommendations.

The next chapter is explicitly devoted to public policy recommendation, so steps completely into the realm of normative analysis. The purpose of the material in Chapters 10 and 11 has been to create a solid foundation for using the exchange model of government and its implications to recommend policy initiatives.

12 Political Ethics and Public Policy

This chapter begins with the premise that societies have the ability to choose the characteristics of their governments. It is not an analysis of the public choice process, however, but a discussion about how individuals within a society would determine what governmental characteristics are desirable – that is, what characteristics they should want to choose. As a starting point, individuals will desire institutions that benefit them, and if social interaction were a zero-sum game, politics would simply amount to trying to balance the interests of some against the interests of others. But social interaction is not a zero-sum game, and productive institutional structures can generate benefits for everyone. The challenges are to identify productive institutional changes, and to identify ways to get them implemented.

When looked at in a political framework, the criterion of agreement naturally suggests itself as a measure of the desirability of public policy proposals. The preceding two chapters have argued that in the abstract, desirable changes are changes that people will agree to, but in a political setting, agreement provides an additional benefit.[1] Agreement is desirable because it makes outcomes politically feasible.

The process of public policy formation can be broken down into two steps. First, desirable policies must be identified. Second, those policies must be approved through the political process in order to be enacted. The contractarian framework produces a close link between these two steps because agreement is the criterion by which the desirability of a policy is established, and agreement is necessary in order to get a policy approved. While agreement at the two stages is not identically the same agreement, it is similar.

Rawlsian Agreement as a Heuristic Device

Agreement behind a veil of ignorance as Rawls described is obviously a heuristic device. It is not intended to be descriptive of any actual agreement in the real world, but rather is intended to suggest a decision-making process in which people abstract from their own narrow self interests when they participate in the process of agreeing on desirable social institutions. The metaphor of agreement behind the veil of ignorance is useful to help visualize how people would evaluate alternative institutions without directly considering their own narrow self interests.

People do not actually agree behind a veil of ignorance, but Rawlsian agreement provides a guide for public policy proposals within a contractarian framework. How can the desirability of a policy proposal be evaluated? From a Rawlsian perspective, the proposal would have to be agreed to by everyone – if everyone abstracts from their own particular interests. Thus, some individuals might be made worse off as a result of a particular proposal, but the contractarian trying to justify such a proposal as desirable would have to say that if those who are harmed would abstract from their own narrow self interests, they would agree that the welfare improvement for those who benefit more than offsets the harm done to those who are made worse off. From a contractarian perspective, this means abstracting from one's own narrow point of view to consider the welfare of all individuals in the group.

Abstraction of this type can be described in theory, but may be difficult in practice. Would it ever be possible for an individuals in the real world to abstract from their own interests in order to make proposals that are in the more general public interest? The possibility is more likely if what is being agreed to is a general framework for collective action – constitutional rules – rather than specific activities to be undertaken and financed collectively.[2] Even here, such abstraction may be difficult.[3]

From a contractarian perspective, one might argue that if people abstracted from their own self interests, they would agree that a certain proposal would be desirable. But there is a second part to the Rawlsian argument that puts additional constraints on the contractarian: agreement is required. Thus, the contractarian must not only decide that a particular proposal would be desirable, but must also persuade others to agree.

Agreement is made easy under the abstraction of the veil of ignorance because if everyone abstracts from their own particular conditions, people are for all practical purposes identical.[4] People do not know whether they will be rich or poor, athletic, intelligent, male or female, what race they will be, and so forth. Behind the veil of ignorance, everyone is the same – a composite of the entire population – so there will be little room for disagreement. But while agreement may be easier to reach behind the Rawlsian veil than in the real world, the criterion of agreement remains.

The utilitarian is freer than the contractarian to assert that a particular proposal is in the public interest and try to see it through. The contractarian is bound by the norm of agreement, and must try to convince others that it is in the public interest. One can imagine a situation where a contractarian would argue that people do not agree with a proposal only because they are not abstracting from their own personal interests, but even then the contractarian should be reluctant to forge ahead, considering the norm of agreement that is at the center of the contractarian model.

Wicksellian Agreement

The Rawlsian model provides a heuristic device within which agreement can be visualized, but not the only heuristic device. Buchanan, in *The Limits of Liberty*, uses the benchmark of renegotiation from anarchy as a criterion for evaluating agreement.[5] Individuals visualize a renegotiation of the social contract from a state of anarchy, and provisions that seem to be likely outcomes in a renegotiation from anarchy would be a part of the agreed-upon social contract.

In this case, rather than individuals visualizing themselves behind a veil of ignorance, they visualize agreeing to a new set of social rules and institutions starting from anarchy, and what people would agree to in this situation meets the test of agreement and therefore desirability. While one might dissect the differences between Rawls' construction and Buchanan's, from a normative standpoint, the set of policy recommendations that would emanate from both would be similar. On the one hand, one would argue, "If people would stand behind a veil of ignorance and abstract from their own personal interests, they would agree to this," and on the other hand would argue, "If a new set of social rules and institutions were to be agreed to starting from a situation of anarchy, this would be something to which people would agree."

Wicksell had a similar idea about using agreement as a benchmark, but wanted to use it more directly in the political process.[6] Recognizing the practical problems of reaching absolute unanimous agreement on anything, Wicksell nevertheless argued for an approximate unanimous agreement on public sector activity. Anything that was truly in the public interest should be able to command approximately unanimous agreement, he reasoned.

Wicksell explicitly recognized that while some proposals might produce aggregate benefits in excess of costs and still not receive unanimous agreement, this could be caused due to a distribution of costs that did not closely reflect the distribution of benefits. For example, some people could be taxed to provide benefits to others. Wicksell's solution was to restructure the costs so that those who received benefits also paid for them. If a proposal truly is in the public interest, the total benefits should exceed the total costs, so it must be possible to restructure the costs such that everyone benefits from any proposal that is in the public interest.

Wicksell's observation is important. Any proposal that is in the public interest should produce benefits in excess of costs, and Wicksell points out that therefore it should be possible to structure proposals that are in the public interest in such a way that everyone actually would agree with them. This does not mean agreement behind a veil of ignorance or agreement by imagining renegotiation from anarchy; this means actual agreement in a political forum. If an actual consensus is not reached, then Wicksell would argue that the costs imposed by the proposal should be reallocated so that those who do not benefit are not made to pay for benefits for those who do. If such a restructuring cannot be found, then Wicksell would argue that the proposal is not actually in the public interest.

Recognition of this principle of Wicksell's might influence what people would agree to in a Rawlsian setting. From behind a veil of ignorance, one might agree that a particular proposal has benefits in excess of costs, but still not agree to the proposal unless the beneficiaries actually paid those costs. A more utilitarian view would weigh the gains to the gainers against the costs to the losers, but the contractarian perspective, which emphasizes agreement, would also look at the distribution of the benefits and costs to see if they could be structured in such a way as to produce more agreement.

Agreement as a Benchmark

The preceding discussion leads to the conclusion that desirable policies are policies on which people agree. Agreement is useful as a benchmark for evaluating public policy for three reasons. First, agreement is an indicator of social welfare. Second, agreement can be used as a benchmark for efficiency. Third, agreement necessary for real world political approval.

The use of agreement as an indicator of social welfare is an implication of an individualistic view of society. A society is nothing more than a collection of individuals, so social welfare can mean nothing more than the welfare of the individuals in a society. Since people are not omniscient, there is no way for one person to know what would improve the welfare of another. Stated differently, individuals are the best judges of their own welfare. It follows that if people agree to a change, they believe it is welfare-enhancing. Using individuals' own evaluations of their welfare, agreement among all individuals in a society indicates an improvement in social welfare.[7]

Whenever one tries to evaluate what social institutions are desirable, a value judgment is involved. Since one cannot directly measure an individual's well-being, any policy recommendation must be the result of using the values of some individual or group to make the evaluation. When agreement is used as the criterion to evaluate social welfare, the values being used are those of the individuals who are affected by the policy proposal. Individuals are evaluating what would be beneficial for themselves rather than having someone else attempt to make that judgment for them.

The use of agreement as an indicator of social welfare is enhanced because of the Wicksell principle discussed in the previous section. Any proposal which produces benefits in excess of costs must be able to be structured in such a way that when the beneficiaries pay for the proposal, everyone would be better off; thus, everyone would agree. Agreement is useful as an indicator of social welfare precisely because it can also be used as a benchmark for efficiency.

Finally, agreement is necessary to make political change. Nobody has the power to implement social change without the assistance of others, and to get the assistance of others requires their agreement. The larger the proportion of people that agree, the easier the change will be to implement. So from a practical standpoint, agreement has much to recommend it as a benchmark for evaluating the desirability of public policy proposals.[8]

Agreement is the key contractarian benchmark for evaluating the desirability of public policy proposals. One might argue in the abstract about how people could agree under hypothetical circumstances, but the benchmark of agreement applies to real-world agreement on real-world proposals as well. Those who propose public policy initiatives do not complete their job if they simply argue that people should agree, or would agree if they understood the proposal or abstracted from their own personal interests. They should, first, look for ways to structure the proposal in such a way as to maximize the political agreement that the proposal can receive, and then argue the case to get others to agree.

Non-Pareto Superior Policy Proposals

Actual agreement is an indicator of the desirability of a public policy proposal. However, there is room within the contractarian framework to advocate the adoption of a policy even if it is unable to secure actual agreement in a political forum. Three reasons why actual agreement might be difficult to acquire for some desirable proposals are that the transactions costs involved in restructuring the costs of a proposal might be too costly, distributional programs always impose costs in excess of benefits on some people, and that some problem with the status quo could prevent a Pareto superior move from being made.

The transactions cost argument is based on the fact that it is costly to redesign the tax structure to allow for almost everyone to benefit from any particular government program. However, when taken as a whole, people could on average, expect to be beneficiaries of government in general. Thus, in the absence of transactions costs, a program that primarily benefits one group could have taxes imposed primarily on that group, while a program primarily benefitting another group would be financed primarily from taxes on that group. However, a single tax structure to raise revenue for all government programs could be more efficient. When viewed over a wide range of government programs, an argument could be made that everyone would agree with the structure of government that collects general taxes for these programs that benefit narrower groups, even though this financial structure would lead every program to have some opponents, at least if people evaluated the programs according to their narrow self interest.[9] But taking a longer view, the costs even out over a large number of programs, and everyone benefits from having a simplified revenue structure.

A second reason why some proposals will not receive unanimous approval in the real world is that redistributional programs by definition take resources from some people and give them to others. If the programs are viewed as social insurance, people from behind the veil of ignorance might agree to such programs, figuring that if they end up destitute, they would want the social system to take care of them. But when the veil is lifted and some people discover that they are very well off, they might protest having income redistributed from them to others. Thus, in the real world, there will not be agreement on something that could be agreed to from behind a veil of ignorance.

Redistribution programs have also been justified based on the argument that redistribution provides benefits to those who are taxed as well as those who are the recipients, but that there is a free rider problem among those who are taxed. People who are well-off want to see that those who are less fortunate are helped out, but have an incentive to free ride and let others help the poor. Thus, to overcome the free rider problem, everyone is forced to contribute, and everyone benefits as a result.[10] But note that this argument implies that there should be agreement in the real world.

If there really is a free rider problem that can be overcome and improve the welfare of both givers and recipients, then everyone should favor it. Thus, the transactions cost argument in the previous paragraph suggests a rationalization for favoring a particular redistribution program even if it is not agreed to in the real world; the free rider argument in this paragraph does not.[11]

Yet another reason why agreement might not be able to be reached in the real world even though the proposed change is in the public interest is that there may be some inherent unfairness in the status quo. Social conditions such as slavery and apartheid are possible examples. If social rules are set up in such a way as to give some group an unfair advantage over others, those who have the advantages would be unlikely to agree to do away with them, and likely would be able to develop arguments justifying those conditions as socially desirable. Needless to say, a value judgment must be made to assert that these conditions are unfair. This is where conceptual agreements, behind a veil of ignorance, or from a state of anarchy, come into their own. While in the real world people consider their own self interests, if they did not know who they would be after the veil was lifted, or if they negotiated a social contract from a condition of anarchy, it is easy to imagine that conditions such as slavery and apartheid would not be agreed to if people did not know in which group they would be once the contract took effect.

This section illustrates that there are ways in which a contractarian model, ultimately based on agreement, can be used to recommend policies even when there is not general agreement on those policies.

Problems with Non-Pareto Superior Policy Proposals

One must be careful when using arguments of the type developed in the previous section, for these arguments amount to saying that people should agree, using some notion of conceptual agreement, even though they actually do not agree.[12] From a normative standpoint, one is on much firmer ground using arguments like those above to try to persuade people to agree rather than using them to justify forcing people to accept policies with which they do not agree.

For example, one might argue with the supporters of apartheid that it is undesirable and would not be agreed to behind a veil of ignorance, or under any other plausible bargaining situation. The contractarian is on strong grounds using this type of argument to persuade those who support apartheid to change their minds. However, some of the foundation of the contractarian model is eroded if the argument is used to try to force people to change against their wishes.

Earlier in the chapter, agreement was argued to be a good benchmark for the desirability of a policy for several reasons. If people agree, it is an indicator of social welfare, but if they are forced to accept some policy, the indicator is gone. It is an indicator of efficiency, but if people are forced, there is no guarantee that the benefits outweigh the costs of the action. Finally, advantages were noted in implementing change through the political process if the desirability of change is agreed upon. All of this shows that the contractarian framework is useful as an intellectual device to try to persuade others about the merits of a particular policy. But when these arguments are used to try to force people to do something that those who are doing the forcing think others should agree to but will not, then much of the intellectual persuasiveness of the contractarian framework is lost.

This framework can be used to try to persuade people to agree with a particular point of view, but an important part of the framework is abandoned when it is used as a justification for forcing people to adopt policies they do not favor.

The Wicksellian Model of Taxation

From the standpoint of practical political implementation, some of these principles of agreement could be incorporated easily into the current political structure in the United States. One argument given earlier for not requiring approximately unanimous agreement on all issues is that the transactions costs associated with putting together a new tax proposal for each spending proposal would be high. However, a new taxing proposal would not have to be drawn up anew for each proposal. All that would be necessary would be to identify the source of revenue.

Every spending proposal costs money, and the money must come from somewhere. One could require that every proposal to spend money explicitly state where the revenues would be raised. For example, Congress might propose to spend $1 million to aid victims of some disaster, such as a hurricane, flood, or earthquake. That money would have to come from somewhere, and prudent budgeting would dictate that the opportunity cost of the funds be taken into account when the spending bill was passed. If no other spending was to be cut at the same time, then the spending bill would explicitly say that the national debt would be increased by $1 million to pay for disaster relief. If, on the other hand, spending would be cut in other areas to pay for it, then those other areas would be explicitly listed in the spending legislation. Alternatively, taxes might be increased, in which case the legislation should say so explicitly.

Thus, after stating the purpose of the spending, the bill would go on to say, for example, that $500,000 would be raised by a temporary one-cent per gallon tax on gasoline, that $300,000 would come from a reduction in defense procurement items (that would be listed specifically in the bill), and that the national debt would be increased by $200,000. This would require nothing more than the status quo, except that legislation would have to explicitly consider the opportunity cost of all spending. This way, people could see what they would have to give up for everything they get. Furthermore, by making the opportunity costs explicit, legislators themselves would be forced to do what they should do anyway, which is consider the costs along with the benefits of legislation.

Once this type of budget is established, spending should then be required to stay within the budget. Assume, for example, that more people than anticipated applied for food stamps, causing the entire budget to be spent before the end of the fiscal year. In this case, Congress would have to legislate additional funds, using the method above, for the program to be able to spend more.[13]

This modest proposal falls far short of Wicksell's criterion of approximate unanimity, but it is Wicksellian in the sense that it requires an explicit accounting of costs and benefits of all legislation. While one might want to do more, it is hard to see the objections to this type of legislation, except from those who want to hide the true cost of government spending.

Desirability and Feasibility

Desirable policy from a normative standpoint will be a function of what is possible, which requires a positive analysis. What would people agree to from behind a veil of ignorance? If they had little knowledge of the real world, one could imagine people agreeing to establish policies with the idea that they would produce desirable results, when in reality the actual effects of those proposals would be undesirable in the eyes of those who originally agreed. People would agree to proposals with undesirable results, following this train of thought, because they did not understand the true consequences of what they had agreed to.

The existence of such people behind the Rawlsian veil of ignorance would violate the spirit of the model. The contractarian model has in mind agreement among people who understand the true consequences of what they agree to, but who are able to abstract from their own self interests. There must be the presumption that those who agree in the contractarian framework agree with full knowledge of the consequences of the proposals they consider.

This opens up the possibility of disagreement in the real world over the consequences of policy proposals in addition to the value judgments behind them. Two people might, for example, have identical values, and yet one could favor a proposal while another opposes it because the two individuals differ in their assessment of the likely actual effects of the proposal.[14] Here again, the criterion of agreement is relevant. It is not sufficient to argue that these people would agree under certain hypothetical circumstances; rather, consistent application of the principle of agreement would demand that these individuals create agreement by convincing others of their point of view.

This is the point where positive analysis becomes relevant in developing agreement on desirable social policy. In the abstract, one can extol the virtues of peace and prosperity, but the real world offers constraints, and everything is not possible. Thus, one must understand the way in which the real world works, and any normative argument meant as a recommendation of a desirable policy in the real world must be consistent with a correct positive analysis of the way in which the world works. A normative position must argue not only that a particular state of affairs is desirable, but also that it is possible. Thus, the positive theory of government that constitutes the bulk of this book lays the foundation for making normative arguments about what constitutes a desirable government. From a practical standpoint, a normative assessment about what is desirable must be selected from among those options that positive analysis shows are feasible.

Legitimacy and Agreement

Part of what goes into determining what is feasible is a technological matter. Can this much output be produced? Is it possible to produce this mix of goods? Under this social system, is there sufficient information for producers to tell whether they are acting efficiently? Are there sufficient incentives for people to produce up to their potential? But part of what is feasible is also a political matter. Agreement is necessary because political implementation cannot be accomplished without it. As a result, policy proposals must have the aura of legitimacy in order to be feasible.

Douglass North's concept of ideology falls squarely into this framework.[15] Ideology is a way of gaining political support for policy proposals.

Murray Edelman discusses the symbolic nature of political institutions in the same way.[16] The democratic election of legislators and the constitutional procedures by which legislation is passed constitute far more than just a process for legislating change. In addition, those institutions convey legitimacy to the outcome of the legislative process. Even if people do not personally agree with the outcome, they recognize it as legitimate because it is the result of a legitimate process. Thus, legitimacy is an important element in securing agreement.

Contrast this contractarian approach with another type of fairness theory, called superfairness by Baumol.[17] Under this idea of superfairness, individuals evaluate what they have relative to others, and if they would be willing to trade positions with someone else, they are defined as having envy. A fair world is defined as one in which there is no envy. This approach does not consider the process by which envy is produced, it does not consider whether there is general agreement with the institutions that govern society, and it does not consider whether those institutions and even the general outcome is considered legitimate.

In contrast, the contractarian framework contains a procedural theory of fairness: fair outcomes are those outcomes that are the result of fair processes. A process not generally accepted as legitimate will not produce results that are generally considered to be fair; in contrast, it people view the process as legitimate, they will be inclined to view the outcome as legitimate. For purposes of public policy espousal, a part of convincing others about the desirability of a policy is convincing them that it is legitimate.

This further reinforces the importance of agreement in the contractarian model. Again, it is not sufficient to argue simply that under certain hypothetical circumstances people would agree. Rather, this argument about hypothetical circumstances must be used to convince people in the real world that they should agree. Without agreement, the proposal will lack the legitimacy that is necessary for a truly desirable policy. The foundation of agreement in the contractarian model is compromised if policies are not actually agreed to. Arguments about hypothetical agreement can be used as persuasive devices, but if they are used to force people to adopt policies against their wishes, the policies will lack the legitimacy they require to be effective.

The Importance of the Status Quo

Buchanan has made the argument that the status quo is important because it is the place from which all changes must be initiated.[18] In the abstract, one might imagine the characteristics of a desirable society, but in the real world, a more desirable society can only be created by changing the existing society. If the concept of agreement is to have anything more than abstract significance, it must be agreement to change the status quo to something people agree is better.

A Pareto superior move clearly qualifies. If some people are made better off and nobody worse off, then social welfare is enhanced and agreement should be relatively easy to reach. Changes that lower the welfare of some people could still reach agreement, if those people who are being made worse off can believe that there are social benefits that offset the sacrifices they are asked to make. People frequently engage voluntarily in charitable actions. The key to producing agreement, then, is to invoke arguments like those presented earlier in the chapter about why a non-Pareto superior move would be socially beneficial. But since any changes must be changes from the status quo, the contractarian model is most powerful when these arguments are used to persuade others to agree rather than when they are used as justifications for coerced change.

Considering the special significance of the status quo, the nature of desirable changes will be dependent upon what currently exists. One cannot in the abstract recommend a certain type of society without recommending how that type of society can be produced from the existing one, and political implementation will be difficult if general agreement cannot be secured to move from the status quo.

Conclusion

Normative concepts are especially relevant to the public sector because public sector institutions are the result of the choices of individuals. In a democracy, a collective decision-making procedure gives every citizen some voice in a society's institutions, but other forms of government are the results of the decisions of smaller groups of individuals, and more to the point, those institutions can be changed if the individuals who make the decisions choose to change them. This being so, it is important to have some normative principles to identify those changes that would be desirable. This chapter has attempted to develop some general guidelines.

Most of the book has been devoted to a positive analysis of government based upon a model of exchange. People interact because they can improve their welfare by doing so, and a positive model of government was developed in which the logic of government institutions was illustrated by showing how people could agree to them. The bargaining process did not impose any constraints on the bargains that could be struck, and the model showed why everyone would agree to have a government that adhered to well-defined constitutional rules. The foundation of that model was agreement.

In a positive setting, agreement is important because it increases wealth and because it produces political institutions that are viewed as legitimate and therefore durable. In a strictly positive setting, governments cannot last long without the perception of legitimacy in the eyes of their citizens. In a positive setting, legitimacy can be produced by unconstrained satisfaction with the government's policies, it can be produced by agreement with the general process by which political decisions are made even if there is some dissatisfaction with specific actions, and it can be produced by force. In any government, a combination of these factors are in operation. But agreement and exchange lie at the foundation of the positive model of government presented here.

This concept of agreement carries over into the normative analysis done in this chapter. Agreement appears desirable as a normative criterion because it uses as its values the values of those who will be governed by particular policies rather than some externally imposed values. Agreement also makes a good normative criterion in light of the positive model of government developed previously. If agreement and exchange are at the foundation of actual government institutions, then there is a consistency between the way that the government works in a positive sense and the way that it should work in a normative sense.

As a practical matter, complete agreement will be difficult to reach on any issue. General principles can be developed, however, to argue that under certain circumstances people should agree about certain policies. The Rawlsian veil of ignorance and Buchanan's construction of anarchistic equilibrium are heuristic devices that enable individuals to imagine what people would agree to if they abstract from their own self-interests. Arguments that people would conceptually agree under these circumstances can then be used as arguments that people should agree in reality.

Agreement is desirable because it makes political outcomes feasible. Policy espousal and political debate is ultimately persuasion that people should favor certain proposals. Nobody can enact policies without general political support. Even the military dictator needs the support of the military, and the military can always be persuaded by others to abandon the dictator, requiring even dictators to create the aura of agreement and legitimacy with the government. Since political debate is persuasion, and since agreement ultimately produces political change, agreement is an appropriate normative criterion for advocating public policy.

The positive principles of agreement and exchange that have provided the foundation for the model of government developed here can therefore be extended into normative principles of political ethics. Desirable political institutions are those institutions on which people can agree. In the real world, one must choose from among those outcomes that are feasible, making positive analysis a necessary prerequisite to normative recommendations. This chapter has argued that agreement is the appropriate criterion to use for evaluating public policy, which fortunately is consistent with the argument that agreement is necessary to implement public policy.

13 Conclusion

The institutions of government are the product of exchange. Individuals perceive opportunities to enhance their welfare by bargaining with others to agree to an institutional structure which provides a well-defined and stable set of rules under which individuals interact. The product of this agreement is a constitution, and the preceding chapters discussed why it is in the interests of individuals to participate in the bargaining process, what terms of agreement would be expected to be found in the resulting constitution, and gave a broad outline explaining how the government produced by the constitution would be expected to operate. For the most part, the analysis was positive in nature, describing how agreement takes place and what emerges from agreement, without passing judgment on the desirability of the resulting agreement. The last several chapters, however, extended the positive analysis to normative issues in an attempt to determine how individuals might identify desirable institutions and constitutional rules.

Because any normative analysis is based ultimately on value judgments, the normative discussion does not follow as a logical conclusion of the positive. Nevertheless, the normative issues are worthwhile to consider for two reasons. First, because both the normative and positive analyses are based on models of exchange and agreement, it is possible to see how normative and positive analyses are related, and it is possible to provide a consistent positive framework for a normative contractarian model. Second, because people choose their governmental institutions, it is always worthwhile to consider how people can decide which institutions they should choose. This is especially true because government institutions are the result of collective choice, so if some shared values can be developed for determining desirable institutions, collective choice and agreement will be easier to produce. Before considering these normative issues further, this concluding chapter will return to the positive analysis of the exchange model of government.

The Exchange Model of Government

All of the preceding analysis has been built on an exchange model of government that depicts governmental institutions as the result of a bargaining process among individuals. The model begins with the observation that all individuals are better off if they can agree to rules governing social interaction. The absence of such rules will produce a Hobbesian anarchy – a war of all against all. Even anarchists who argue that government is unnecessary or counterproductive do so by making the argument that social institutions will be produced by voluntary agreements among individuals.[1]

In any exchange where individuals agree on rules of social interaction, some individuals will be in a stronger bargaining position than others. Individuals who are physically stronger would be in a stronger bargaining position, for example, because they can threaten to harm individuals who will not agree to their terms. Individuals who are more productive will also be in a better bargaining position, because agreement with them will result in greater gains from trade and more overall welfare for the group. Weak and unproductive individuals will be in a poor bargaining position, and unless others grant them more equality in the bargaining process, they would be likely to end up with fewer rights in the resulting bargain. The result of an exchange model of government is not necessarily equality of rights.[2]

In a purely economic framework, it makes sense for some people to specialize in protecting individuals' rights while others specialize in producing goods and services, but there is more to the creation of government than comparative advantage and gains from trade. Those who run the government have the ability to force the citizens of government to comply with the government's rules and to exclude others from using force in a similar manner. This gives those who run the government a degree of monopoly power, and their use of monopoly power to charge monopoly prices for their services makes running the government a profitable endeavor.

The bargaining process that produces government begins with individuals in unequal bargaining positions. Those in strong bargaining positions can demand that those in weaker positions turn over a portion of their incomes to the stronger group. This stronger group becomes government, and institutionalizes the tribute paid to them in the form of taxes. Once the government establishes this arrangement and receives its income from its citizens, it has an incentive to protect them, because in so doing, it is protecting its own source of income. The primary outcome of this exchange model is a government that exchanges protection for tribute.

Clubs and Governments

The traditional public finance model of government suggests that some public goods that will not be produced unless done so collectively, and that because of the free rider problem, everyone is better off paying taxes and having the government produce public goods. In this model, government is like a club that produces benefits for its members. The analogy between clubs and governments, suggested by Buchanan,[3] is furthered by the Rawlsian contractarian model of the state, in which government is the product of agreement among the governed. The model developed here, while it has a clear contractarian foundation, also draws a clear distinction between a model of clubs and a model of governments.

In the theory of clubs, a club exists to produce public goods for its members, but why should anyone in government want to produce public goods? In the exchange model of government developed here, those in government want to protect their source of income, which is the foundation for the exchange of protection for tribute. Public goods are produced to ensure a future stream of income to the government, and can be sold at monopoly prices. The protection that the government produces for its side of the bargain enables the government to use coercion, giving it a permanent advantage in the bargaining process. There is exchange, but the terms are biased to favor those in government.

Clubs are voluntary organizations, whereas governments are coercive. This observation applies regardless of how much individuals like their governments, or how much they agree with their government's policies. One can quit a club if one does not like its rules, but government uses force against those who do not want to play by its rules. Consider the production of national defense in the two models. In the club model, national defense is produced as a public good to benefit its members; in the government model, national defense is the result of a compulsory exchange of protection for tribute, which enables the government to protect its source of income. There may be some similarities between clubs and governments, but a theory of clubs is not a theory of governments.

Constitutional Rules

This exchange of protection for tribute must be institutionalized within the constitutional rules of a society in order to ensure that the citizens are willing to invest in their productive abilities. If the government took income from citizens without relying on a constitutional rule to do so, even if it produced protection for them, citizens would have little incentive to be productive. Why produce anything today if it is likely that the government will take it tomorrow? Why invest in future productive capacity if it is likely that the government will appropriate the fruits of that investment?

Thus, optimal constitutional rules for a productive society will promise limited taxation, both for the benefit of citizens and for the benefit of those who run the government and profit from the revenue it collects.

Constitutional limits to taxation give citizens an incentive to be productive because they have some promise that they will be able to keep a share of their output, and that share is defined ahead of time through the constitution. The government benefits because citizens have an incentive to be more productive, and a more productive population means greater income for the government that shares in that productivity. One difference between taxation and theft is that taxation imposes a clearly defined burden on the taxpayer, leaving an incentive to produce in the future so that the government can have a steady future stream of revenue.

The argument extends from taxation to rules governing other forms of social interaction. Individuals receive benefits from institutionalizing the rules of social interaction into constitutional rules. That way, individuals have some assurance that their rights which others observe today will remain intact in the future, and the long term contract establishes a social setting in which everyone has an incentive to be more productive. Thus, the agreement that emerges from the exchange model of government is a set of constitutional rules. Some of these rules might be embodied in a written constitution, but even where a written constitution exists, much of the agreement on constitutional rules will exist in a less formal setting, such as the common law, or unwritten norms regarding the limits of acceptable action. Regardless of its particular form, the product of the exchange model of government is a set of constitutional rules that has similarities with the social contract in the social contract theory of the state.

Constitutions and Competition

One of the benefits received by those who run the government is that they can charge a monopoly price for the government's services. The lure of monopoly profits creates competition for the right to run the government, which means that those who are in government must establish a way to keep potential competitors from displacing them. If potential competitors can be eliminated from competing, then the existing government will be free to collect monopoly profits; however, it will be costly to discourage competitors, and the costs of controlling competitors must be weighed against the benefits of monopoly profits.

The existence of a stable constitution plays a role in controlling competition, because it provides evidence from the existing government about what conditions citizens can expect if the existing government remains in power. Potential competitors can make promises to citizens about what they could expect from a new government, but these untested promises must stand against the actual evidence from the status quo under the existing government. This provides the existing government with the fundamental advantage of incumbency: the comparison of actual conditions now with the possibly unattainable promises of challengers.

Because of the potential to reap monopoly profits, challengers will always want to run the government. If the current government offered no guarantee about what the future would be like under its rule, then there would be no reason for citizens to accept the rule of the current government rather than the promises of a challenger. The existence of a stable constitution provides that promise, and lowers the cost to those in the existing government of keeping challengers from replacing them.

This analysis has placed much importance on the role of perceived legitimacy in the survival prospects of a government. Governments can force individuals to comply with their rules, but governments incur costs when they use force, and are able to secure compliance in large degree because most people comply with government without being forced. Citizens may feel coerced in that the government would take action against them if they did not comply with the government's rules, but no government has sufficient resources to force everyone to do as the government wants. Governments rely on the voluntary cooperation of most people, although possibly under the threat of force.

One way to get people to comply is to marshall sufficient resources in a police force, so that people comply out of fear of the consequences if they do not. Another way is to convince people that the demands of government are legitimate, and that they should comply regardless of whether they are forced. The government still uses force against those that do not comply, to encourage cooperation, but if the government's demands are viewed as legitimate, the government can use fewer resources to enforce its rules.

One function of democratic government is to give the government the image of legitimacy. One might object to the policies of government leaders, but those policies can be defended on the basis that the leaders were popularly elected to determine those policies. Thus, democracy can make unpopular policies appear legitimate nonetheless, which lowers the cost of enforcing those policies.

Competition and Monopoly in Government

Potential competition can come from many sources. Any government is at risk from overthrow from both internal and external threats. Foreign aggressors and military coups are examples. In addition, democratic governments are at risk of being voted out at election time. Those who run the government can reap monopoly profits from their activities, but competition places a constraint on the amount of profit they can collect, and in the limit may push the returns to governing down to a competitive level.

In an insightful article, Harold Demsetz argued that natural monopolies can be made to produce competitive results without direct regulation by allowing potential monopolists to bid for the right to become the monopoly producer.[4] The process of competing for the right to be the monopoly supplier pushes the return to the monopolist down to the competitive level. This same type of competition can occur in politics as potential political leaders compete for the right to be chosen to run the monopoly government.[5] Sufficient competition will eliminate all monopoly profits to those in government.

From the standpoint of the citizens, they would prefer a government that enforces constitutional rules, but at the lowest possible cost, so factors that increase the competition for the right to govern will benefit them. Conversely, those in government would prefer to erect barriers to entry that limit competition and enhance their abilities to reap monopoly profits.

Government by Agreement

The positive and normative parts of this volume share the common element of being based on agreement. The exchange model of government depicts government institutions as the outcome of a bargaining process, making agreement an important element in determining the characteristics of governmental institutions. Adopting an individualistic view of the public interest, agreement can also be used as the criterion for evaluating the desirability of alternative social institutions. The public interest is nothing more than a combination of all of the individual interests of the people who make up the public. There is no reason to believe that others can evaluate the welfare of individuals more accurately than those individuals themselves, so proposals that are in the public interest are proposals with which individuals agree.

In a normative setting, actual agreement among individuals may not always be the appropriate criterion to evaluate alternative institutions, as the previous chapter noted. For example, if the status quo gives some individuals an unjust advantage, one would not expect the advantaged individuals to agree easily to give up their advantages. Thus, criteria such as agreement behind a Rawlsian veil of ignorance might identify more desirable institutions than the criterion of actual agreement.

The link between the positive and normative models developed here is that they are both based on agreement, and this provides a foundation for making normative judgments more than if normative criteria are simply presented with no foundations in positive models of government.

Agreement and Public Policy

The normative use of agreement as a criterion for desirable public policy can be defended because, first, it relies on the value judgments of those who are affected by the policy rather than on some outside evaluation of the policy, and second, because ultimately agreement in a political forum will be needed to implement the policy. As just noted, the concept of agreement can be applied without making the argument that the policy proposal actually makes everyone better off. Using the Rawlsian model of agreement, one can argue that if everyone abstracted from their own personal interests, they would agree with the proposal. However, the argument cannot stop there. The one making the argument must go on to convince others that the argument is true. Thus, the concept of agreement is used as a device to argue the merits of a proposal and ultimately to get others to agree.

Ironically, arguments about agreement have been used to justify coercive government actions, using the rationale that people would agree to be coerced. In producing public goods, for example, there is an incentive to be a free rider, so everyone would benefit if everyone was forced to contribute to produce the good.[6] The agreement argument is being misused here; properly used, the argument would be made to convince everyone to agree to have the government produce the public good using taxation, as argued by Wicksell,[7] rather than using the argument as a justification for coercing people. In a normative setting, the criterion of agreement can be defended most strongly when it is used to convince others to come to an actual agreement.

In the real world political environment, agreement must always be forged among some group in order to implement public policy. No individual can implement policy alone, although in dictatorships the group that must agree might be limited to the state police force which enforces the dictator's rules. Even then, without some perception of legitimacy, it will be difficult to get people to comply with the dictator's demands. In a democracy, agreement must be even more widespread. Anyone advocating some policy change cannot simply make the argument that it is desirable and expect that it will be implemented. Others must be convinced in order to get the support for the proposal. In this sense, regardless of the theoretical foundation for the normative argument, all advocates become contractarians to a degree.

One might argue that a policy is desirable because it protects the natural rights of individuals, or that it enhances social welfare from a utilitarian perspective, or that people who abstract from their personal interests would agree to it, but in order for the argument to advance from being a strictly academic argument to one that will have an impact in the real world of politics, the person making the argument must get others to agree. In the real world of politics, agreement is the ultimate criterion of social choice.

Desirable Political Institutions

Having advanced a positive theory of government, and having advanced a normative theory regarding the choice of governmental institutions, the next step is to identify desirable institutional changes that could be implemented. The theory developed here discusses the general foundations of government rather than its institutional details, so policy recommendations from this analysis will be very general. Nevertheless, some guidelines do suggest themselves.

Constitutional Rules
The importance of constitutional rules as a foundation for government was emphasized as an important outcome of the exchange model of government. The tax structure, discussed earlier in the chapter, provides a good illustration of the principle. The government receives its income from taxing its citizens, and then has an incentive to protect them to protect its own income. However, the taxes the government will collect must be clearly defined in order to leave citizens with the incentive to be productive. Even a revenue-maximizing government has an incentive to place constitutional limits on its power to tax in order to retain incentives for productivity among its citizens.[8]

Note the difference between a constitutional limit on the government's ability to tax and a more academic policy of changing the tax structure to reflect current knowledge about optimal taxation. Under the latter policy, individuals are uncertain about what innovations might appear regarding optimal taxation, so cannot be sure what the tax structure might look like in the future. Thus, prudent individuals must plan for a large number of contingencies, most of which will never occur. The constitutional tax rule, while it may not reflect current thinking on optimal taxation, so may not be optimal in a static sense, provides better incentives in a dynamic setting. Of course, if a truly superior tax system were designed, then the designers could convince citizens to alter the tax constitution for the public good. In this setting, the change would occur because it was agreed to, rather than because those in charge had the discretion to change things.

The constitutional argument applies well beyond tax policy, to government in general. In the long-running debate about the desirability of rules versus discretion in monetary policy, the constitutional framework argues for rules. If monetary authorities can use discretion to adjust monetary policy for what they perceive is the public interest, then the general public is faced with uncertainty about prices, interest rates, and so forth. One type of monetary rule would be to stabilize the price level, and another would be to stabilize some specified interest rate, while another would be to stabilize the growth rate of the money supply. While a comparison of the merits of these various rules is beyond the scope of the present work, choosing some rule rather than leaving monetary policy to the discretion of the central bank offers a more stable and predictable environment.

Similar arguments can be made about other areas of governmental policy. Fiscal policy, redistributive policies, and the legal environment are but some of the areas in which clear constitutional rules produce a more stable society and enhance its long-run productivity. The arguments presented here do not constitute specific public policy recommendations, but rather more general institutional recommendations. Whatever policies one advocates, desirable policies will be more desirable if they are institutionalized into a stable constitutional rule, rather than being subject to political reversal.[9]

In a more general sense, this discussion argues against a reliance on comparative statics models to draw conclusions about social welfare. In the real world, the choice is not among various alternative states of the world, but rather between the status quo or various changes to the status quo. One of the costs of change is the possible undermining of the constitutional framework, so just because a society would be better off if it had adopted policy B rather than policy A does not mean it would be better off changing from A to B once A is already adopted as the status quo.

Competition in Government

Another area of analysis that can produce general policy recommendations is the model of government as monopolist. The exchange model of government depicts the result of the bargaining process as a monopoly government that produces protection, and likely other outputs as well. Government uses its monopoly powers to charge monopoly prices, which is why being in a position to run the government is desirable. Government is modelled here in a very general sense, and the results of the model apply to dictatorships as well as democracies. Those who have the power of government are better off the more monopoly power they can exercise, while the citizens subject to government power are better off if the political environment is more competitive so that they can receive a more competitive bundle of services (including rights that the government protects) at more competitive prices.

One way in which monopoly power of government can be reduced is through intergovernmental competition. At the state and national level, this suggests producing all public sector output at the lowest level of government possible. This contrasts with the trend toward centralization in the United States. Furthermore, in a more international economy, multi-national corporations can take advantage of intergovernmental competition among nations. Historically, the threat of war has been one factor limiting multinational corporations and international intergovernmental competition. Corporations could be afraid of losing their assets to unfriendly governments during hostilities. A more peaceful international climate will promote intergovernmental competition, along with advances in transportation and communication. Multinational corporations can take advantage of intergovernmental competition to lower the monopoly power of government in any one nation.

Additional policy implications involve making entry into existing governments more competitive. Entry can take place in several ways – war, revolution, and democratic election are examples. While most readers will immediately accept the desirability of democratic election over violent methods of entry, it is worth noting that within this model, democratic elections are desirable because, first, they allow some continuity in constitutional rules, with the advantages just discussed, and second, the resource cost of changing governments this way probably will be lower and will be more concentrated on those who want to compete. In a dictatorship, potential new entrants will have to expend resources to attempt overthrowing the current government by force; likewise, the current government must protect itself by expending resources on military and police protection to prevent forceful overthrow. This imposes costs on all citizens through taxation, possible conscription, and possible threats to life and property during hostilities.

With democratic government, violent overthrow is still possible, but democratic institutions give potential challengers a way to channel resources into political campaigns rather than violent activity in their attempts to replace the existing government. This reduces the amount of resources the existing government must devote to police protection to protect itself from overthrow, and channels resources for these competitive activities into campaigns for election where those most interested in running the government use their own resources to compete for political power.

Another advantage of democracy in the modern political environment is that it produces legitimacy for the existing government's actions. If the government is democratically elected, then the government can argue that even those who disagree with government policies still should go along with them, because they are the will of the majority. While democracy lends several advantages to those with political power, it also has the drawback that it is relatively easy to replace elected leaders. Those in government would prefer to retain the advantages given to them by democracy, but give themselves more security at the same time.

The result is that democratic governments attempt to erect barriers to entry to keep potential competitors out. Campaign finance laws, the franking privilege, staffs paid for by taxpayer money, and increased media exposure are examples of factors that create barriers to entry for challengers. As a consequence, for many elected offices, there is little chance for a challenger to unseat the incumbent. In the U.S. House of Representatives, for example, over 95 percent of incumbents who run again for their seats are reelected.

Increased security means that incumbents have more monopoly power, allowing them to profit more from their production of public sector goods and services. A clear policy implication is that citizens would benefit from a reduction in the barriers to entry into political office.

Dimensions of Political Competition

When people think about political competition in democracies, the image that typically comes to mind is electoral competition. Parties and candidates compete with each other for elected office. However, as the discussion above makes clear, competition between incumbents and challengers is likely to be a more significant dimension of political competition than competition among candidates or parties.

In a typical election, a candidate from one party runs against a candidate from another, making it look like sides are drawn along party lines. Often, the election will also pit an incumbent against a challenger, and the coalition of incumbents against challengers is a more significant political tie than the coalition of one party against another. Once elected, incumbents have a history of creating barriers to entry to keep challengers from office. If party competition were more significant, those in a minority party would have an incentive to work to dismantle barriers to entry to allow more of their fellow party members a fair chance to be elected and increase the chances of their party becoming a majority. Yet incumbents of all parties work to create barriers to entry, even though this works against the best interests of the minority party. Incumbents are incumbents first, and party members second.[10]

This does not deny that competition among parties is significant. Certainly politicians identify with their parties and legislative coalitions are often formed along party lines. This is more true in European than in American politics because typically, the party can decide which candidate will represent it, while in the United States, candidates can choose to run with a certain party affiliation without the party's approval. However, American politics used to be more party-oriented, but incumbents have worked to erect barriers to entry that have lessened the influence of parties and of party competition, and have raised the influence of incumbency.[11] This threat exists in any democracy.

When people observe a typical election, they see an incumbent from one party run against a challenger from another. What they notice is that one party is competing against another, but they do not notice the more significant competition of incumbent against challenger. One of the important features of the model developed here is that it emphasizes the importance of the coalition of incumbents in democratic governments who erect barriers to entry to try to prevent challengers from becoming a part of the government. This competition of incumbents against challengers is even more problematic because when challengers do win, they switch coalitions and become incumbents the next time there is an election.

Institutions and Outcomes

The importance of institutional factors in determining the outcome of a political process will depend upon the setting. In situations where bargaining among decision-makers would be extremely costly, institutions will be very important in determining the outcome, whereas in settings where bargaining would be relatively easy, the specific institutional setting will be less influential.

Most models of democratic processes focus on the high bargaining cost settings. Examples include the election of representatives to a legislature, state-wide referenda, and on a more theoretical plane, the cyclical majority models of democratic decision-making. When it is difficult for participants to bargain with each other, they are forced to interact following the rules of the existing political institutions, and the outcome of the political process can often be determined by the institutional framework within which the decision is made. Under the old system where party leaders chose their presidential candidates, it is unlikely that Jimmy Carter, Ronald Reagan, of Michael Dukakis would have been their party's candidates, but under the primary system, they were chosen. Likewise, under state-wide referenda, voters can only vote for or against what is stated on the ballot, and have no way to express their preference intensities or make marginal changes in the issues to be voted on. The cyclical majority model clearly shows how the outcome of an election can be determined by the institutional framework.

In a setting with low bargaining costs, such as with decisions made in a legislature, all legislators can bargain with each other, and even when preference rankings suggest a cyclical majority, such an outcome is unlikely. The reason is that the group can bargain and exchange votes so that the group can select the outcome most highly valued by the group members.[12] The small numbers case operates like a market, and will tend to maximize the value of its output to those who are able to participate in the exchange.[13]

The structure of political institutions is an important determinant of political outcomes when large numbers of participants are involved, which effectively precludes bargaining. In small groups, however, exchange occurs so that, first, participants are able to choose the most valuable outcome, and second, the particular institutional environment is less important. Institutions can make it more or less costly to bargain, but in the small numbers setting, individuals can make agreements outside of the formal institutional apparatus. Theories that describe the outcomes of political institutions, such as theories about special interest politics or majority voting, are more applicable to settings with a large number of political participants, where institutions influence outcomes greatly, rather than small number settings where individuals can trade with each other.

Models of instability in majority rule will apply to large number settings, rather than small number settings where bargaining is possible. Thus, instability in selecting candidates does not necessarily translate into instability in policies selected by those who are elected. Considering the incentives and institutions, determinate public policy could be produced even with cycles among candidates for elected office.

There is more than just an analogy between political exchange and market exchange. Trade is taking place in both cases, so political exchange is more than "like a market:" it is a market. The same economic tools used to analyze exchange of goods and services apply to exchange in political markets as well. In academic analysis, there is often a tendency to give too much weight to the institutional setting in a small numbers case, and to take insufficient account of the influence that bargaining has over the ultimate outcome. The economic foundations of government are important when analyzing legislative decision-making processes.

Building on the Foundations

The purpose for developing this model of government has been to explore the economic foundations on which a complete theory of government could be built. If successful, this effort will contribute to the foundation, but has added relatively little to the superstructure. To continue with this analogy, after this effort the building will not look much different, but it will be on more solid footing.

There are two academic reasons why this type of exploration might be useful. First, if the building is not on a solid foundation to begin with, the construction of a more substantial foundation can keep the building from collapsing. There seems to be little immediate danger of this, however; economic models of politics are readily accepted and the area of public choice is substantial and growing. The second reason for adding to the foundation is to support a more substantial superstructure than currently exists. The building appears the same today, but the additional foundation allows for future expansion. Perhaps in this way, the models in this book can be useful for further developing the theory of public choice.

There is a practical reason for studying the theory of political institutions as well. Governments are the result of human design, and can be changed by human design. The better their operation is understood, the greater will be the chances that public sector institutions will be improved.

Notes

Chapter 1

1. James M. Buchanan, *The Limits of Liberty: Between Anarchy and Leviathan* (Chicago: University of Chicago Press, 1975).
2. Robert Nozick, *Anarchy, State, and Utopia* (New York: Basic Books, 1974).
3. John Rawls, *A Theory of Justice* (Cambridge, Mass.: Belknap, 1971).
4. Scott Gordon, "The New Contractarians," *Journal of Political Economy* 84, No. 3 (June 1976), pp. 573–590, criticizes what he perceives as the attempt to derive normative principles from positive analysis in this line of work.
5. See James M. Buchanan, "Public Finance and Public Choice," *National Tax Journal* 28 (December 1975), pp. 383–394.
6. As an example of a group that was willing to consider the social contract theory as a positive theory, Sir Ernest Barker notes in his introduction to *Social Contract* (New York & London: Oxford University Press, 1960) that in England "the house of Lords, as a part of the Convention Parliament, had agreed by 55 votes to 46 that there was an original contract between the King and the people" (p. xxii).
7. Rawls, *A Theory of Justice*, and Buchanan, *The Limits of Liberty*, cited earlier.
8. This does not necessarily imply that the antitrust laws are in the public interest, or were intended to be. Bruce Benson, M. L. Greenhut, and Randall Holcombe, "Interest Groups and the Antitrust Paradox," *Cato Journal* 6, No. 3 (Winter 1987), pp. 801–817, argue that the antitrust laws were the result of special interest politics. Robert Higgs, *Crisis and Leviathan: Critical Episodes in the Growth of American Government* (New York: Oxford University Press, 1987), argues that there was a change in the dominant ideology around the beginning of the 20th century that resulted in more government involvement in the economy, lending support to the idea that the value judgments of individuals do affect the activities of government.
9. Armen A. Alchian, "Uncertainty, Evolution, and Economic Theory," *Journal of Political Economy* 58 (1950), pp. 211–221.
10. Israel M. Kirzner, *Competition and Entrepreneurship* (Chicago: University of Chicago Press, 1973).
11. Oliver E. Williamson, "A Comparison of Alternative Approaches to Economic Organization," *Journal of Institutional and Theoretical Economics* 146, No. 1 (March 1990), pp. 61–71, discusses the differences between the economic analysis of contracts and of constitutions, and

produces an interesting general taxonomy of the economic analysis of institutions.

12. The incentive would not exist in a socialist economy in which all investment belongs to the state, but the point remains the same. The government imposes a stable institutional structure that gives people the incentive to behave in a certain way.

13. For example, James M. Buchanan and Richard E. Wagner, *Democracy in Deficit: The Political Legacy of Lord Keynes* (New York: Academic Press, 1977) argue that balanced budgets were a part of the fiscal constitution before the general acceptance of Keynesian economic principles. The discussion of constitutional rules is couched within this framework throughout this book, so constitutional rules are broader than just the written constitution.

14. This distinction was made clearly by James M. Buchanan and Gordon Tullock, *The Calculus of Consent* (Ann Arbor: University of Michigan Press, 1962), who developed a general model of constitutions. Buchanan's *Limits of Liberty*, cited earlier, carries this line of reasoning further. See also Geoffrey Brennan and James M. Buchanan, *The Reason of Rules: Constitutional Political Economy* (Cambridge: Cambridge University Press, 1985).

15. Thomas Hobbes, *Leviathan* (New York: E.P. Dutton, 1950, orig. 1651) discusses government in exactly this framework, with those in government having powers not granted to ordinary citizens, for the benefit of the citizens. As to whether government must have a monopoly over the use of force, Robert Nozick, *Anarchy, State, and Utopia* (New York: Basic Books, 1974) argues that monopoly government is natural and unavoidable, while Murray N. Rothbard, *For a New Liberty* (New York: Macmillan, 1973) argues that competitive markets could protect individual rights better than monopoly government.

Chapter 2

1. This definition roughly corresponds to that of Wesley Hohfeld, *Fundamental Legal Conceptions* (1923; Westport, Conn.: Greenwood Press, 1978). See David D. Gordon, "Morality and Rights," *Humane Studies Review* 5, No. 3 (Spring 1988), pp. 1–2, 17–22, for a discussion and a bibliographic essay on morality and rights.

2. See John Umbeck, "Might Makes Rights: A Theory of the Foundation and Initial Distribution of Property Rights," *Economic Inquiry* 19, No. 1 (January 1981), pp. 38–59, for a discussion of rights in this context.

3. This idea is discussed in the opening pages of Ludwig von Mises, *Human Action*, 3rd rev. ed. (Chicago: Henry Regnery Company, 1966). Additional discussion of the idea appears in Randall G. Holcombe,

Economic Models and Methodology (Westport, Conn.: Greenwood Press, 1989), chapter 7.

4. Thomas Hobbes, *Leviathan* (New York: E.P. Dutton, 1950 (orig. 1651)), p. 104.

5. *Leviathan*, p. 104.

6. Along these lines, see David Gauthier, *Morals By Agreement* (Oxford: Clarendon Press, 1986). Some, such as Murray Rothbard, *For a New Liberty* (New York: Macmillan, 1973), argue that anarchy would develop market institutions that would make it more productive than a society with government; however, rights are observed in Rothbard's anarchy.

7. Buchanan, *The Limits of Liberty: Between Anarchy and Leviathan* (Chicago: University of Chicago Press, 1975).

8. Robert Nozick, *Anarchy, State, and Utopia* (New York: Basic Books, 1974).

9. Robert C. Ellickson, "A Critique of Economic and Sociological Theories of Social Control," *Journal of Legal Studies* 16, No. 1 (January 1987), pp. 67–99. has suggested that the law and economics literature has overstated the importance of laws as methods of social control, and that social norms tend to evolve that are wealth maximizing rules even though they are not laws. Ellickson goes on to note that such norms do not always distribute the gains from Pareto superior improvements equally.

10. This is especially true of Rawls and Buchanan, and to a lesser degree Nozick. None of those theories, for example, provides for the possibility that some individuals will find their rights subordinated to others through institutions such as slavery.

11. Both Rawls and Buchanan have detailed models explaining what they mean by agreement with the social contract. The concept of agreement is discussed at length later in the book.

12. For a discussion, see Henry Sumner Maine, *Ancient Law* (New York: Henry Holt and Company, 1888), and Maine, *Early Law and Custom* (New York: Henry Holt and Company, 1886).

13. Maine, *Ancient Law*, pp. 121–126.

14. See Maine, *Ancient Law*, Chapter 4, "The Modern History of the Law of Nature," and Richard A. Posner, "A Theory of Primitive Society, with Special Reference to Law," *Journal of Law & Economics* 23, No. 1 (April 1980), pp. 1–53.

15. This point is emphasized by Leland B. Yeager, "Rights, Contract, and Utility in Policy Analysis," *Cato Journal* 5, No. 1 (Summer 1985), pp. 259–294, who notes that regardless of how much one agrees with the policies of one's government, the fundamental relationship between the state and its citizens is coercive.

16. Around major league baseball parks in inner cities, residents will offer to watch the car of a baseball fan during the game, in exchange for a fee. Is this a threat or a promise?

17. Bruce Benson, "An Institutional Explanation for Corruption of Criminal Justice Officials," *Cato Journal* 8, No. 1 (Spring/Summer 1988), pp. 139–163, discusses the emergence of black markets and the incentives for corruption when government tries to prevent economic exchange.

18. Hernando de Soto, *The Other Path* (New York: Harper & Row, 1989).

19. The reason such prohibitive regulation exists is that existing owners of housing and businesses use the political process to establish regulations protecting their positions from competition by newcomers. The regulations have created a system that is ripe for bribery and corruption, and is very inefficient. De Soto's book describes the problems in detail.

20. See Tibor Machan, *Individuals and Their Rights* (La Salle, Illinois: Open Court, 1989), who considers rights as a purely normative concept.

21. The compensation is not a reward for good behavior, but rather an incentive to act in such a way that they not lose their jobs and the associated rents.

22. See, however, Amartya Sen, "Rational Fools: A Critique of the Behavioral Foundations of Economic Theory," *Philosophy and Public Affairs* 6 (Summer 1977), pp. 317–344, on the idea of dual utility functions.

23. See James M. Buchanan, "Public Finance and Public Choice," *National Tax Journal* 28 (December 1975), pp. 383–394, who describes this as the fundamental premise of public choice. George J. Stigler, "The theory of Economic Regulation," *Bell Journal of Economics and Management Science* 2 (Spring 1971), pp. 2–21, spawned a new literature on regulation by explaining it as the outcome of individual self-interested behavior rather than legislation in the public interest. However, Steven Kelman, "Public Choice and Public Spirit," *The Public Interest* 87 (Spring 1987), pp. 80–94, argues that this type of analysis is damaging to society because it undermines the norm of public spiritedness, so becomes a self-fulfilling prophecy that causes government to act less in the public interest.

24. One might argue that such behavior has a biological origin. Following the publication of Edward O. Wilson's *Sociobiology* (Cambridge: Harvard University Press, 1975), economists developed an interest in biological origins of economic behavior. For a discussion, see Gary S. Becker, "Altruism, Egoism, and Genetic Fitness: Economics and Sociobiology," *Journal of Economic Literature* 14, No. 3 (September 1976), pp. 817–826, Jack Hirshleifer, "Shakespere vs. Becker on Altruism: The Importance of Having the Last Word," *Journal of Economic Literature* 15, No. 2 (June 1977), pp. 500–502, Gordon Tullock, "Economics and Sociobiology: A Comment," *Journal of Economic Literature* 15, No. 2 (June 1977), pp. 502–506, and Gary S. Becker, "Reply to Hisrshleifer and Tullock," *Journal of Economic*

Literature 15, No. 2 (June 1977), pp. 506–507. Regardless of the possibility of a biological origin, the challenge for the present argument is to explain why people will identify with certain groups to further group interests. Of course, biological models might apply without any genetic foundation, due to the competitive process. See Armen A. Alchian, "Uncertainty, Evolution, and Economic Theory," *Journal of Political Economy* 58 (1950), pp. 211–221 for an insightful discussion.

25. Adam Smith, *The Wealth of Nations* (New York: Random House, Modern Library, 1937), begins his treatise with a discussion of the benefits of the division of labor.

26. Robert Axelrod, *The Evolution of Cooperation* (New York: Basic Books, 1984).

27. Douglass C. North, *Structure and Change in Economic History* (New York: W.W. Norton & Company, 1981), especially chapter 5.

28. The economics literature has some discussion of ideology as an alternative to narrow self-interested behavior. See, for examples, James B. Kau and Paul H. Rubin, "Self-Interest, Ideology, and Logrolling in Congressional Voting," *Journal of Law & Economics* 22 (October 1979), pp. 365–384, Joseph P. Kalt and Mark A. Zupan, "Capture and Ideology in the Theory of Politics," *American Economic Review* 74 (June 1984), pp. 279–300, and Sam Peltzman, "Constituent Interest and Congressional Voting," *Journal of Law & Economics* 27, No. 1 (April 1984), pp. 181–210.

29. Margaret Levi, *Of Rule and Revenue* (Berkeley: University of California Press, 1988).

30. Murray Edelman, *The Symbolic Uses of Politics* (Urbana: University of Illinois Press, 1964).

31. Buchanan, *The Limits of Liberty*, argues for a concept of agreement in his social contract theory that implies agreement if the individual does not think he or she could expect to do better in a renegotiation. The issue is considered in more detail in the chapters dealing directly with the social contract theory.

32. David Gauthier, *Morals By Agreement* (Oxford: Clarendon Press, 1986), discusses moral behavior – which might be considered to be at least part of the observance of the rights of others – as behavior which is not self-interested. While the possibility of moral behavior that is not self-interested must be recognized, Gauthier does note that moral behavior is desirable because it enables cooperation among others in society. This cooperation is socially desirable even though it may impose costs directly on the individual. A different view is put forward by Robert Axelrod, *The Evolution of Cooperation* (New York: Basic Books, 1984), who depicts cooperative behavior as self-interested. The views of Gauthier and Axelrod are not necessarily inconsistent, but this theory of rights follows Axelrod's lead. Additional justification is provided by Geoffrey Brennan and James M. Buchanan, "Predictive

Power and the Choice Among Regimes," in *Explorations into Constitutional Economics* (College Station: Texas A&M University Press, 1989). Brennan and Buchanan argue for models of self-interest when analyzing public sector institutions so that institutions can be designed to guard against such behavior, rather than because such behavior is necessarily descriptive.

33. An application of the distinction is found in Randall G. Holcombe, "Applied Fairness Theory: Comment," *American Economic Review* 73 (December 1983), pp. 1153–1156, commenting on William J. Baumol, "Applied Fairness Theory and Rationing Policy," *American Economic Review* 72 (September 1982), pp. 639–651.

34. Posner's "A Theory of Primitive Society, with Special Reference to Law," and North's *Structure and Change in Economic History*, are examples of this type of theory.

35. Yeager, "Rights, Contract, and Utility in Policy Espousal."

36. This is not the type of utilitarianism Yeager espouses. It is, however, the common view of applied utilitarianism. See, for example, Paul G. Hare, ed., *Surveys in Public Sector Economics* (Oxford: Basil Blackwell, 1988), for a collection of readings using the utilitarian framework.

37. David Gauthier, *Morals By Agreement* (Oxford: Clarendon Press, 1986), p. 221, points out that there is no fixed set of rights in a utilitarian framework, since one's rights depend upon what arrangements maximize social welfare. One could easily imagine a change in circumstances which would require some people to give up some rights they previously enjoyed in order to benefit others and improve social welfare. The same is true in the economic theory of rights: a change in bargaining power can change the rights a person is able to claim and defend.

38. Natural rights theorists tend to focus on rights as opportunities rather than entitlements. For some examples, see Ayn Rand, "Man's Rights," in *The Virtue of Selfishness* (New York: New American Library, 1961), and Murray Rothbard, *The Ethics of Liberty* (Atlantic Highlands, N.J.: Humanities Press, 1982). Another application is liberalism as defined by Sen. See, for example, Amartya Sen, "Liberty, Unanimity, and Rights," *Economica* 43 (August 1976), pp. 217–245.

39. James M. Buchanan and Gordon Tullock, *The Calculus of Consent* (Ann Arbor: University of Michigan Press, 1962).

40. The phraseology was deliberately chosen to be provocative in the same way as Paul A. Samuelson's "The Pure Theory of Public Expenditure," *Review of Economics and Statistics* 36 (November 1954), pp. 387–389. Samuelson later modified the tile to call it "a theory" rather than "the theory" in "A Diagrammatic Exposition of a Theory of Public Expenditure," *Review of Economics and Statistics* 37 (November 1955), pp. 350–356," in response to comments that there were other theories of public expenditure. The reader is invited

to consider how other purely economic theories of rights might be developed.

41. *The Calculus of Consent*, p. 7.
42. Ronald H. Coase, "The Problem of Social Cost," *Journal of Law & Economics* 3 (October 1960), pp. 1–44.
43. See James M. Buchanan, "The Relevance of Pareto Optimality," *Journal of Conflict Resolution* (November 1962), pp. 341–354, on the relevance of Pareto optimality to institutional changes.
44. Skee Axelrod, *The Evolution of Cooperation*, for a related discussion.
45. The model of Alchian, "Uncertainty, Evolution, and Economic Theory," is an example of the way that the analogy of biological evolution has been used to understand social evolution.
46. See Steven N. S. Cheung, "China in Transition: Where is She Heading Now?" *Contemporary Policy Issues* 4, No. 4 (October 1986), pp. 1–11, who argues that China has gone past the point of no return in extending rights to its citizens. Cheung's idea that it would not be possible to take back certain rights once extended paints an optimistic picture about the future of individual rights in general. Both Milton Friedman, *Capitalism and Freedom* (Chicago: University of Chicago Press, 1962), and Freidrich A. Hayek, *The Road to Serfdom* (London: George Routledge & Sons, 1944), argue the interdependence of rights structures and economic performance. Gerald W. Scully, "The Institutional Framework and Economic Development," *Journal of Political Economy* 96, No. 3 (June 1988), pp. 652–662, finds an empirical relationship supporting the views of Friedman and Hayek.

Chapter 3

1. Charles A. Beard, *An Economic Interpretation of the Constitution* (New York: Macmillan, 1913), argues that the U.S. Constitution was written in a manner that protected the wealth of its authors. This is much more of a direct economic motivation than the more public-spirited idea of writing a constitution to promote the wealth of nations, and Beard's hypothesis has remained controversial. Robert A., McGuire and Robert L. Ohsfeldt, "Self-Interest, Agency Theory, and Voting Behavior: The Ratification of the United States Constitution," *American Economic Review* 79, No. 1 (March 1989), pp. 219–234 consider this same issue.
2. Thomas Hobbes, *Leviathan* (New York: E.P. Dutton, 1950, orig. 1651).
3. F. A. Hayek's discussion on the use of knowledge in society was intended to show why market economies are more productive than centrally planned economies, but Hayek's argument applies to slave societies as well. See Hayek's "The Use of Knowledge in Society," *American Economic Review* 35, No. 4 (September 1945), pp. 519–530.

4. See Steven N. S. Cheung, "Transaction Costs, Risk Aversion, and the Choice of Contractual Arrangements," *Journal of Law & Economics* 12, No. 1 (April 1969), pp. 23–42, for a discussion of the efficiency aspects of arrangements of this type.

5. The resulting bargain must at least be one in which both persons gain relative to a natural distribution that would exist without the agreement. This idea of a natural distribution was developed in Winston C. Bush, "Individual Welfare in Anarchy," Chapter 1 in Gordon Tullock, ed., *Explorations in the Theory of Anarchy* (Blacksburg, Va.: Center for Study of Public Choice, 1972), is used in James M. Buchanan's *The Limits of Liberty* (Chicago: University of Chicago Press, 1975), and is explored in greater detail by David Gauthier, *Morals By Agreement* (Oxford: Clarendon Press, 1986).

6. Often, such enduring agreements are more a part of social norms than political agreement, although they still are likely to be the outcome of at least implicit agreement. How else would norms become established? See Robert Sudgen, "Spontaneous Order," *Journal of Economic Perspectives* 3, No. 4 (Fall 1989), pp. 85–97, and Jon Elster, "Social Norms and Economic Theory," *Journal of Economic Perspectives* 3, No. 4 (Fall 1989), pp. 99–117, for a discussion.

7. James M. Buchanan and Gordon Tullock, *The Calculus of Consent* (Ann Arbor: University of Michigan Press, 19620, and John Rawls, *A Theory of Justice* (Cambridge, Mass.: Belknap, 1971).

8. Gordon Tullock, *The Social Dilemma* (Blacksburg, Va.: University Publications, 1974), discusses similar issues and arrives at similar conclusions. See especially his discussion on pp. 7–8.

9. James S. Coleman, *Foundations of Social Theory* (Cambridge, Mass.: Harvard University Press, 1990), p. 53.

10. Even within societies, the strong have been able to use the threat of violence to enforce the rights to which they believed they were entitled. See, for example, E. Adamson Hoebel, *The Law of Primitive Man: A Study in Comparative Legal Dynamics* (Cambridge, Mass.: Harvard University Press, 1954), especially Chapter 7 and his discussion of Comanche law.

11. Robert Nozick, *Anarchy, State, and Utopia* (New York: Basic Books, 1974) models government as built on the natural monopoly characteristic of the production of protective services, but Murray Rothbard, *For a New Liberty* (New York: Macmillan, 1973) argues that protective services could be produced in a competitive setting.

12. Harold Demsetz, "Why Regulate Utilities?" *Journal of Law & Economics* 11 (1968), pp. 55–65, explains how this can be the case with utilities that produce in natural monopoly markets. Gordon Tullock, "Entry Barriers in Politics," *American Economic Review* 55, No. 2 (March 1965), pp. 458–466, has developed a model similar to Demestz's, but explicitly applied to electoral politics.

13. This point is made in the very insightful analysis of politics by Murray

Edelman, *The Symbolic Uses of Politics* (Urbana: University of Illinois Press, 1964).

14. Douglass C. North, *Structure and Change in Economic History* (New York: W.W. Norton & Company, 1981), and "Ideology and Political/Economic Institutions," *Cato Journal*, Spring/Summer 1988, 8, 15–28.

15. See, for examples, James B. Kau and Paul H. Rubin, "Self-Interest, Ideology, and Logrolling in Congressional Voting," *Journal of Law & Economics* 22 (October 1979), pp. 365–384, Joseph P. Kalt and Mark A. Zupan, "Capture and Ideology in the Theory of Politics," *American Economic Review* 74 (June 1984), pp. 279–300, Sam Peltzman, "Constituent Interest and Congressional Voting," *Journal of Law & Economics* 27, No. 1 (April 1984), pp. 181–210. North's concept of legitimacy is explored and extended by Justin Yifu Lin, "An Economic Theory of Institutional Change: Induced and Imposed Change," *Cato Journal* 9, No. 1 (Spring/Summer 1989), pp. 1–33.

16. William A. Niskanen, "Conditions Affecting the Survival of Constitutional Rules," *Constitutional Political Economy* 1, No. 2 (Spring/Summer 1990), pp. 53–62, discusses some conditions affecting the survival of constitutional rules, and wonders why they seem to last as long as they do. This discussion suggests that long-term stability of constitutional rules benefits those in power, at promoting at least some degree of longevity.

17. R. G. Holcombe, "A Contractarian Model of the Decline in Classical Liberalism," *Public Choice* 35, No. 3 (1980), pp. 260–274, discusses Buchanan's device of renegotiation from anarchy at greater length.

18. Hobbes, *Leviathan*, pp. 142–143.

19. Hobbes, *Leviathan*, p. 143.

20. This ignores the possibility of bargaining strength exercised if an individual is willing to hold out for favorable treatment. This might be possible with the unanimity in *The Calculus of Consent*, but probably not behind the Rawlsian veil of ignorance, because nobody knows their place in society until after the constitution is drawn up.

21. Robert Nozick, *Anarchy, State, and Utopia* (New York: Basic Books, 1974).

22. Nozick relies on unanimity less than the others, seeing that there may be a free rider problem with regard to government, and creating a role for government coercion to overcome the free rider problem. These people in Nozick's model do not "agree to be coerced," as would be the case if a unanimous decision rule is required, as in *The Calculus of Consent* and *A Theory of Justice*.

23. Charles M. Tiebout, "A Pure Theory of Local Expenditures," *Journal of Political Economy* 64 (October 1956), pp. 416–424.

24. Knut Wicksell, "A New Principle of Just Taxation" (1896), pp. 72–118 in Richard A. Musgrave and Alan T. Peacock, eds., *Classics in the Theory of Public Finance* (New York: St. Martin's Press, 1967).

25. Leland B. Yeager, "Rights, Contract, and Utility in Policy Analysis," *Cato Journal* 5, No. 1 (Summer 1985), pp. 259–294, criticizes modern contractarians generally, and Buchanan in particular, for the use of conceptual agreement to signify agreement when actual agreement could never take place.

26. If Nozick's minimal state is optimal, one would have to rule out a prisoners' dilemma situation in which individual bargains could lead to a state of the world that is inferior to another state of the world that could be judged superior by unanimous agreement. However, a Hobbesian view would be that it is only the existence of potential prisoners' dilemma situations which justify the existence of government in the first place.

27. See Randall G. Holcombe, "Non-Optimal Unanimous Agreement," *Public Choice* 48, No. 3 (1986), pp. 229–244, for a discussion of unanimous agreement under less-than-unanimity rule.

28. Hobbes, *Leviathan*, p. 147.

29. The role of alternatives is present in Buchanan's *Limits of Liberty* but not in *The Calculus of Consent* or *A Theory of Justice*.

30. Conceptual agreement in contractarian theories has been criticized by Leland B. Yeager, "Rights, Contract, and Utility in Policy Analysis," cited above. In some societies, agreement may have been more direct. For example, Harold J. Berman, *Law and Revolution: The Formation of the Western Legal Tradition* (Cambridge: Harvard University Press, 1983) suggests that in cities formed in Europe in the 1050–1150 time period, it was common for all residents to collectively affirm their agreement with the city rules.

31. William A. Niskanen, in several works, modeled bureaucratic output as the result of a bargaining process between a bureau and its sponsor. See "The Peculiar Economics of Bureaucracy," *American Economic Review* 58 (May 1968), pp. 293–305, *Bureaucracy and Representative Government* (Chicago and New York: Aldine-Atherton, 1971), and "Bureaucrats and Politicians," *Journal of Law & Economics* 18 (December 1975), pp. 617–643. While it is a different bargain, the modelling philosophy of this chapter is the same.

32. Nozick, in *Anarchy, State, and Utopia*, models government as evolving from private contracts to provide protective services. The institutions become government when it is no longer viewed as legitimate for citizens to terminate the contract for protective services, or for the protective service to announce a change in the terms of its service without the agreement of its clients. In a market setting, the provider of the service could unilaterally change the service as it sees fit, and the customer could either continue or not with the new terms. In a government setting, a well-defined procedure must be followed if the change is to be viewed as legitimate.

33. Increasing government monopoly power as a result of increased security of incumbents is discussed by Randall G. Holcombe and James

D. Gwartney, "Political Parties and the Legislative Principal-Agent Relationship," *Journal of Institutional and Theoretical Economics* 145, No. 4 (December 1989), pp. 669–675.

34. Randolph S. Bourne, *War and the Intellectuals* (New York: Harper & Row, 1964), called war the health of the state.

35. I have never heard Frank Knight say this, but I have frequently heard James Buchanan say that Frank Knight said it.

Chapter 4

1. The title of Bruce L. Benson, "A Note on Corruption by Public Officials: The Black Market for Property Rights," *Journal of Libertarian Studies* 5, No. 3 (Summer 1981), pp. 305–311, explains these differential rights in just the terms used here. There is a market for rights. See also "Corruption in Law Enforcement: One Consequence of 'The Tragedy of the Commons' Arising with Public Allocation Processes," *International Review of Law and Economics* 8 (1988), pp. 73–84, and "An Institutional Explanation for Corruption of Criminal Justice Officials," *Cato Journal* 8, No. 1 (Spring/Summer 1988), pp. 139–163, by the same author, and Benson and John Baden, "The Political Economy of Governmental Corruption: The Logic of Underground Government," *Journal of Legal Studies* 14 (June 1985), pp. 391–410.

2. One might want to consider, in this context, what the difference is between corruption and special interest legislation. In both cases people are using the power of the political process for their own private ends.

3. Oliver E. Williamson, *The Economic Institutions of Capitalism*. New York: The Free Press, 1985, discusses opportunism at some length and methods by which contracts can be made to deal with the problem. He devotes two chapters to the idea of credible commitments, of which the political institutions discussed later in the chapter can be viewed as examples.

4. Thomas Schwartz, "The Universal-Instability Theorem," *Public Choice* 37, No. 3 (1981), pp. 487–501, develops a model that illustrates the similarity of market exchange and political exchange in this regard.

5. See Robert Axelrod, *The Evolution of Cooperation* (New York: Basic Books, 1984), for a discussion of iterated prisoners' dilemma games.

6. This type of model of social institutions is described by Earl A. Thompson and Roger L. Faith, "A Pure Theory of Strategic Behavior and Social Institutions," *American Economic Review* 71, No. 3 (June 1981), pp. 366–380.

7. Gordon Tullock, "The Welfare Costs of Tariffs, Monopolies, and Theft," *Western Economic Journal* 5 (June 1967), pp. 224–232, discusses these. It is interesting to note the parallel Tullock draws between tariffs and theft. The efficiency losses that exist because people try to protect themselves from theft also exist because people

try to avoid taxation, but the fact that there is a welfare cost in each case does not alter the fact that neither tax burdens nor rights are absolute. Economists use lump-sum taxation as a model of ideal efficient taxation, and perhaps just as an ideal efficient tax does not exist, an ideal efficient rights structure does not exist either.

8. The prominent article by Isaac Ehrlich, "The Deterrent Effect of Capital Punishment: A Question of Life and Death," *American Economic Review* 65, No. 3 (June 1975), pp. 397–417, suggests that the deterrent effect of capital punishment saves more victims' lives than the number of murderers executed.

9. More resources are used to protect the life of the president than the all-night convenience store clerk. This is another example where some people are granted more extensive rights than others.

10. The notion of the legal system providing unconditional rights is embodied in victim compensation laws that specify that the state provide compensation for crime victims.

11. Robert Nozick, *Anarchy, State, and Utopia* (New York: Basic Books, 1974).

12. In this small number setting, the allocation of the right is likely to be optimal if transaction costs are low, following Ronald H. Coase, "The Problem of Social Cost," *Journal of Law & Economics* 3 (October 1960), pp. 1–44.

13. This incentive to share in the gains from trade could far overshadow the power to protect rights. Robert Axelrod, *The Evolution of Cooperation* (New York: Basic Books, 1984), has argued how the incentive for cooperation over the long run can be more important than the transitory gains that could be reaped through noncooperative behavior.

14. This construction was used in Randall G. Holcombe, "A Contractarian Model of the Decline in Classical Liberalism," *Public Choice* 35, No. 3 (1980), pp. 260–274, to depict the social contract theory in James M. Buchanan, *The Limits of Liberty: Between Anarchy and Leviathan* (Chicago: University of Chicago Press, 1975). The present application does not require the same concept of agreement as is found in the social contract theory.

15. Hans-Jorg Schmidt-Trenz, "The State of Nature in the Shadow of Contract Formation: Adding a Missing Link to J. M. Buchanan's Social Contract Theory," *Public Choice* 62, No. 3 (September 1989), pp. 237–251, argues that the point of anarchistic equilibrium, point A in Figure 4.3, is a function of the type of bargaining that will take place to produce the social contract. The model developed here does not rely on point A being in a specific location, so is not affected by Schmidt-Trenz's observation. His more general point about the outcome of the bargain being a function of the type of bargaining that takes place is relevant to this model, however.

16. This static model depicts a rights structure at a point in time, which might change over time. Dan Usher, "The Dynastic Cycles and the

Stationary State," *American Economic Review* 79, No. 5 (December 1989), pp. 1031– 1044, develops a dynamic model that depicts a constant evolution rather than a steady state. The comparative statics framework might capture an instant in this dynamic model, but does not have dynamic elements built in.

17. Freidrich A. Hayek, "The Use of Knowledge in Society," *American Economic Review* 35, No. 4 (September 1945), pp. 519–530.

18. Thus, the results of human action but not of human design will not always produce the most efficient institutions.

Chapter 5

1. The fiscal exchange model of government is described by James M. Buchanan, "Taxation in Fiscal Exchange," *Journal of Public Economics* 6 (July-August 1976), pp. 17–29.

2. In my textbook, *Public Sector Economics* (Belmont, California: Wadsworth, 1988), chapter 5 discusses collective decision-making in a framework that applies to clubs as well as governments. This is a standard way of approaching collective decision-making in public choice theory.

3. James M. Buchanan, "An Economic Theory of Clubs," *Economica* (February 1965), pp. 1–14.

4. Sir Ernest Barker, *Social Contract* (New York & London: Oxford University Press, 1960), traces the origins of the social contract theory to Plato.

5. James M. Buchanan, *The Limits of Liberty: Between Anarchy and Leviathan* (Chicago: University of Chicago Press, 1975).

6. John Rawls, *A Theory of Justice* (Cambridge: Belknap Press, 1971).

7. On this point, it is interesting to note that Barker, *Social Contract*, p. xxii, reports that "the House of Lords, as a part of the Convention of Parliament, had agreed by 55 votes to 46 that there was an original contract between the King and the People."

8. Some criticisms are presented by Scott Gordon, "The New Contractarians," *Journal of Political Economy* 84, No. 3 (June 1976), pp. 573–590, and Leland B. Yeager, "Rights, Contract, and Utility in Policy Espousal," *Cato Journal* 5, No. 1 (Summer 1985), pp. 259–294. Gordon's review article included Rawls and Buchanan as well as Robert Nozick, *Anarchy, State, and Utopia* (New York: Basic Books, 1974), although Gordon finds Nozick's brand of contractarianism to be significantly different at its foundations than that of Rawls and Buchanan. Yeager's critique of contractarianism cites Buchanan's *Limits of Liberty* and Randall G. Holcombe's *Public Finance and the Political Process* (Carbondale: Southern Illinois University Press, 1983) for examples of contractarian arguments.

9. See, for example, Murray N. Rothbard, *Conceived in Liberty*, vol. 3, p. 350, where he argues about the American revolution that " . . . the revolution was genuinely and enthusiastically supported by the great majority of the American population. It was a true people's war . . . American rebels certainly could not have concluded the first successful war of national liberation in history . . . unless they had commanded the support of the American people." One would hardly say that this constitutes a social contract, but it does suggest general support for the establishment of the U.S. government at the time of the nation's founding, and by a writer who is normally very critical of government.

10. See Bernard H. Siegan, "Non-Zoning in Houston," *Journal of Law & Economics* 13, No. 1 (April 1979), pp. 71–147.

11. Robert A. Dahl, *Democracy and Its Critics* (New Haven: Yale University Press, 1989), p. 42. Note that this definition is given as Dahl explains the arguments of another writer, but Dahl accepts the definition and goes on to explain why it may be desirable for the state to act coercively. On page 107, Dahl defines government by saying that "The decisionmakers who make binding decisions constitute the *government* of the association" (original emphasis). Dahl thus defines government as a group of people, but explicitly notes that this definition could apply to the governing institutions of a voluntary organization as well as a state.

12. Note that Dahl is not as interested in delineating state activity from other collective activity, but rather in promoting democracy. But while noting that voluntary organizations have governing structures, Dahl concentrates on democracy within the state. See also his *Democracy, Liberty, and Equality* (Oxford: Oxford University Press, 1986) and *A Preface to Economic Democracy* (Berkeley: University of California Press, 1985) for similar views on government.

13. Dahl, *Modern Political Analysis*, 3rd ed. (Englewood Cliffs, N.J.: Prentice-Hall, 1976), p. 10.

14. Max Weber, *The Theory of Social and Economic Organization*, translated by A.M. Henderson and Talcott Parsons (Oxford: Oxford University Press, 1947), p. 154.

15. This definition is the opening sentence of Rand's essay, "The Nature of Government," in *The Virtue of Selfishness* (New York: New American Library, 1961). It seems considerably more enlightening than the dictionary definition (from *Webster's New World Dictionary*, College Edition, 1968), the exercise of authority over an organization, institution, state, district, etc.; direction; control; rule; management. Following this definition, it would make sense to talk about the government of a bridge club, but without implying that the bridge club is a government.

16. Weber's definition seems to be commonly accepted among individuals studying government. Yet another adopter of his definition is Richard

D. Auster and Morris Silver, *The State as a Firm: Economic Forces in Political Development* (Boston: Martinus Nijhoff, 1979), p. 21.

17. Carl Joachim Friedrich, *Man and His Government: An Empirical Theory of Politics* (New York: McGraw-Hill, 1963), p. 182.

18. Friedrich, *Man and His Government*, p. 550 also defines state to include the government and a sense of nationalism among the individuals ruled by the government.

19. One might argue that a gunman could enter the restaurant and demand dinner without conforming to the dress code, but those working at the restaurant could still refuse to serve the gunman. Even if the gunman was successful, governments are frequently attacked in the real world, but such encroachments do not make them lose their status of being governments, unless they are completely overthrown.

20. Murray N. Rothbard, *The Ethics of Liberty* (Atlantic Highlands, N.J.: Humanities Press, 1982), pp. 162–163.

21. *The Ethics of Liberty*, p. 171.

22. Extensions of the argument at this point might take two directions. First, ambiguous cases might be considered. For example, is an electric utility a government because it can use the right of eminent domain to confiscate private property? I would argue that it is not, but that the utility is exercising a right granted by a government, but from the definition above there is a fine distinction that could be argued both ways. Second, cases where governments or non-governments appear not to fit the definition could be considered. The involuntary neighborhood association is an example of an organization classified as a government under this definition but is not normally considered a government. Conversely, the governments of people who do not have fixed territorial claims are unambiguously excluded under this definition. The chapter's argument must be that they are not governments in the true sense of the word, but are voluntary associations. Such groups would include the PLO, nomadic tribes, bands of gypsies, and motorcycle gangs.

23. Note that while they do not define government in this way, Geoffrey Bennan and James M. Buchanan, *The Power to Tax: Analytical Foundations of a Fiscal Constitution* (Cambridge: Cambridge University Press, 1980), are concerned with ways in which to constitutionally constrain the government from abusing its powers of taxation.

24. This notion of coercion is consistent with that described by Dahl, *Democracy and Its Critics*. See page 44, for example.

25. Charles M. Tiebout, "A Pure Theory of Local Expenditures," *Journal of Political Economy* 64 (October 1956), pp. 416–424.

26. For a discussion, see James M. Buchanan and Charles J. Goetz, "Efficiency Limits of Fiscal Mobility: An Assessment of the Tiebout Model," *Journal of Public Economics* 1 (1972), pp. 25–43.

Chapter 6

1. The theory of contestable markets extends the competitive model beyond cases where actual alternatives exist to cases where barriers to entry are low making potential competition easy. See William J. Baumol, "Contestable Markets: An Uprising in the Theory of Industry Structure," *American Economic Review* 72, No. 1 (March 1982), pp. 1–15, and William J. Baumol, John C. Panzar, and Robert D. Willig, *Contestable Markets and the Theory of Industry Structure.* New York: Harcourt Brace Jovanovich, 1982.

2. Models by Douglass C. North, *Structure and Change in Economic History* (New York: W.W. Norton & Company, 1981) and Margaret Levi, *Of Rule and Revenue* (Berkeley: University of California Press, 1988) depict government as a profit maximizer along the same lines as the neoclassical firm. See also Richard D. Auster and Morris Silver, *The State as a Firm: Economic Forces in Political Development* (Boston: Martinus Nijhoff, 1979), chapter 5, for an analysis of the monopoly powers of government.

3. See Charles M. Tiebout, "A Pure Theory of Local Expenditures," *Journal of Political Economy* 64 (October 1956), pp. 416–424.

4. Thus, for example, the Pareto optimal redistribution suggested by Harold M. Hochman and James D. Rodgers, "Pareto Optimal Redistribution," *American Economic Review* 59 (September 1969), pp. 542–557, would be coercive because people are forced to contribute, even if to overcome a free rider problem that everyone recognizes.

5. Robert Nozick, *Anarchy, State, and Utopia.* New York: Basic Books, 1974.

6. Harold Demsetz, "Why Regulate Utilities?" *Journal of Law & Economics* 11 (1968), pp. 55–65.

7. Gordon Tullock, "Entry Barriers in Politics," *American Economic Review* 55, No. 2 (March 1965), pp. 458–466, discusses entry barriers in democracies. See also W. Mark Crain, Randall Holcombe, and Robert Tollison, "Monopoly Aspects of Political Parties," *Atlantic Economic Journal* 7, No. 2 (July 1979), pp. 54–58 for a discussion.

8. Anthony Downs, *An Economic Theory of Democracy* (New York: Harper & Row, 1957).

9. See Duncan Black, *The Theory of Committees and Elections* (Cambridge: Cambridge University Press, 1958) for a discussion of the committee model and Howard R. Bowen, "The Interpretation of Voting in the Allocation of Economic Resources," *Quarterly Journal of Economics* 58 (November 1943), pp. 27–48, for a development of the model in a referendum setting.

10. See Randall G. Holcombe, "The Median Voter Model in Public Choice Theory," *Public Choice* 61, No. 2 (1989), pp. 115–125, for a discussion of the model and its use in public choice.

11. William H. Riker, in *The Theory of Political Coalitions* (New Haven: Yale University Press, 1962), challenges the view that politicians

maximize votes, instead arguing that they seek the minimum winning coalition. In other words, they get the minimum number of votes necessary, not the maximum number they can. In the context of the competitive model, the distinction is irrelevant because the vote-maximizing strategy is able to capture only a bare majority of the votes. Thus, in the competitive model, Riker's strategy and Downs' strategy would be the same.

12. See, however, Donald Wittman, "Why Democracies Produce Efficient Results," *Journal of Political Economy* 97, No. 6 (December 1989), pp. 1395–1424, who questions whether strong support from a few is really politically advantageous enough to offset weak opposition from a substantial majority.

13. This type of model is developed by Barry R. Weingast, Kenneth A. Shepsle, and Christopher Johnsen, "The Political Economy of Benefits and Costs: A Neoclassical Approach to Distributive Politics," *Journal of Political Economy* 89, No. 4 (August 1981), pp. 642–664, and Randall G. Holcombe, *An Economic Analysis of Democracy* (Carbondale: Southern Illinois University Press, 1985).

14. Margaret Levi, *Of Rule and Revenue* (Berkeley: University of California Press, 1988) builds agency costs into her model of politics.

15. See Glenn R. Parker, "Looking Toward Reelection: Revising Assumptions About the Factors Motivating Congressional Behavior," *Public Choice* 63, No. 3, (December 1989), pp. 237–252, for a discussion of discretionary activity of legislators.

16. This proposition will be familiar to students of microeconomic theory, so will not be demonstrated here. Unfamiliar and curious readers can see the argument in any microeconomics textbook. One example is George J. Stigler, *The Theory of Price*, 4th ed. (New York: Macmillan, 1987), pp. 228–232.

17. The exception to this statement occurs when reapportionment causes a state to lose representatives, in which case there is the potential for incumbents to run against each other.

18. This idea is discussed persuasively in W. Mark Crain, "On the Structure and Stability of Political Markets," *Journal of Political Economy* 85, No. 4 (August 1977), pp. 829–842.

19. There is a literature on ideological voting that deals with this issue. For examples, see James B. Kau and Paul H. Rubin, "Self-Interest, Ideology, and Logrolling in Congressional Voting," *Journal of Law & Economics* 22 (October 1979), pp. 365–384, Joseph P. Kalt and Mark A. Zupan, "Capture and Ideology in the Theory of Politics," *American Economic Review* 74 (June 1984), pp. 279–300, and Sam Peltzman, "Constituent Interest and Congressional Voting," *Journal of Law & Economics* 27, No. 1 (April 1984), pp. 181–210.

20. Models describing the role of senior members in this way are found in Barry R. Weingast and William J. Marshall, "The Industrial Organiza-

tion of Congress; or, Why Legislatures, Like Firms, Are Not Organized as Markets," *Journal of Political Economy* 96, No. 1 (February 1988), pp. 132–163, and Kenneth J. Koford, "Centralized Vote Trading," *Public Choice* 39, No. 2 (1982), pp. 245–268.

21. This is the argument made in Randall G. Holcombe, "A Note on Seniority and Political Competition," *Public Choice* 61, No. 3 (1989), pp. 285–288.

22. Jody Lipford and Bruce Yandle, "Exploring Dominant State Governments," *Journal of Institutional and Theoretical Economics* 146, No 4 (December 1990), pp. 561–575, examine state governments in the United States and find that states more dominated by a single party have greater control of state and local tax revenues. This provides evidence that interparty competition does have some effect.

23. This line of reasoning could be discussed extensively. For example, Milton Friedman, *Capitalism and Freedom* (Chicago: University of Chicago Press, 1962) and Milton and Rose Friedman, *Free to Choose* (New York: Harcourt Brace Jovanovich, 1980) suggest that political freedom is associated with improved economic performance, as does Freidrich A. Hayek, *The Road to Serfdom* (London: George Routledge & Sons, 1944). Others, Ayn Rand, "Man's Rights," in *The Virtue of Selfishness*) New York: New American Library, 1961) being an example, argue that while political freedom produces economic prosperity as a by-product, the rights people have should not be justified by their economic consequences. Any theory of natural rights, as for example, Murray Rothbard, *The Ethics of Liberty* (Atlantic Highlands, N.J.: Humanities Press, 1982) would concur. While this line of reasoning might be questioned for many reasons other than those discussed in Chapter 2, it can stand here as a working hypothesis.

24. Richard B. McKenzie and Robert J. Staaf, "Revenue Sharing and Monopoly Government," *Public Choice* 33, No. 3 (1978), pp. 93–97, discuss this idea.

25. George J. Stigler, "The Theory of Economic Regulation," *Bell Journal of Economics and Management Science* 2 (Spring 1971), pp. 2–21. However, Gordon Tullock, "The Transitional Gains Trap," *Bell Journal of Economics* 6 (Autumn 1975), pp. 671–678, discusses the possibility that these benefits will be competed away over time. Such competition can be the result of what economists call rent seeking. The seminal articles on rent seeking are Gordon Tullock, "The Welfare Costs of Tariffs, Monopolies, and Theft," *Western Economic Journal* 5 (June 1967), pp. 224–232, Anne O. Kreuger, "The Political Economy of the Rent-Seeking Society," *American Economic Review* 64 (June 1974), pp. 291–303, and Richard A. Posner, "The Social Costs of Monopoly and Regulation," *Journal of Political Economy* 83 (August 1975), pp. 807–827.

26. Gregg A. Jarrell, "The Demand for State Regulation of the Electric Utility Industry," *Journal of Law & Economics* 21, No. 3 (October

1978), pp. 269–295, argues that regulated utilities wanted to be regulated to free them from competition from other utilities.

27. See Randall G. Holcombe and Lora P. Holcombe, "The Market for Regulation," *Journal of Institutional and Theoretical Economics* 142, No. 4 (December 1986), pp. 684–696, for a discussion of the way in which the market provides for regulatory activity if the government does not get involved.

28. See Richard A. Posner, "Taxation by Regulation," *Bell Journal of Economics and Management Science* 2 (Spring 1971), pp. 22–50.

29. Sam Peltzman, "Toward a More General Theory of Regulation," *Journal of Law & Economics* 19 (August 1976), explores this line of reasoning.

30. Bruce L. Benson has done extensive analysis of corruption from an economic standpoint. For examples, see his "Corruption in Law Enforcement: One Consequence of 'The Tragedy of the Commons' Arising with Public Allocation Processes," *International Review of Law and Economics* 8 (1988), pp. 73–84, "An Institutional Explanation for Corruption of Criminal Justice Officials," *Cato Journal* 8, No. 1 (Spring/Summer 1988), pp. 139–163, "A Note on Corruption by Public Officials: The Black Market for Property Rights," *Journal of Libertarian Studies* 5, No. 3 (Summer 1981), pp. 305–311, and with John Baden, "The Political Economy of Governmental Corruption: The Logic of Underground Government," *Journal of Legal Studies* 14 (June 1985), pp. 391–410.

31. This idea appears in Thomas C. Schelling, "Economic Analysis of Organized Crime," in the President's Commission on Law Enforcement and the Administration of Justice *Task Force Report: Organized Crime*. U.S. Government Printing Office, Washington, D.C., 1967. See also Peter Reuter, "Police Regulation of Illegal Gambling: Frustrations of Symbolic Enforcement," *The Annals of the American Academy of Political and Social Science*, No. 474 (July 1984), pp. 36–47.

32. This line of reasoning with regard to the secret ballot is discussed by Gary M. Anderson and Robert D. Tollison, "Democracy, Interest Groups, and the Price of Votes," *Cato Journal* 8, No. 1 (Spring/Summer 1988), pp. 53–70.

Chapter 7

1. Charles M. Tiebout, "A Pure Theory of Local Expenditures," *Journal of Political Economy* 64 (October 1956), pp. 416–424.

2. The model of Robert Nozick, *Anarchy, State, and Utopia* (New York: Basic Books, 1974), argues that individuals freely contracting from a state of anarchy will produce monopoly government.

3. The term "right" is used here in a purely positive setting, as in Chapter 2. It means that someone or some group claims to be the

government, and that others honor the claim. It says nothing about the moral correctness of the claim.

4. Margaret Levi, *Of Rule and Revenue* (Berkeley: University of California Press, 1988) describes government as a monopoly and looks into issues such as the discount rate and time horizon that leaders might have, given their possibilities of being replaced. Shorter time horizons can have an obvious effect on government policy.

5. This could be viewed in the framework of Murray Edelman, *The Symbolic Uses of Politics* (Urbana: University of Illinois Press, 1964), perhaps arguing that democratic institutions provide a symbol of political choice and grant legitimacy to the existing government, which removes some of the ability of challengers to mount revolutions. The existing government, after all, was chosen by the people.

6. This risk-return trade-off is modeled in Guilio M. Gallarotti, "Legitimacy as a Capital Asset of the State," *Public Choice* 63, No. 1 (October 1989), pp. 43–61. Directly following Gallarotti's article is John Mbaku and Chris Paul, "Political Instability in Africa: A Rent-Seeking Approach," *Public Choice* 63, No. 1 (October 1989), pp. 63–72, who argue that Arican instability is due to rent-seeking dictators that accept risk in search of higher returns from governing.

7. This point is made by James M. Buchanan, "Politics, Policy, and the Pigouvian Margins," *Economica* n.s. 29 (February 1962), pp. 17–28.

8. This definition follows Paul A. Samuelson, "The Pure Theory of Public Expenditure," *Review of Economics and Statistics* 36 (November 1954), pp. 387–389, and "A Diagrammatic Exposition of a Theory of Public Expenditure," *Review of Economics and Statistics* 37 (November 1955), pp. 350–356. The definition is a standard one used by economists.

9. The conditions under which the median voter will prefer the optimal level of output are discussed more fully in Randall G. Holcombe, *Public Finance and the Political Process* (Carbondale: Southern Illinois University Press, 1983), ch. 2. On this issue, see also Robin Barlow, "Efficiency Aspects of Local School Finance," *Journal of Political Economy* 78 (September-October 1970), pp. 1028–1040, and "Efficiency Aspects of Local School Finance: Reply," *Journal of Political Economy* 81 (January-February 1973), pp. 192–202.

10. The idea is developed in Erik Lindahl, "Just Taxation – A Positive Solution" (1919), pp. 168–176 in Richard A. Musgrave and Alan T. Peacock, eds., *Classics in the Theory of Public Finance* (New York: St. Martin's Press, 1967).

11. An argument can be made that Lindahl equilibrium is in some cases not equitable. See Arthur T. Denzau and Robert J. Mackay, "Benefit Shares and Majority Voting," *American Economic Review* 66 (March 1976), pp. 69–76.

12. This is discussed in Holcombe, *Public Finance and the Political Process*, ch. 2.

13. This may not quite be true if there is some division of taxes that appears to be naturally fair. Such a point of natural agreement is sometimes called a Schelling point after the analysis in Thomas C. Schelling, *The Strategy of Conflict* (Cambridge, Mass.: Harvard University Press, 1960). Even so, it may be that the Lindahl equilibrium division is also the Schelling point.

14. Knut Wicksell, "A New Principle of Just Taxation" (1896), pp. 72–118 in Richard A. Musgrave and Alan T. Peacock, eds., *Classics in the Theory of Public Finance* (New York: St. Martin's Press, 1967).

15. Anthony Downs, *An Economic Theory of Democracy* (New York: Harper & Row, 1957).

16. See, for examples Richard D. McKelvey, "Intransitivities in Multi Dimensional Voting Models and Some Implications for Agenda Control," *Journal of Economic Theory* 12, No. 3 (June 1976), pp. 472–482, and "General Conditions for Global Intrasitivities in Formal Voting Models," *Econometrica* 47, No. 5 (September 1979), pp. 1085–1112. McKelvey's models provoked renewed interest in the issue of stability in formal voting models.

17. An overview of some of the questions asked of this type of model can be found in Gordon Tullock, "Why So Much Stability?" *Public Choice* 37, No. 2 (1982), pp. 189–202, Charles K. Rowley, "The Relevance of the Median Voter Theorem," *Journal of Institutional and Theoretical Economics* 140, No. 1 (1984), pp. 104–126, and Randall G. Holcombe, "The Median Voter Model in Public Choice Theory," *Public Choice* 61, No. 2 (1989), pp. 115–125. Holcombe, *An Economic Analysis of Democracy* (Carbondale: Southern Illinois University Press, 1985), is largely devoded to an analysis of this model.

18. The first section of Kenneth J. Arrow's influential *Social Choice and Individual Values*, 2nd. ed. (New Haven: Yale University Press, 1963) discusses the problem.

19. This is demonstrated by Charles R. Plott, "A Notion of Equilibrium and Its Possibility under Majority Rule," *American Economic Review* 62, No. 4 (September 1967), pp. 787–806, and a special case of Plott's equilibrium is demonstrated by Gordon Tullock, "The General Irrelevance of the General Impossibility Theorem," *Quarterly Journal of Economics* 81, No. 2 (May 1967), pp. 256–270.

20. A suggestion for improvement is given by T. Nicolaus Tideman and Gordon Tullock, "A New and Superior Process for Making Social Choices," *Journal of Political Economy* 84 (December 1976), pp. 1145–1160. They explain a public goods pricing system developed by Edward H. Clarke, "Multipart Pricing of Public Goods," *Public Choice* 11 (Fall 1971), pp. 17–33, which produces a Lindahl equilibrium.

21. Kenneth J. Arrow, *Social Choice and Individual Values* (New Haven: Yale University Press, 1951).

22. In considering the literature spawned by McKelvey's paper, William

H. Riker, "Implications from the Disequilibrium of Majority Rule for the Study of Institutions," *American Political Science Review* 74, No. 2 (June 1980), pp. 432–446, concluded that a unique and stable political equilibrium could not be produced in the same sense as a unique and stable market equilibrium.

23. However, see Tideman and Tullock, "A New and Superior Process for Making Social Choices," cited above, for an example of such a system. The informational requirements and other complexities make it apparent why implementation would be difficult from a practical standpoint.

24. James M. Buchanan and Gordon Tullock, *The Calculus of Consent* (Ann Arbor: University of Michigan Press, 1962), discuss the efficiency of logrolling in this context.

25. Ronald H. Coase, "The Problem of Social Cost," *Journal of Law & Economics* 3 (October 1960), pp. 1–44.

26. See Kenneth A. Shepsle and Barry R. Weingast, "Structure-Induced Equilibrium and Legislative Choice," *Public Choice* 37, No. 3 (1981), pp. 503–519, for a discussion.

27. Mancur Olson, Jr., *The Logic of Collective Action* (New York: Shocken Books, 1965), used the distinction between large and small groups to drive his theory of collective action.

28. See, for examples, Kenneth J. Koford, "Centralized Vote Trading," *Public Choice* 39, No. 2 (1982), pp. 245–268, who develops a model in which party leaders act as middlemen in the exchange, and Barry Weingast, Kenneth A. Shepsle, and Christopher Johnsen, "The Political Economy of Benefits and Costs: A Neoclassical Approach to Distributive Politics," *Journal of Political Economy* 89, No. 4 (August 1981), pp. 642–664, who present a model in which coalitions form to exchange votes on special interest projects.

29. Weingast, Shepsle, and Johnsen, "The Political Economy of Benefits and Costs: A Neoclassical Approach to Distributive Politics," cited above, and Holcombe, *An Economic Analysis of Democracy*, also cited above, give accounts of this model.

30. This line of reasoning is explored by James B. Kau and Paul H. Rubin, "Self-Interest, Ideology, and Logrolling in Congressional Voting," *Journal of Law & Economics* 22 (October 1979), pp. 365–384, Joseph P. Kalt and Mark A. Zupan, "Capture and Ideology in the Theory of Politics," *American Economic Review* 74 (June 1984), pp. 279–300, and Sam Peltzman, "Constituent Interest and Congressional Voting," *Journal of Law & Economics* 27, No. 1 (April 1984), pp. 181–210.

31. Motivations and rewards for ideological voting are discussed by Amihai Glazer and Bernard Grofman, "Why Representatives are Ideologists though Voters are Not," *Public Choice* 61, No. 1 (April 1989), pp. 29–39, and William R. Dugan and Michael C. Munger, "The Rationality of Ideology," *Journal of Law & Economics* 32, No. 1 (April 1989), pp. 119–142.

32. Referenda are an exception to this statement. Implications of popular voting on referenda are discussed in the next section. The literature on agenda control has discussed referendum voting in some detail. See, for examples, Randall G. Holcombe, "An Empirical Test of the Median Voter Model," *Economic Inquiry* 18, No. 2 (April 1980), pp. 260–274, Holcombe, *Public Finance and the Political Process* (Carbondale: Southern Illinois University Press, 1983), Thomas Romer and Howard Rosenthal, "Political Resource Allocation, Controlled Agendas, and the Status Quo," *Public Choice* 33, No. 4 (1978), pp. 27–43, and Romer and Rosenthal, "Median Voters or Budget Maximizers: Evidence from School Expenditure Referenda," *Economic Inquiry* 20, No. 4 (October 1982), pp. 556–578.

33. Donald J. Saari, and Jill van Newenhizen, "The Problem of Indeterminacy in Approval, Multiple, and Truncated Voting Systems," *Public Choice* 59, No. 2 (November 1988), pp. 101–120, use the analogy of a roulette wheel to describe the outcome of majority rule voting.

34. James M. Buchanan, "Social Choice, Democracy, and Free Markets," *Journal of Political Economy* 62 (1954), pp. 114–123.

35. Votes are the medium of exchange, but not the unit of account. Votes on different issues can have different values, so trade is more like barter with IOUs than monetary exchange.

Chapter 8

1. Thomas Hobbes, *Leviathan* (New York: E.P. Dutton, 1950, orig. 1651), sees government as the solution to an unpleasant existence under anarchy. Murray Rothbard, *For a New Liberty* (New York: Macmillan, 1973), sees the possibility of protective firms in an anarchistic setting that make government unnecessary. In the model of Robert Nozick, *Anarchy, State, and Utopia* (New York: Basic Books, 1974), protective firms evolve into a minimal government.

2. This follows along with the assumptions of John Rawls, *A Theory of Justice* (Cambridge, Mass.: Belknap, 1971), and James M. Buchanan, *The Limits of Liberty: Between Anarchy and Leviathan* (Chicago: University of Chicago Press, 1975). The framework of Figure 8.1 and its representation of anarchistic equilibrium is close to Buchanan's depiction of agreement with the social contract.

3. While there is a parallel here between the theory and the development of the U.S. Constitution, Charles A. Beard, *An Economic Interpretation of the Constitution of the United States* (New York: Macmillan, 1913) argues that the Constitution was not written behind a veil of uncertainty, but rather was written to protect the interests of wealthy individuals in the United States.

4. This accounts for important differences in legal reasoning and economic reasoning. The differences are discussed in Randall G. Holcombe,

Public Finance and the Political Process (Carbondale: Southern Illinois University Press, 1983) Chapter 9, "Economic Efficiency and the Evolution of the Common Law," and Holcombe, *Economic Models and Methodology* (Westport, Conn.: Greenwood Press, 1989), where differences in inductive and deductive reasoning are discussed extensively.

5. While this section contrasts the flexibility of the common law with more rigid constitutional rules, there are other differences as well. In an insightful article, Louis De Alessi and Robert Staaf, "The Common Law Process: Efficiency or Order?" *Constitutional Political Economy* 2, No. 1 (Winter 1991), pp. 107–126, note that the common law allows contracting around its provisions, whereas statutory law does not.

6. Richard A. Posner, *Economic Analysis of Law* (Boston: Little, Brown, 1972), describes the common law as if the court were acting in order to create efficient economic incentives. Paul H. Rubin, "Why is the Common Law Efficient?" *Journal of Legal Studies* 6, No. 1 (January 1977), pp. 51–63, George L. Priest, "The Common Law Process and the Selection of Efficient Rules," *Journal of Legal Studies* 6, No. 1 (January 1977), pp. 65–82, and Holcombe, *Public Finance and the Political Process*, Chapter 9, "Economic Efficiency and the Evolution of the Common Law," all discuss models of the efficient development of common law.

7. Friedrich Hayek's work has been especially concerned with unintended consequences, both when they are beneficial and when they are not. In relation to the current discussion, see his *Law, Legislation, and Liberty*, 3 vols. (Chicago: University of Chicago Press, 1973, 1976, 1979).

8. Adam Smith, *The Wealth of Nations* (New York: Random House, Modern Library, 1937).

9. Whether their economic well-being was increased as a result of these programs is a matter of debate. For an exposition of the viewpoint that it was not, see Charles Murray, *Losing Ground* (New York: Basic Books, 1984).

10. Paul A. Samuelson, "The Pure Theory of Public Expenditure," *Review of Economics and Statistics* 36 (November 1954), pp. 387–389, and "A Diagrammatic Exposition of a Theory of Public Expenditure," *Review of Economics and Statistics* 37 (November 1955), pp. 350–356.

11. James M. Buchanan, "An Economic Theory of Clubs," *Economica* (February 1965), pp. 1–14.

12. Harold M. Hochman and James D. Rodgers, "Pareto Optimal Redistribution," *American Economic Review* 59 (September 1969), pp. 542–557.

13. Leland Yeager, "Rights, Contract, and Utility in Policy Analysis," *Cato Journal* 5, No. 1 (Summer 1985), pp. 259–294, criticizes the contractarian model on this ground.

14. Douglass C. North, "Ideology and Political/Economic Institutions," *Cato Journal*, Spring/Summer 1988, 8, 15–28, and *Structure and*

Change in Economic History (New York: W.W. Norton & Company, 1981).

15. Murray Edelman, *The Symbolic Uses of Politics* (Urbana: University of Illinois Press, 1964), insightfully discusses the symbolic value of political institutions and the way that they convey legitimacy to government.

16. Harold J. Berman, *Law and Revolution: The Formation of the Western Legal Tradition* (Cambridge: Harvard University Press, 1983), p. 38.

17. See Bruce L. Benson, *The Enterprise of Law: Justice Without the State* (San Francisco: Pacific Research Institute, 1990), for a discussion of the development of law outside of the framework of government.

Chapter 9

1. See, for example, William J. Baumol, "Applied Fairness Theory and Rationing Policy," *American Economic Review* 72 (September 1982), pp. 639–651, and Randall G. Holcombe, "Applied Fairness Theory: Comment," *American Economic Review* 73 (December 1983), pp. 1153–1156, for differing views on fair pricing.

2. William A. Niskanen, "The Peculiar Economics of Bureaucracy," *American Economic Review* 58 (May 1968), pp. 293–305, introduces his theory, which was elaborated in *Bureaucracy and Representative Government* (Chicago and New York: Aldine-Atherton, 1971), and extended in "Bureaucrats and Politicians," *Journal of Law & Economics* 18 (December 1975), pp. 617–643.

3. This criticism of Niskanen's suggestions appears in Earl A. Thompson, "Review of Niskanen's *Bureaucracy and Representative Government*," *Journal of Economic Literature* 11 (September 1973), pp. 950–953.

4. Harold M. Hochman and James D. Rodgers, "Pareto Optimal Redistribution," *American Economic Review* 59 (September 1969), pp. 542–557, suggest that people can be better off if the government forces them to contribute to redistributive programs, for example.

5. Charles M. Tiebout, "A Pure Theory of Local Expenditures," *Journal of Political Economy* 64 (October 1956), pp. 416–424.

6. Some of the limits of the Tiebout model are discussed by James M. Buchanan and Charles J. Goetz, "Efficiency Limits of Fiscal Mobility: An Assessment of the Tiebout Model," *Journal of Public Economics* 1 (1972), pp. 25–43.

7. This is discussed in Richard B. McKenzie and Robert J. Staaf, "Revenue Sharing and Monopoly Government," *Public Choice* 33, No. 3 (1978), pp. 93–97.

8. Harold Hotelling, "Stability in Competition," *Economic Journal* 39 (March 1929), pp. 41–57 was the springboard for Anthony Downs, *An Economic Theory of Democracy* (New York: Harper & Row, 1957).

9. This aspect of political competition is discussed by Gordon Tullock,

"Entry Barriers in Politics," *American Economic Review* 55, No. 2 (March 1965), pp. 458–466. Tullock's model is similar to that of Harold Demsetz, "Why Regulate Utilities?" *Journal of Law & Economics* 11 (1968), pp. 55–65, who applies the argument to competition for a natural monopoly. W. Mark Crain, Randall Holcombe, and Robert Tollison, "Monopoly Aspects of Political Parties," *Atlantic Economic Journal* 7, No. 2 (July 1979), pp. 54–58, discuss competition for the right to be a political monopolist further.

10. Demsetz, "Why Regulate Utilities?" cited earlier.

11. His essay, "The State," in Randolph S. Bourne, *War and the Intellectuals* (New York: Harper & Row, 1964), argues, "Government is obviously composed of common and unsanctified men, and thus is a legitimate object of criticism and even contempt . . . . The republican state has almost no trappings to appeal to the common man's emotions . . . . With the shock of war, however, the State comes into its own . . . The patriot loses all sense of the distinction between State, nation and government . . . . For war is essentially the health of the State" (pp. 65–69).

12. This phenomenon is carefully documented by Alan T. Peacock and Jack Wiseman, *The Growth of Public Expenditure in the United Kingdom* (Princeton: Princeton University Press, 1961). See also Robert Higgs, *Crisis and Leviathan: Critical Episodes in the Growth of American Government* (New York: Oxford University Press, 1987) for a slightly different interpretation.

13. Mancur Olson, Jr., *The Rise and Decline of Nations* (New Haven: Yale University Press, 1982).

14. See Harold J. Berman, *Law and Revolution: The Formation of the Western Legal Tradition* (Cambridge: Harvard University Press, 1983) for a discussion.

15. Armen Alchian and William R. Allen, *University Economics*, 3rd ed. (Belmont, California: Wadsworth, 1972), p. 7. In a latter work, they tone down their statement, arguing, "Although many social scientists (including economists) will offer all sorts of ethical assessments, what economic *theory* says must be distinguished from what an individual economist may prefer. The former is what counts, not the latter." (original emphasis) Armen Alchian and William R. Allen, *Exchange and Production: Competition, Coordination, and Control*, 2nd ed. (Belmont, California: Wadsworth, 1977), p. 19.

16. A discussion of choice subject to constraints and choice of constraints is given by James M. Buchanan, "Rational Choice Models," Chapter 3, and Chapter 5, "Constitutional Economics," in *Explorations into Constitutional Economics* (College Station: Texas A&M University Press, 1989).

17. John Maynard Keynes ended his book, *The General Theory of Employment, Interest, and Money* (New York: Harcourt Brace, 1936) by arguing, "the ideas of economists and political philosophers, both

when they are right and when they are wrong, are more powerful than is commonly understood. Indeed the world is ruled by little else (p. 383).

18. Work such as Friedrich Hayek's *The Road to Serfdom* (London: George Routledge & Sons, 1944) and Milton Friedman's *Capitalism and Freedom* (Chicago: University of Chicago Press, 1962) argue for social engineering in this sense, but argue that societies should be designed with less government. Neither Friedman nor Hayek fall in the group of individuals normally considered social engineers, yet they do promote ideas for redesigning government.

19. Politicians and leaders of popular uprisings such as occurred on campuses in the late 1960s understand this principle. Such leaders will argue vigorously against current policies, and many agree that change is needed. They refer only vaguely if at all to their specific proposals for change, knowing that they can get much more popular support by being against the status quo than in favor of a specific replacement.

Chapter 10

1. This notion of agreement is similar to that used by James M. Buchanan, *The Limits of Liberty* (Chicago: University of Chicago Press, 1975). Buchanan had individuals consider whether they would expect to be better off if the social contract were renegotiated from anarchy.

2. One model of this type is Harold M. Hochman and James D. Rodgers, "Pareto Optimal Redistribution," *American Economic Review* 59 (September 1969), pp. 542–557, which uses the idea that one person's utility enters into another's utility function, thereby making altruistic behavior benefit both the donor and the recipient. The literature on sociobilology, pioneered by Edward O. Wilson, *Sociobiology* (Cambridge: Harvard University Press, 1975), has spilled into economics to a limited extent. See Gary S. Becker, "Altruism, Egoism, and Genetic Fitness: Economics and Sociobiology," *Journal of Economic Literature* 14, No. 3 (September 1976), pp. 817–826, and his "Reply to Hirshleifer and Tullock," *Journal of Economic Literature* 15, No. 2 (June 1977), pp. 507–507, which replies to Jack Hirshleifer, "Shakespere vs. Becker on Altruism: The Importance of Having the Last Word," *Journal of Economic Literature* 15, No. 2 (June 1977), pp. 500–502, and Gordon Tullock, "Economics and Sociobiology: A Comment," *Journal of Economic Literature* 15, No. 2 (June 1977), pp. 502–506.

3. See Robert Higgs, *Crisis and Leviathan: Critical Episodes in the Growth of American Government* (New York: Oxford University Press, 1987), for an argument of this type.

4. See Carl Joachim Friedrich, *Constitutional Government and Democracy* (Boston: Ginn and Company, 1950), pp. 14–15 for a discussion.

5. Murray Edelman, *The Symbolic Uses of Politics* (Urbana: University of Illinois Press, 1964).

6. This line of reasoning follows that of Hochman and Rodgers, "Pareto Optimal Redistribution," cited earlier.

7. Douglass C. North, *Structure and Change in Economic History* (New York: W.W. Norton & Company, 1981).

8. See, for examples, James B. Kau and Paul H. Rubin, "Self-Interest, Ideology, and Logrolling in Congressional Voting," *Journal of Law & Economics* 22 (October 1979), pp. 365–384, Joseph P. Kalt and Mark A. Zupan, "Capture and Ideology in the Theory of Politics," *American Economic Review* 74 (June 1984), pp. 279–300, and Sam Peltzman, "Constituent Interest and Congressional Voting," *Journal of Law & Economics* 27, No. 1 (April 1984), pp. 181–210.

9. Friedrich Hayek has incorporated the theme of the evolution of efficient institutions "as a result of human action but not of human design" throughout his work. See, for example, his *Studies in Philosophy, Politics, and Economics* (Chicago: University of Chicago Press, 1969). Armen A. Alchian, "Uncertainty, Evolution, and Economic Theory," *Journal of Political Economy* 58 (1950), pp. 211–221, discusses this idea with regard to firms in the private sector.

10. An overview of various criteria is given in Randall G. Holcombe, "Social Welfare," pp. 159–185 in John Creedy, ed., *Foundations of Economic Thought* (Oxford: Basil Blackwell, 1990).

11. Among modern contractarians, this premise is especially evident in Buchanan *The Limits of Liberty*, which compares the well-being of individuals living under a social contract with a much less desirable position of anarchistic equilibrium. Randall G. Holcombe "A Contractarian Model of the Decline in Classical Liberalism," *Public Choice* 35, No. 3 (1980), pp. 260–274, analyzes this model of the social contract.

12. Leland B. Yeager, "Rights, Contract, and Utility in Policy Analysis," *Cato Journal* 5, No. 1 (Summer 1985), p. 271. The references in Yeager's quotation are to Randall G. Holcombe, *Public Finance and the Political Process* (Carbondale: Southern Illinois University Press, 1983), and James M. Buchanan, *The Limits of Liberty* (Chicago: University of Chicago Press, 1975).

13. Yeager, "Rights, Contract, and Utility," p. 272.

14. Tibor Machan, "Individualism and the Problem of Political Authority," *The Monist* 66, No. 4 (October 1983), pp. 500–516, makes this point. See also Machan's *Individuals and Their Rights* (La Salle, Illinois: Open Court, 1989).

15. The fiction does act as a constraint, binding the degree to which the Court can depart from previous interpretations of the Constitution.

16. Credit is often given to Anthony Downs, *An Economic Theory of Democracy* (New York: Harper & Row, 1957). for this insight.

17. See Steven Kelman, "'Public Choice' and Public Spirit," *The Public*

Interest 87 (Spring 1987), pp. 80–94, who argues that damage is being done because public choice analysis is overturning this fiction.

18. Charles M. Tiebout, "A Pure Theory of Local Expenditures," *Journal of Political Economy* 64 (October 1956), pp. 416–424.

19. This idea is explored in Donald J. Boudreaux and Randall G. Holcombe, "Government by Contract," *Public Finance Quarterly* 17, No. 3 (June 1989), pp. 264–280. See also Spencer Heath MacCallum, *The Art of Community* (Menlo Park: Institute for Humane Studies, 1970), for a discussion of the way in which optimal community arrangements can be developed through the market process.

20. Oliver E. Williamson, *The Economic Institutions of Capitalism* (New York: The Free Press, 1985), pp. 35–39 discusses the company town. Contrast this will MacCallum, *The Art of Community*, which discusses the benefits of having a single owner for property in an area.

21. Harold J. Berman, *Law and Revolution: The Formation of the Western Legal Tradition* (Cambridge: Harvard University Press, 1983), p. 384.

22. Berman, *Law and Revolution*, p. 393.

23. James M. Buchanan, "Utopia, the Minimal State, and Entitlement," *Public Choice* 23 (Fall 1975), pp. 121–126, discusses Rawls' views on the criteria on which people would be likely to agree.

24. See James M. Buchanan, "A Contractarian Paradigm for Applying Economic Theory," *American Economic Review* 65, No. 2 (May 1975), pp. 225–230, for a comparison with other approaches.

25. See James M. Buchanan and Richard E. Wagner, *Democracy in Deficit: The Political Legacy of Lord Keynes* (New York: Academic Press, 1977).

Chapter 11

1. The economist's understanding of the positive-normative distinction comes from Milton Friedman's *Essays in Positive Economics* (Chicago: University of Chicago Press, 1953). This discussion stays within Friedman's framework. See Randall G. Holcombe, *Economic Models and Methodology* (New York: Greenwood, 1989), ch. 5, for a discussion of Friedman's positivism.

2. One might object that a minimum wage law will not cause unemployment, contrary to what is stated in this paragraph. The point of the example does not rely on a minimum wage law creating unemployment, however, but on laws of social interaction determining the effect of a minimum wage law. The example is only a concrete illustration of the point that one cannot generate certain types of behaviors from individuals in a society simply by passing a law that people act in certain ways.

3. This theme appears in the opening pages of Ludwig von Mises, *Human Action*, 3rd rev. ed. (Chicago: Henry Regnery Company, 1966). On

this general theme, see Richard E. Wagner, *To Promote the General Welfare: Market Processes Vs. Political Transfers* (San Francisco: Pacific Research Institute, 1989), who discusses the legal mandating of rights that sometimes are inconsistent with the laws of social science.

4. James M. Buchanan and Gordon Tullock, *The Calculus of Consent* (Ann Arbor: University of Michigan Press, 1962), ch. 6.

5. The social welfare function is justified by Paul A. Samuelson, "Social Indifference Curves," *Quarterly Journal of Economics* 70 (1956), pp. 1–22. The methodology of using social welfare function maximization as a guide to policy choice is illustrated in most of the contributions to Paul G. Hare, ed., *Surveys in Public Sector Economics* (Oxford: Basil Blackwell, 1988). While this methodology has had its critics, the Hare volume shows that it retained its popularity in some circles well into the 1980s.

6. See Hare, ed., *Surveys in Public Sector Economics*, cited above, for an example.

7. Leland B. Yeager, "Rights, Contract, and Utility in Policy Analysis," *Cato Journal* 5, No. 1 (Summer 1985), pp. 259–294, discusses utilitarianism from the perspective of a rule utilitarian, but clearly, as Hare, ed., *Surveys in Public Sector Economics* indicates, act utilitarianism is not uncommon among economists.

8. J. Charles King, "Contract, Utility, and the Evaluation of Institutions," *Cato Journal* 8, No. 1 (Spring/Summer 1988), pp. 29–52, agrees with this statement, arguing that the differences between Yeager's utilitarianism and Buchanan's contractarian are philosophical. Politically, he says, they are in agreement, but Yeager's views come from that of an observer and Buchanan's from that of a participant in the political process.

9. Murray, Charles, *Losing Ground* (New York: Basic Books, 1984).

10. Friedrich A. Hayek, *The Road to Serfdom* (London: George Routledge & Sons, 1944).

11. Milton Friedman, *Capitalism and Freedom* (Chicago: University of Chicago Press, 1962), and with Rose Friedman, *Free to Choose* (New York: Harcourt Brace Jovanovich, 1980).

12. This point is made by David Friedman, "Many, Few, One: Social Harmony and the Shrunken Choice Set," *American Economic Review* 70, No. 1 (March 1980), pp. 225–232. A similar point is made by James M. Buchanan and Viktor Vanberg, "Interests and Theories in Constitutional Choice," *Journal of Theoretical Politics* 1 (January 1989), pp. 49–62.

13. The consideration of institutional changes that could improve everyone's welfare is what James M. Buchanan calls the relevance of Pareto optimality in "The Relevance of Pareto Optimality," *Journal of Conflict Resolution* (November 1962), pp. 341–354.

14. Tibor Machan, *Individuals and Their Rights* (La Salle, Illinois: Open Court, 1989) discusses natural rights from an ethical standpoint.

15. Machan, *Individuals and Their Rights*, develops the natural rights

agument differently. He argues that rights make sense only in a social setting. However, his theory of natural rights is consistent with the discussion in this section.

16. See Armen A. Alchian, "Some Economics of Property Rights," *Il Politico* 30, No. 4 (1965), pp. 816–829.

17. See, for example, Murray N. Rothbard, *The Ethics of Liberty* (Atlantic Highlands, N.J.: Humanities Press, 1982), and the works of Ayn Rand. In novel form, Rand's *Atlas Shrugged* (New York: Random House, 1957) espouses her philosophy. Rand's theory of natural rights is explicitly developed in her essay, "Man's Rights," in *The Virtue of Selfishness* (New York: New American Library, 1961). See also Machan's *Individuals and Their Rights*, referenced earlier.

18. See, for examples, Richard Posner, *Economic Analysis of Law* (Boston: Little, Brown and Company, 1972), Paul H. Rubin, "Why is the Common Law Efficient?" *Journal of Legal Studies* 6 No. 1 (January 1977), pp. 51–73, George L. Priest, "The Common Law Process and the Selection of Efficient Rules," *Journal of Legal Studies* 6 no. 1 (January 1977), pp. 65–82, and Randall G. Holcombe, "Economic Efficiency and the Evolution of the Common Law," chapter 9 in *Public Finance and the Political Process* (Carbondale: Southern Illinois University Press, 1983). An insightful description of the way in which efficient outcomes can be "the result of human action, but not of human design," is found in Chapter 6 of F. A. Hayek's *Studies in Philosophy, Politics, and Economics* (New York: Simon and Schuster, 1967). Hayek applies this concept to the law in *Law, Legislation, and Liberty*, Vol. I (Chicago: University of Chicago Press, 1973), where he traces the idea to many earlier thinkers. Bruce Benson, *The Enterprise of Law: Justice Without the State* (San Francisco: Pacific Research Institute, 1990), discusses the evolution of law outside of governmentally imposed legislation.

19. Paul H. Rubin, "Why is the Common Law Efficient?" cited above.

20. Armen A. Alchian, "Uncertainty, Evolution, and Economic Theory," *Journal of Political Economy* 58 (1950), pp. 211–221, explains why this is so even if they do not intend to act efficiently.

21. Bruce L. Benson, "An Institutional Explanation for Corruption of Criminal Justice Officials," *Cato Journal* 8, No. 1 (Spring/Summer 1988), pp. 139–163.

22. Public choice has made much of the notion of rationally ignorant voters, who are rationally ignorant because their opinions do not influence public policy.

23. Anthony Downs, *An Economic Theory of Democracy* (New York: Harper & Row, 1957) explained the theory of rational ignorance on the part of voters. See also Edelman, *The Symbolic Uses of Politics*, for a development of this theme.

24. Ludwig von Mises, *Human Action*, Third Revised Edition (Chicago: Henry Regnery Company, 1966) suggests that purposeful action by

itself is evidence of an individual attempting to further his self-interest.

25. James M. Buchanan, in *The Limits of Liberty* (Chicago: University of Chicago Press, 1975), develops a more involved theory where the status quo is legitimized through the distribution that would exist in anarchy, but his theory is in the spirit of this analysis. Also along these lines, and developed from Buchanan's model is Randall G. Holcombe, "A Contractarian Model of the Decline in Classical Liberalism," *Public Choice* 35, No. 3 (1980), pp. 277–286.

26. See Thomas C. Schelling, *The Strategy of Conflict* (Cambridge: Harvard University Press, 1960). With regard to the perceived legitimacy of the status quo, it is interesting to note that this is very true with regard to what society views as "just" prices. Just prices are historical prices. Threats of price controls on oil arose in the 1970s when the price of oil rises (why should a gallon of gasoline cost less than a gallon of milk?), and threats of economy-wide price controls arise when prices in general increase. The same is true for price decreases, as for example, farm price supports to keep farm prices from falling. Society seems to accept the status quo as just.

27. However, J. M. Buchanan and Gordon Tullock, *The Calculus of Consent* (Ann Arbor: University of Michigan Press, 1962) have demonstrated that Pareto optimal decision rules do not necessarily imply that every individual decision will make everyone better off. The question here, then, is voluntary agreement with the rules of society.

Chapter 12

1. The term ethics in the title of this chapter is not meant to imply some moral justification for public policy, but rather a political justification that can achieve wide agreement. The foundation of the contractarian framework is agreement, directly implying that people would agree to policies meeting the contractarian test. As a moral issue, the contractarian model is more complex than what is being addressed here. See David Gauthier, *Morals By Agreement* (Oxford: Clarendon Press, 1986), for an application of the contractarian model to moral issues, and Russell Hardin, "Contractarianism: Wistful Thinking," *Constitutional Political Economy* 1, No. 2 (Spring/Summer 1990), pp. 35–52, for a critique.

2. An argument along these lines is made by James M. Buchanan and Gordon Tullock, *The Calculus of Consent* (Ann Arbor: University of Michigan Press, 1962), chapter 6.

3. For example, Charles A. Beard, *An Economic Interpretation of the Constitution of the United States* (New York: Macmillan, 1913) argues that the U.S. Constitution was drawn up to protect the economic interests of the founding fathers.

4. See Scott Gordon, "The New Contractarians," *Journal of Political Economy* 84, No. 3 (June 1976), pp. 573–590, who makes this observation about the Rawlsian construction.

5. James M. Buchanan, *The Limits of Liberty: Between Anarchy and Leviathan* (Chicago: University of Chicago Press, 1975).

6. Knut Wicksell, "A New Principle of Just Taxation" (1896), pp. 72–118 in Richard A. Musgrave and Alan T. Peacock, eds., *Classics in the Theory of Public Finance* (New York: St. Martin's Press, 1967).

7. Buchanan and Tullock, in *The Calculus of Consent*, stress this individualistic point of view.

8. Richard E. Wagner, *To Promote the General Welfare: Market Processes Vs. Political Transfers* (San Francisco: Pacific Research Institute, 1989), compares the contractarian framework with a more utilitarian concept of social welfare, siding with the contractarian model for reasons like those given here. See also his "Agency, Economic Calculation, and Constitutional Construction," in Charles K. Rowley, Robert D. Tollison, and Gordon Tullock, eds., *The Political Economy of Rent-Seeking* (Boston: Kluwer Academic Publishers, 1988), pp. 423–443.

9. The logic of this argument follows Buchanan and Tullock, *The Calculus of Consent*, chapter 6, where they develop the argument that people could agree to a less than unanimous decision rule, even though they know that sometimes the result will be decisions that go against their narrow self interests.

10. This argument is developed by Harold M. Hochman and James D. Rodgers, "Pareto Optimal Redistribution," *American Economic Review* 59 (September 1969), pp. 542–557.

11. For an excellent discussion of the redistribution issue, see Edgar K. Browning, "Inequality and Poverty," *Southern Economic Journal* 55, No. 4 (April 1989), pp. 819–830.

12. See Leland B. Yeager, "Rights, Contract, and Utility in Policy Analysis," *Cato Journal* 5, No. 1 (Summer 1985), pp. 259–294, for a critique of the contractarian model along these lines.

13. One could imagine that under such a financial regime, it would be desirable to establish a contingency fund so that Congress could appropriate money from the previously established fund. Perhaps the legislation might also require a repayment. For example, if the gas tax revenues would come in too slowly for effective disaster relief in the earlier example, Congress to approve immediate spending from the fund (or from an increase in the debt), with funds to be repaid out of the proceeds of a temporary gas tax.

14. David Friedman, "Many, Few, One: Social Harmony and the Shrunken Choice Set," *American Economic Review* 70, No. 1 (March 1980), pp. 225–232, argues that most apparently normative disagreements are really positive disagreements, following the argument given here.

15. Douglass C. North, "Ideology and Political/Economic Institutions," *Cato Journal*, Spring/Summer 1988, 8, 15–28.

16. Murray Edelman, *The Symbolic Uses of Politics* (Urbana: University of Illinois Press, 1964).
17. William J. Baumol, "Applied Fairness Theory and Rationing Policy," *American Economic Review* 72 (September 1982), pp. 639–651, and *Superfairness* (Cambridge, Mass.: MIT Press, 1986). For a critique of this approach along slightly different lines than is offered here, see Randall G. Holcombe, "Applied Fairness Theory: Comment," *American Economic Review* 73 (December 1983), pp. 1153–1156.
18. James M. Buchanan, *The Limits of Liberty: Between Anarchy and Leviathan* (Chicago: University of Chicago Press, 1975), pp. 77–82.

Chapter 13

1. See, for example, Murray N. Rothbard, *For a New Liberty* (New York: Macmillan, 1973).
2. It was noted before, and worth remarking again, that in the last half of the 20th century, physically handicapped individuals have been granted more and more rights, while the mentally handicapped have seemed to suffer a decline in their rights. Mentally handicapped people are more frequently left to take care of themselves, even if they end up homeless, while physically handicapped people have increased rights in the form of reserved handicapped parking, access to public transportation and buildings, computer-assisted work environments, and so forth. Increasingly, productive work is mental labor that can be done by physically handicapped individuals rather than physical labor that can be done by mentally handicapped individuals. It is no coincidence that the rights of the physically handicapped have increased along with their productivity, while the rights of the mentally handicapped have decreased as their potential to be productive has also decreased.
3. James M. Buchanan, "An Economic Theory of Clubs," *Economica* (February 1965), pp. 1–14.
4. Harold Demsetz, "Why Regulate Utilities?" *Journal of Law & Economics* 11 (1968), pp. 55–65.
5. Gordon Tullock, "Entry Barriers in Politics," *American Economic Review* 55, No. 2 (March 1965), pp. 458–466, develops a model along the lines of Demsetz's, which describes a process of competition for the right to be the monopoly supplier of legislation.
6. Harold M. Hochman and James D. Rodgers, "Pareto Optimal Redistribution," *American Economic Review* 59 (September 1969), pp. 542–557, make this argument with regard to income redistribution policies.
7. Knut Wicksell, "A New Principle of Just Taxation" (1896), pp. 72–118 in Richard A. Musgrave and Alan T. Peacock, eds., *Classics in the Theory of Public Finance.* New York: St. Martin's Press, 1967.
8. This might not be true if the government did not expect to be in power

long. Cases like this are discussed in an insightful manner by Margaret Levi, *Of Rule and Revenue* (Berkeley: University of California Press, 1988).

9. Stability offers another benefit as well. If policies are easily reversed through the political system, some people will devote resources to trying to change them, while others will be forced to devote resources toward trying to maintain the status quo. These rent-seeking expenditures can be conserved if the political environment is more stable.

10. See Randall G. Holcombe, "Barriers to Entry and Political Competition," *Journal of Theoretical Politics* 3, No. 2 (April 1991), pp. 231–240, for further development of this theme.

11. For a further discussion along these lines, see Glenn R. Parker, "Looking Toward Reelection: Revising Assumptions About the Factors Motivating Congressional Behavior," *Public Choice* 63, No. 3 (December 1989), pp. 237–252. See also Randall G. Holcombe, "A Note on Seniority and Political Competition," *Public Choice* 61, No. 3 (1989), pp. 285–288.

12. The perception of political exchange in this way is largely attributable to James M.Buchanan and Gordon Tullock, *The Calculus of Consent* (Ann Arbor: University of Michigan Press, 1962).

13. This statement is nothing more than an application of the Coase theorem, developed by Ronald H. Coase, "The Problem of Social Cost," *Journal of Law & Economics* 3 (October 1960), pp. 1–44.

Bibliography

Alchian, Armen A., "Some Economics of Property Rights," *Il Politico* 30, No. 4 (1965), pp. 816–829.

——, "Uncertainty, Evolution, and Economic Theory," *Journal of Political Economy* 58 (1950), pp. 211–221.

——, and William R. Allen, *Exchange and Production: Competition, Coordination, and Control*, 2nd ed. Belmont, California: Wadsworth, 1977.

——, and ——, *University Economics*, 3rd ed. Belmont, California: Wadsworth, 1972.

Anderson, Gary M., and Robert D. Tollison, "Democracy, Interest Groups, and the Price of Votes," *Cato Journal* 8, No. 1 (Spring/Summer 1988), pp. 53–70.

Arrow, Kenneth J., *Social Choice and Individual Values*, 2nd. ed. New Haven: Yale University Press, 1963. First edition 1951.

Auster, Richard D., and Morris Silver, *The State as a Firm: Economic Forces in Political Development*. Boston: Martinus Nijhoff, 1979.

Axelrod, Robert, *The Evolution of Cooperation*. New York: Basic Books, 1984.

Barker, Sir Ernest, *Social Contract*. New York & London: Oxford University Press, 1960.

Barlow, Robin, "Efficiency Aspects of Local School Finance," *Journal of Political Economy* 78 (September-October 1970), pp. 1028–1040.

——, "Efficiency Aspects of Local School Finance: Reply," *Journal of Political Economy* 81 (January-February 1973), pp. 192–202.

Baumol, William J., "Applied Fairness Theory and Rationing Policy," *American Economic Review* 72 (September 1982), pp. 639–651.

——, "Contestable Markets: An Uprising in the Theory of Industry Structure," *American Economic Review* 72, No. 1 (March 1982), pp. 1–15.

——, *Superfairness*. Cambridge, Mass.: MIT Press, 1986.

Baumol, William J., John C. Panzar, and Robert D. Willig, *Contestable Markets and the Theory of Industry Structure*. New York: Harcourt Brace Jovanovich, 1982.

Beard, Charles A., *An Economic Interpretation of the Constitution of the United States*. New York: MacMillan, 1913.

Becker, Gary S., "Altruism, Egoism, and Genetic Fitness: Economics and Sociobiology," *Journal of Economic Literature* 14, No. 3 (September 1976), pp. 817–826.

——, "Reply to Hirshleifer and Tullock," *Journal of Economic Literature* 15, No. 2 (June 1977), pp. 507–507.

Benson, Bruce L., "Corruption in Law Enforcement: One Consequence of

'The Tragedy of the Commons' Arising with Public Allocation Processes," *International Review of Law and Economics* 8 (1988), pp. 73–84.

——, *The Enterprise of Law: Justice Without the State.* San Francisco: Pacific Research Institute, 1990.

——, "An Institutional Explanation for Corruption of Criminal Justice Officials," *Cato Journal* 8, No. 1 (Spring/Summer 1988), pp. 139–163.

——, "A Note on Corruption by Public Officials: The Black Market for Property Rights," *Journal of Libertarian Studies* 5, No. 3 (Summer 1981), pp. 305–311.

——, and John Baden, "The Political Economy of Governmental Corruption: The Logic of Underground Government," *Journal of Legal Studies* 14 (June 1985), pp. 391–410.

Benson, Bruce, M. L. Greenhut, and Randall Holcombe, "Interest Groups and the Antitrust Paradox," *Cato Journal* 6, No. 3 (Winter 1987), pp. 801–817.

Berman, Harold J., *Law and Revolution: The Formation of the Western Legal Tradition.* Cambridge: Harvard University Press, 1983.

Black, Duncan, *The Theory of Committees and Elections.* Cambridge: Cambridge University Press, 1958.

Boudreaux, Donald J., and Randall G. Holcombe, "Government by Contract," *Public Finance Quarterly* 17, No. 3 (June 1989), pp. 264–280.

Bourne, Randolph S., *War and the Intellectuals.* New York: Harper & Row, 1964.

Bowen Howard R., "The Interpretation of Voting in the Allocation of Economic Resources," *Quarterly Journal of Economics* 58 (November 1943), pp. 27–48.

Brennan, Geoffrey, and James M. Buchanan, *The Power to Tax: Analytical Foundations of a Fiscal Constitution.* Cambridge: Cambridge University Press, 1980.

——, and ——, *The Reason of Rules: Constitutional Political Economy.* Cambridge: Cambridge University Press, 1985.

Browning, Edgar K., "Inequality and Poverty," *Southern Economic Journal* 55, No. 4 (April 1989), pp. 819–830.

Buchanan, James M., "A Contractarian Paradigm for Applying Economic Theory," *American Economic Review* 65, No. 2 (May 1975), pp. 225–230.

——, "An Economic Theory of Clubs," *Economica* (February 1965), pp. 1–14.

——, *Explorations into Constitutional Economics.* College Station: Texas A&M University Press, 1989.

——, *The Limits of Liberty: Between Anarchy and Leviathan.* Chicago: University of Chicago Press, 1975.

——, "Politics, Policy, and the Pigouvian Margins," *Economica* n.s. 29 (February 1962), pp. 17–28.

——, "Public Finance and Public Choice," *National Tax Journal* 28 (December 1975), pp. 383–394.

——, "The Relevance of Pareto Optimality," *Journal of Conflict Resolution*

(November 1962), pp. 341–354.

——, "Social Choice, Democracy, and Free Markets," *Journal of Political Economy* 62 (1954), pp. 114–123.

——, "Taxation in Fiscal Exchange," *Journal of Public Economics* 6 (July-August 1976), pp. 17–29.

——, "Utopia, the Minimal State, and Entitlement," *Public Choice* 23 (Fall 1975), pp. 121–126.

Buchanan, James M., and Charles J. Goetz, "Efficiency Limits of Fiscal Mobility: An Assessment of the Tiebout Model," *Journal of Public Economics* 1 (1972), pp. 25–43.

Buchanan, James M., and Gordon Tullock, *The Calculus of Consent.* Ann Arbor: University of Michigan Press, 1962.

Buchanan, James M., and Viktor Vanberg, "Interests and Theories in Constitutional Choice," *Journal of Theoretical Politics* 1 (January 1989), pp. 49–62.

Buchanan, James M., and Richard E. Wagner, *Democracy in Deficit: The Political Legacy of Lord Keynes.* New York: Academic Press, 1977.

Bush, Winston C., "Individual Welfare in Anarchy," Chapter 1 in Gordon Tullock, ed., *Explorations in the Theory of Anarchy.* Blacksburg, Va.: Center for Study of Public Choice, 1972.

Cheung, Steven N.S., "Transaction Costs, Risk Aversion, and the Choice of Contractual Arrangements," *Journal of Law & Economics* 12, No. 1 (April 1969), pp. 23–42.

——, "China in Transition: Where is She Heading Now?" *Contemporary Policy Issues* 4, No. 4 (October 1986), pp. 1–11.

Clarke, Edward H., "Multipart Pricing of Public Goods," *Public Choice* 11 (Fall 1971), pp. 17–33.

Coase, Ronald H., "The Problem of Social Cost," *Journal of Law & Economics* 3 (October 1960), pp. 1–44.

Coleman, James S., *Foundations of Social Theory.* Cambridge, Mass.: Harvard University Press, 1990.

Crain, W. Mark, "On the Structure and Stability of Political Markets," *Journal of Political Economy* 85, No. 4 (August 1977), pp. 829–842.

Crain, W. Mark, Randall Holcombe, and Robert Tollison, "Monopoly Aspects of Political Parties," *Atlantic Economic Journal* 7, No. 2 (July 1979), pp. 54–58.

Creedy, John, ed. *Foundations of Economic Thought.* Oxford: Basil Blackwell, 1990.

Dahl, Robert A., *Democracy and Its Critics.* New Haven: Yale Univeristy Press, 1989.

——, *Democracy, Liberty, and Equality.* Oxford: Oxford University Press, 1986.

——, *Modern Political Analysis*, 3rd ed. Englewood Cliffs, N.J.: Prentice-Hall, 1976.

——, *A Preface to Economic Democracy.* Berkeley: University of California Press, 1985.

De Alessi, Louis, and Robert Staaf, "The Common Law Process: Efficiency or Order?" *Constitutional Political Economy* 2, No. 1 (Winter 1991), pp. 107–126.

Demsetz, Harold, "Why Regulate Utilities?" *Journal of Law & Economics* 11 (1968), pp. 55–65.

Denzau, Arthur T., and Robert J. Mackay, "Benefit Shares and Majority Voting," *American Economic Review* 66 (March 1976), pp. 69–76.

Downs, Anthony, *An Economic Theory of Democracy*. New York: Harper & Row, 1957.

Dugan, William R., and Michael C. Munger, "The Rationality of Ideology," *Journal of Law & Economics* 32, No. 1 (April 1989), pp. 119–142.

Edelman, Murray, *The Symbolic Uses of Politics*. Urbana: University of Illinois Press, 1964.

Ehrlich, Isaac, "The Deterrent Effect of Capital Punishment: A Question of Life and Death," *American Economic Review* 65, No. 3 (June 1975), pp. 397–417.

Ellickson, Robert C., "A Critique of Economic and Sociological Theories of Social Control," *Journal of Legal Studies* 16, No. 1 (January 1987), pp. 67–99.

Elster, Jon, "Social Norms and Economic Theory," *Journal of Economic Perspectives* 3, No. 4 (Fall 1989), pp. 99–117.

Fogel, Robert William, and Stanley L. Engerman, *Time on the Cross: The Economics of American Slavery*. Boston: Little, Brown and Co., 1974.

Friedman, David, "Many, Few, One: Social Harmony and the Shrunken Choice Set," *American Economic Review* 70, No. 1 (March 1980), pp. 225–232.

Friedman, Milton, *Capitalism and Freedom*. Chicago: University of Chicago Press, 1962.

———, *Essays in Positive Economics*. Chicago: University of Chicago Press, 1953.

Friedman, Milton, and Rose Friedman, *Free to Choose*. New York: Harcourt Brace Jovanovich, 1980.

Friedrich, Carl Joachim, *Constitutional Government and Democracy*. Boston: Ginn and Company, 1950.

———, *Man and His Government: An Empirical Theory of Politics*. New York: McGraw-Hill, 1963.

Gallarotti, Guilio M., "Legitimacy as a Capital Asset of the State," *Public Choice* 63, No. 1 (October 1989), pp. 43–61.

Gauthier, David, *Morals By Agreement*. Oxford: Clarendon Press, 1986.

Glazer, Amihai, and Bernard Grofman, "Why Representatives are Ideologists though Voters are Not," *Public Choice* 61, No. 1 (April 1989), pp. 29–39.

Gordon, David D., "Morality and Rights," *Humane Studies Review* 5, No. 3 (Spring 1988), pp. 1–2, 17–22.

Gordon, Scott, "The New Contractarians," *Journal of Political Economy* 84, No. 3 (June 1976), pp. 573–590.

Hardin, Russell, "Contractarianism: Wistful Thinking," *Constitutional Political Economy* 1, No. 2 (Spring/Summer 1990), pp. 35–52.

Hare, Paul G., ed., *Surveys in Public Sector Economics*. Oxford: Basil Blackwell, 1988.

Hayek, Friedrich A., *The Constitution of Liberty*. Chicago: Henry Regnery, 1972.

——, *Law, Legislation, and Liberty*, 3 vols. Chicago: University of Chicago Press, 1973, 1976, 1979.

——, *The Road to Serfdom*. London: George Routledge & Sons, 1944.

——, "The Use of Knowledge in Society," *American Economic Review* 35, no. 4 (September 1945), pp. 519–530.

——, *Studies in Philosophy, Politics, and Economics*. Chicago: University of Chicago Press, 1969.

Higgs, Robert, *Crisis and Leviathan: Critical Episodes in the Growth of American Government*. New York: Oxford University Press, 1987.

Hirshleifer, Jack, "Shakespere vs. Becker on Altruism: The Importance of Having the Last Word," *Journal of Economic Literature* 15, No. 2 (June 1977), pp. 500–502.

Hochman, Harold M., and James D. Rodgers, "Pareto Optimal Redistribution," *American Economic Review* 59 (September 1969), pp. 542–557.

Hobbes, Thomas, *Leviathan*. New York: E.P. Dutton, 1950 (orig. 1651).

Hoebel, E. Adamson, *The Law of Primitive Man: A Study in Comparative Legal Dynamics*. Cambridge, Mass.: Harvard University Press, 1954.

Hohfeld, Wesley, *Fundamental Legal Conceptions* (1923; Westport, Conn.: Greenwood Press, 1978).

Holcombe, Randall G., "Applied Fairness Theory: Comment," *American Economic Review* 73 (December 1983), pp. 1153–1156.

——, "Barriers to Entry and Political Competition," *Journal of Theoretical Politics* 3, No. 2 (April 1991), pp. 231–240.

——, "A Contractarian Model of the Decline in Classical Liberalism," *Public Choice* 35, No. 3 (1980), pp. 260–274.

——, *An Economic Analysis of Democracy*. Carbondale: Southern Illinois University Press, 1985.

——, *Economic Models and Methodology*. New York: Greenwood Press, 1989.

——, "An Empirical Test of the Median Voter Model," *Economic Inquiry* 18, No. 2 (April 1980), pp. 260–274.

——, "The Median Voter Model in Public Choice Theory," *Public Choice* 61, No. 2 (1989), pp. 115–125.

——, "Non-Optimal Unanimous Agreement," *Public Choice* 48, No. 3 (1986), pp. 229–244.

——, "A Note on Seniority and Political Competition," *Public Choice* 61, No. 3 (1989), pp. 285–288.

——, *Public Finance and the Political Process*. Carbondale: Southern Illinois University Press, 1983.

——, *Public Sector Economics*. Belmont, California: Wadsworth, 1988.

——, "Social Welfare," pp. 159–185 in John Creedy, ed., *Foundations of Economic Thought*. Oxford: Basil Blackwell, 1990.

Holcombe, Randall G., and James D. Gwartney, "Political Parties and the Legislative Principal-Agent Relationship," *Journal of Institutional and Theoretical Economics* 145, No. 4 (December 1989), pp. 669–675.

Holcombe, Randall G., and Lora P. Holcombe, "The Market for Regulation," *Journal of Institutional and Theoretical Economics* 142, No. 4 (December 1986), pp. 684–696.

Hotelling, Harold, "Stability in Competition," *Economic Journal* 39 (March 1929), pp. 41–57.

Jarrell, Gregg A., "The Demand for State Regulation of the Electric Utility Industry," *Journal of Law & Economics* 21, No. 3 (October 1978), pp. 269–295.

Kalt, Joseph P., and Mark A. Zupan, "Capture and Ideology in the Theory of Politics," *American Economic Review* 74 (June 1984), pp. 279–300.

Kau, James B., and Paul H. Rubin, "Self-Interest, Ideology, and Logrolling in Congressional Voting," *Journal of Law & Economics* 22 (October 1979), pp. 365–384.

Kelman, Steven, "Public Choice' and Public Spirit," *The Public Interest* 87 (Spring 1987), pp. 80–94.

Keynes, John Maynard, *The General Theory of Employment, Interest, and Money*. New York: Harcout Brace, 1936.

King, J. Charles, "Contract, Utility, and the Evaluation of Institutions," *Cato Journal* 8, No. 1 (Spring/Summer 1988), pp. 29–52.

Kirzner, Israel M., *Competition and Entrepreneurship*. Chicago: University of Chicago Press, 1973.

Koford, Kenneth J., "Centralized Vote Trading," *Public Choice* 39, No. 2 (1982), pp. 245–268.

Kreuger, Anne O., "The Political Economy of the Rent-Seeking Society," *American Economic Review* 64 (June 1974), pp. 291–303.

Levi, Margaret, *Of Rule and Revenue*. Berkeley: University of California Press, 1988.

Lin, Justin Yifu, "An Economic Theory of Institutional Change: Induced and Imposed Change," *Cato Journal* 9, No. 1 (Spring/Summer 1989), pp. 1–33.

Lindahl, Erik, "Just Taxation – A Positive Solution" (1919), pp. 168–176 in Richard A. Musgrave and Alan T. Peacock, eds., *Classics in the Theory of Public Finance*. New York: St. Martin's Press, 1967.

Lipford, Jody, and Bruce Yandle, "Exploring Dominant State Governments," *Journal of Institutional and Theoretical Economics* 146, No 4 (December 1990), pp. 561–575.

MacCallum, Spencer Heath, *The Art of Community*. Menlo Park: Institute for Humane Studies, 1970.

Machan, Tibor, "Individualism and the Problem of Political Authority," *The Monist* 66, No. 4 (October 1983), pp. 500–516.

——, *Individuals and Their Rights*. La Salle, Illinois: Open Court, 1989.

Maine, Henry Sumner, *Ancient Law*. New York: Henry Holt and Company, 1888.

——, *Early Law and Custom*. New York: Henry Holt and Company, 1886.

Mbaku, John, and Chris Paul, "Political Instability in Africa: A Rent-Seeking Approach," *Public Choice* 63, No. 1 (October 1989), pp. 63–72.

McGuire, Robert A., and Robert L. Ohsfeldt, "Self-Interest, Agency Theory, and Voting Behavior: The Ratification of the United States Constitution," *American Economic Review* 79, No. 1 (March 1989), pp. 219–234.

McKelvey, Richard D., "General Conditions for Global Intrasitivities in Formal Voting Models," *Econometrica* 47, No. 5 (September 1979), pp. 1085–1112.

——, "Intransitivities in Multi Dimensional Voting Models and Some Implications for Agenda Control," *Journal of Economic Theory* 12, No. 3 (June 1976), pp. 472–482.

McKenzie, Richard B., and Robert J. Staaf, "Revenue Sharing and Monopoly Government," *Public Choice* 33, No. 3 (1978), pp. 93–97.

Mises, Ludwig von, *Human Action*, 3rd rev. ed. Chicago: Henry Regnery Company, 1966.

Murray, Charles, *Losing Ground*. New York: Basic Books, 1984.

Niskanen, William A., "Bureaucrats and Politicians," *Journal of Law & Economics* 18 (December 1975), pp. 617–643.

——, *Bureaucracy and Representative Government*. Chicago and New York: Aldine-Atherton, 1971.

——, "Conditions Affecting the Survival of Constitutional Rules," *Constitutional Political Economy* 1, No. 2 (Spring/Summer 1990), pp. 53–62.

——, "The Peculiar Economics of Bureaucracy," *American Economic Review* 58 (May 1968), pp. 293–305.

North, Douglass C., "Ideology and Political/Economic Institutions," *Cato Journal*, Spring/Summer 1988, 8, 15–28.

——, *Structure and Change in Economic History*. New York: W.W. Norton & Company, 1981.

Nozick, Robert, *Anarchy, State, and Utopia*. New York: Basic Books, 1974.

Olson, Mancur, Jr., *The Logic of Collective Action*. New York: Schocken Books, 1965.

——, *The Rise and Decline of Nations*. New Haven: Yale University Press, 1982.

Parker, Glenn R., "Looking Toward Reelection: Revising Assumptions About the Factors Motivating Congressional Behavior," *Public Choice* 63, No. 3 (December 1989), pp. 237–252.

Peacock, Alan T., and Jack Wiseman, *The Growth of Public Expenditure in the United Kingdom*. Princeton: Princeton University Press, 1961.

Peltzman, Sam, "Constituent Interest and Congressional Voting," *Journal of Law & Economics* 27, No. 1 (April 1984), pp. 181–210.

——, "Toward a More General Theory of Regulation," *Journal of Law & Economics* 19 (August 1976), pp. 211–240.

Plott, Charles R., "A Notion of Equilibrium and Its Possibility under Majority Rule," *American Economic Review* 62, No. 4 (September 1967), pp. 787–806.

Posner, Richard A., *Economic Analysis of Law*. Boston: Little, Brown, 1972.

——, "The Social Costs of Monopoly and Regulation," *Journal of Political Economy* 83 (August 1975), pp. 807–827.

——, "Taxation by Regulation," *Bell Journal of Economics and Management Science* 2 (Spring 1971), pp. 22–50.

——, "A Theory of Primitive Society, with Special Reference to Law," *Journal of Law & Economics* 23, No. 1 (April 1980), pp. 1–53.

Priest, George L., "The Common Law Process and the Selection of Efficient Rules," *Journal of Legal Studies* 6, No. 1 (January 1977), pp. 65–82.

Rand, Ayn, *Atlas Shrugged*. New York: Random House, 1957.

——, *The Virtue of Selfishness*. New York: New American Library, 1961.

Rawls, John, *A Theory of Justice*. Cambridge, Mass.: Belknap, 1971.

Reuter, Peter, "Police Regulation of Illegal Gambling: Frustrations of Symbolic Enforcement," *The Annals of the American Academy of Political and Social Science*, No. 474 (July 1984), pp. 36–47.

Riker, William H., "Implications from the Disequilibrium of Majority Rule for the Study of Institutions," *American Political Science Review* 74, No. 2 (June 1980), pp. 432–446.

——, *The Theory of Political Coalitions*. New Haven: Yale University Press, 1962.

Romer, Thomas, and Howard Rosenthal, "Political Resource Allocation, Controlled Agendas, and the Status Quo," *Public Choice* 33, No. 4 (1978), pp. 27–43.

——, and ——, "Median Voters or Budget Maximizers: Evidence from School Expenditure Referenda," *Economic Inquiry* 20, no. 4 (October 1982), pp. 556–578.

Rothbard, Murray N. *Conceived in Liberty*, 4 vols. New Rochelle, N.Y.: Arlington House, 1975, 1975, 1976, 1979.

——, *The Ethics of Liberty*. Atlantic Highlands, N.J.: Humanities Press, 1982.

——, *For a New Liberty*. New York: Macmillan, 1973.

Rowley, Charles K., "The Relevance of the Median Voter Theorem," *Journal of Institutional and Theoretical Economics* 140, No. 1 (1984), pp. 104–126.

Rowley, Charles K., Robert D. Tollison, and Gordon Tullock, eds., *The Political Economy of Rent-Seeking*. Boston: Kluwer Academic Publishers, 1988.

Rubin, Paul H., "Why is the Common Law Efficient?" *Journal of Legal Studies* 6, No. 1 (January 1977), pp. 51–63.

Saari, Donald J., and Jill van Newenhizen, "The Problem of Indeterminacy in Approval, Multiple, and Truncated Voting Systems," *Public Choice* 59, No. 2 (November 1988), pp. 101–120.

Samuelson, Paul A., "The Pure Theory of Public Expenditure," *Review of Economics and Statistics* 36 (November 1954), pp. 387–389.

——, "A Diagrammatic Exposition of a Theory of Public Expenditure," *Review of Economics and Statistics* 37 (November 1955), pp. 350–356.

——, "Social Indifference Curves," *Quarterly Journal of Economics* 70

(1956), pp. 1–22.

Schelling, Thomas C., *The Strategy of Conflict*. Cambridge, Mass.: Harvard University Press, 1960.

——, "Economic Analysis of Organized Crime," in the President's Commission on Law Enforcement and the Administration of Justice *Task Force Report: Organized Crime*. U.S. Government Printing Office, Washington, D.C., 1967.

Schmidt-Trenz, Hans-Jorg, "The State of Nature in the Shadow of Contract Formation: Adding a Missing Link to J.M. Buchanan's Social Contract Theory," *Public Choice* 62, No. 3 (September 1989), pp. 237–251.

Schwartz, Thomas, "The Universal-Instability Theorem," *Public Choice* 37, No. 3 (1981), pp. 487–501.

Scully, Gerald W., "The Institutional Framework and Economic Development," *Journal of Political Economy* 96, No. 3 (June 1988), pp. 652–662.

Sen, Amartya, "Liberty, Unanimity, and Rights," *Economica* 43 (August 1976), pp. 217–245.

——, "Rational Fools: A Critique of the Behavioral Foundations of Economic Theory," *Philosophy and Public Affairs* 6 (Summer 1977), pp. 317–344.

Shepsle, Kenneth A., and Barry R. Weingast, "Structure-Induced Equilibrium and Legislative Choice," *Public Choice* 37, No. 3 (1981), pp. 503–519.

Siegan, Bernard H., "Non-Zoning in Houston," *Journal of Law & Economics* 13, No. 1 (April 1979), pp. 71–147.

Smith, Adam, *The Wealth of Nations*. New York: Random House, Modern Library, 1937.

Soto, Hernando de, *The Other Path*. New York: Harper & Row, 1989.

Stigler, George J., "The Theory of Economic Regulation," *Bell Journal of Economics and Management Science* 2 (Spring 1971), pp. 2–21.

——, *The Theory of Price*, 4th ed. New York: Macmillan, 1987.

Sudgen, Robert, "Spontaneous Order," *Journal of Economic Perspectives* 3, No. 4 (Fall 1989), pp. 85–97.

Thompson, Earl A., "Review of Niskanen's *Bureaucracy and Representative Government*," *Journal of Economic Literature* 11 (September 1973), pp. 950–953.

Thompson, Earl A., and Roger L. Faith, "A Pure Theory of Strategic Behavior and Social Institutions," *American Economic Review* 71, No. 3 (June 1981), pp. 366–380.

Tideman, T. Nicolaus, and Gordon Tullock, "A New and Superior Process for Making Social Choices," *Journal of Political Economy* 84 (December 1976), pp. 1145–1160.

Tiebout, Charles M., "A Pure Theory of Local Expenditures," *Journal of Political Economy* 64 (October 1956), pp. 416–424.

Tullock, Gordon, "Economics and Sociobiology: A Comment," *Journal of Economic Literature* 15, No. 2 (June 1977), pp. 502–506.

——, "Entry Barriers in Politics," *American Economic Review* 55, No. 2 (March 1965), pp. 458–466.

——, ed., *Explorations in the Theory of Anarchy*. Blacksburg, Va.: Center for

Study of Public Choice, 1972.

———, "The General Irrelevance of the General Impossibility Theorem," *Quarterly Journal of Economics* 81, No. 2 (May 1967), pp. 256–270.

———, *The Social Dilemma: The Economics of War and Revolution.* Blacksburg, Va.: University Publications, 1974.

———, "The Transitional Gains Trap," *Bell Journal of Economics* 6 (Autumn 1975), pp. 671–678.

———, "The Welfare Costs of Tariffs, Monopolies, and Theft," *Western Economic Journal* 5 (June 1967), pp. 224–232.

———, "Why So Much Stability?" *Public Choice* 37, No. 2 (1982), pp. 189–202.

Umbeck, John, "Might Makes Rights: A Theory of the Foundation and Initial Distribution of Property Rights," *Economic Inquiry* 19, No. 1 (January 1981), pp. 38–59.

Usher, Dan, "The Dynastic Cycle and the Stationary State," *American Economic Review* 79, No. 5 (December 1989), pp. 1031–1044.

Wagner, Richard E., "Agency, Economic Calculation, and Constitutional Construction," in Charles K. Rowley, Robert D. Tollison, and Gordon Tullock, eds., *The Political Economy of Rent-Seeking.* Boston: Kluwer Academic Publishers, 1988, pp. 423–443.

———, *To Promote the General Welfare: Market Processes Vs. Political Transfers.* San Francisco: Pacific Research Institute, 1989.

Weber, Max, *The Theory of Social and Economic Organization*, trans. A.M. Henderson and Talcott Parsons. Oxford: Oxford University Press, 1947.

Weingast, Barry R., and William J. Marshall, "The Industrial Organization of Congress; or, Why Legislatures, Like Firms, Are Not Organized as Markets," *Journal of Political Economy* 96, No. 1 (February 1988), pp. 132–163.

Weingast, Barry, Kenneth A. Shepsle, and Christopher Johnsen, "The Political Economy of Benefits and Costs: A Neoclassical Approach to Distributive Politics," *Journal of Political Economy* 89, No. 4 (August 1981), pp. 642–664.

Wicksell, Knut, "A New Principle of Just Taxation" (1896), pp. 72–118 in Richard A. Musgrave and Alan T. Peacock, eds., *Classics in the Theory of Public Finance.* New York: St. Martin's Press, 1967.

Williamson, Oliver E., "A Comparison of Alternative Approaches to Economic Organization," *Journal of Institutional and Theoretical Economics* 146, No. 1 (March 1990), pp. 61–71.

———, *The Economic Institutions of Capitalism.* New York: The Free Press, 1985.

Wilson, Edward O., *Sociobiology.* Cambridge: Harvard University Press, 1975.

Wittman, Donald, "Why Democracies Produce Efficient Results," *Journal of Political Economy* 97, No. 6 (December 1989), pp. 1395–1424.

Yeager, Leland B., "Rights, Contract, and Utility in Policy Analysis," *Cato Journal* 5, No. 1 (Summer 1985), pp. 259–294.

Index

Agreement
  conceptual vs. actual, 165–6, 178
  and ideology, 162–3
  implied, 168–70
  importance of, 155–6
  and legitimacy, 157–60, 173,
    205–206
  normative application of, 175–8,
    199–200
  normative vs. positive concepts
    of, 163–5
  with postconstitutional decisions,
    166–7
  and the public interest, 215–16
  and the social contract, 164, 165–7
  and the status quo, 207
  as the ultimate criterion of social
    choice, 217
  Wicksellian, 198–9
Alchian, Armen A., 6, 151–2, 228, 230,
  251, 254
Allen, William R., 151–2
Altruism
  and legitimacy of government, 158
  and rights, 22–6
Amin, Idi, 48
Anarchy
  and division of labor, 135
  emergence of government from,
    32–3, 36
  negotiation in, 44, 62–9, 129–30
  rights in, 33–5
Anderson, Gary M., 242
Arrow, Kenneth J., 119, 125, 244
Auster, Richard D., 238, 239
Axelrod, Robert, 24, 228, 230, 234, 235

Baden, John, 234, 242
Barker, Sir Ernest, 224, 236
Barlow, Robin, 243
Barriers to entry, 95, 98–9, 142
  and democratic voting, 145–6

seniority as, 99–100
Baumol, William J., 206, 229, 239, 248
Beard, Charles A., 230, 246, 255
Becker, Gary S., 227, 250
Benson, Bruce L., 192, 227, 234, 242,
  248, 254
Berman, Harold J., 140, 175, 233, 249
Black, Duncan, 239
Boudreaux, Donald J., 252
Bourne, Randolph S., 147, 234
Bowen, Howard R., 239
Brennan, Geoffrey, 228, 238
Browning, Edgar K., 256
Buchanan, James M., 2–3, 14, 17, 27,
  28, 33, 43, 44, 45, 46, 47, 73,
  125, 138, 166, 171–3, 183, 198,
  206, 212, 225, 227, 228, 230, 233,
  235, 236, 238, 243, 245, 246, 247,
  248, 249, 250, 251, 252, 255,
  256, 258

Cartel
  government as, 95–6, 98–9
  and federalism, 103–4
Caste system, *see* rights structures
Cheung, Steven N.S., 230, 231
Circular reference, *see* reference, circular
Clubs
  economic theory of, 73–4
  and governments, 74–9, 211–12
  as voluntary organizations, 72, 74
Coase, Ronald H., 27, 235, 258
Coase theorem, 69, 121, 125, 126
Coercion
  and agreement, 7, 25, 47, 161–2
  as force, 157
  of free riders, 138–9
  by government, 36, 92–4
  and rights, 60–61
Coleman, James S., 35
Common law
  evolution of, 131–2

and rights, 17
Competition
    among potential governments, 38–9
    between incumbents and non-
        incumbents, 101–2, 220–1
    electoral, 96, 145–6
    and government growth, 148–9
    intergovernmental, 103–4, 143–5
    in markets vs. politics, 113
    vs. monopoly in government, 219
    for the right to be dictator, 111
    and special interests, 97–8
Compromise, 1, 113, 116–19
Constitutional rules
    as foundation for government, 7–8, 33
    and legitimacy, 40–41
    as social contract, 41–3
Consensus
    as a foundation for government,
        215–17
    and Lindahl equilibrium, 116, 118–19
Constitutions
    as barriers to political entry, 213–14
    characteristics of, 50–1
    as constraints, 129–31, 150–51
    evolution of, 132–8
    as foundation of government, 217–18
    ideally created, 131
    and mobility, 89, 146
    and monopoly government, 51–2,
        212–13
    restrictive covenants as, 174
Contractarianism, *see* social contract
Corruption
    as exchange, 54
    as regulation, 106–7
Crain, W. Mark, 239, 240, 249
Cycles
    and the American primary system,
        124–5
    and institutions, 221
    in politics, 119–24

Dahl, Robert, 80, 238
Demsetz, Harold, 95, 146–7, 215, 231
Denzau, Arthur T., 243
Dictatorship
    compared to democracy, 11, 112,
        219–20

and military force, 137
    perceived legitimacy of, 208, 217
Downs, Anthony, 96, 97, 116, 123, 145,
        251, 254
Dugan, William R., 245

Easement, legal recognition of, 57
Edelman, Murray, 25, 161, 206, 231–2,
        248, 254
Ehrlich, Isaac, 235
Elections as political competition,
        38–9, 93
Ellickson, Robert C., 226
Exchange model of government,
        32–4, 92
Exchange in politics and markets, 223

Faith, Roger L., 234
Federalism
    and government cartels, 103–4
    and intergovernmental competition,
        219
Fictions
    and agreement, 170–71
    in common law, 132
    and the normative basis for
        government, 192–4
Free riders, 138
Friedman, David, 253, 256
Friedman, Milton, 188, 230, 241,
        250, 252
Friedman, Rose, 241
Friedrich, Carl Joachim, 80, 250

Gallarotti, Guilio M., 243
Gauthier, David, 226, 228, 229, 255
Glazer, Amihai, 245
Goetz, Charles J., 238, 248
Gordon, Scott, 256
Government
    as a cartel, 95, 96, 98–9
    as a coercive institution, 3–4,
        38–9, 74
    definition of, 84, 90
    as an economic institution, 6–7
    efficiency of, 143
    growth of, 148–9
    as a monopolist, 9–10, 37–8, 51–2,
        92–109

as recipient of tribute, 36
as the result of human design, 151–3, 182
Grofman, Bernard, 245
Gwartney, James D., 233–4

Hardin, Russell, 255
Hare, Paul G., 229, 253
Hayek, Friedrich A., 67, 188, 230, 241, 247, 250, 251, 254
Higgs, Robert, 249, 250
Hirshleifer, Jack, 227, 250
Hobbes, Thomas, 13, 32, 42, 44–5, 47, 48, 128
Hochman, Harold M., 138, 239, 248, 250, 251, 256, 257
Hoebel, E. Adamson, 231
Hohfield, Wesley, 225
Holcombe, Lora P., 242
Holcombe, Randall G., 225, 229, 232, 233, 234, 235, 239, 240, 241, 242, 243, 244, 245, 246, 247–8, 249, 251, 252, 254, 255, 257, 258
Hotelling, Harold, 145
Houston, Texas, 79

Ideology
    and group identification, 25
    and legitimacy, 40, 139, 162–3
    and political exchange, 123
Intergovernmental competition
    see competition, intergovernmental
    see also Tiebout, Charles M.

Jarrell, Gregg A., 241
Johnson, Christopher, 240, 245

Kalt, Joseph P., 232, 240, 245, 251
Kau, James B., 232, 240, 245, 251
Kelman, Steven, 227
Keynes, John Maynard, 249
King, J. Charles, 253
Kirzner, Israel M., 6
Knight, Frank, 52
Koford, Kenneth J., 241, 245
Kreuger, Anne O., 241

Law
    development of, 17

fictions in, 17, 132
implied agreement in, 169–70
    see also common law
    see also natural law
Laws of social science, 12–13, 29–30
Legitimacy
    and agreement, 157–60
    and constitutional rules, 40–41
    and cooperation with government, 25, 138–9, 214
    of democratic governments, 161, 163, 214, 220
    and Eastern European governments, 48
    production of, 160–61
    and public policy, 205–6
    of the social contract, 42
Levi, Margaret, 25, 239, 240, 243, 258
Lin, Justin Yifu, 232
Lindahl equilibrium, 113–16, 126
Lindahl taxes as public policy, 203–4
Lipford, Jody, 241
Logrolling, 122

Machan, Tibor, 226, 251–3, 254
Mackay, Robert J., 243
Marshall, William J., 240
Maine, Henry Sumner, 226
McCallum, Spencer Heath, 252
McKelvey, Richard D., 123, 244
McKenzie, Richard B., 241, 248
Mises, Ludwig von, 29, 225, 252, 254
Monarchy, 111
Monopoly
    caste system as, 70
    and constitutional evolution, 133, 148
    constitutional rules and, 51–2
    and the definition of government, 80–82
    and dictatorship, 112
    and division of labor, 135
    government as, 9–10, 37–8, 92–109
    natural, 94–5
    see also barriers to entry
Munger, Michael, 245
Murray, Charles, 188, 247

Natural law, 191–2
    and rights, 17

Natural rights, *see* rights, natural
Newenhizen, Jill van, 246
Niskanen, William A., 50, 143, 232
Normative analysis and the public sector,
    5–6, 180
Normative vs. positive concepts of
    agreement, 163–5
North, Douglass, 25, 40, 48, 139, 162,
    205, 229, 239
Nozick, Robert, 2, 14, 17, 27, 46, 47, 59,
    94, 231, 233, 242, 246

Olson, Mancur, Jr., 148, 245

Panzar, John C., 239
Parker, Glenn R., 258
Paul, Chris, 243
Peacock, Alan T., 249
Peltzman, Sam, 232, 240, 242, 245, 251
Peru, underground economy in, 18–20
Plott, Charles R., 244
Political competition, *see* competition
Positive vs. normative
    and design of constitutional
        rules, 151–2
    disagreements, 188–9
    theories of government, 2–6
    theories of rights, 12–13, 26
Posner, Richard A., 226, 229, 241, 242,
    247, 254
Priest, George L., 247–254
Primitive societies, rights in, 17
Procedural theories of rights, 26–29
Protection for tribute
    and development of rights, 18
    enforcement of, 102
    as foundation for government,
        35–7, 219
    as fundamental contract, 8–9, 41, 211

Rand, Ayn, 80, 229, 241, 254
Rational ignorance, 97, 105
Rawls, John, 2, 3, 4, 17, 27, 28, 33, 43,
    44, 45, 46, 47, 171–3, 246
Reference, circular, *see* circular
    reference
Regulation, 105–6
Restrictive covenants, 76–9, 86, 174
Reuter, Peter, 242

Revolution, 111–12, 137–8
    as political competition, 38–9
    and the rise of nations, 148
Rights
    of aliens, 16
    in anarchy, 34–5
    of animals, 16
    of children, 16
    as constitutional rules, 8–11
    and contractarianism, 27–9
    definition of, 11
    and efficiency, 27
    equality of, 14–15, 17, 211
    in families, 17
    government protection of, 18–20,
        60–61
    and legal institutions, 57–8
    of handicapped persons, 16
    and monopoly government, 103
    natural, 11–12, 189–91
    observation of, as prisoners'
        dilemma, 56–7
    and opportunistic behavior, 54–5
    origins of, 14–16
    positive vs. normative theories of,
        12–13, 20–21, 26, 27–9, 30
    in primitive societies, 17
    procedural theory of, 26, 29
    and the public interest, 22
    and shirking, 67
    and slavery, 15, 28
    and social contract, 18
    and the status quo, 193
    and technological change, 16, 67
    unanimous approval of, 14–15, 27
Rights structures
    cooperative vs. caste, 64–9
    natural, 189–91
Riker, William H., 239–40, 244–5
Rodgers, James D., 138, 239, 248, 250,
    251, 256, 257
Romer, Thomas, 246
Rosenthal, Howard, 246
Rothbard, Murray N., 83–4, 226, 229,
    231, 237, 241, 254, 257
Rowley, Charles K., 244
Rules vs. discretion, 218
Rubin, Paul H., 191, 232, 240, 245, 247,
    251, 254

Saari, Donald J., 246
Samuelson, Paul A., 138, 229, 243, 253
Schelling, Thomas C., 193, 242, 244
Schmidt-Trenz, Hans-Jorg, 235
Schwartz, Thomas, 234
Scully, Gerald W., 230
Secret ballot, 107–8, 122
Sen, Amartya, 227, 229
Seniority system, 99–100
Shepsle, Kenneth A., 240, 245
Siegan, Bernard H., 237
Silver, Morris, 238, 239
Slavery, 15, 28, 33, 64, 202
  and natural rights, 189, 190
Smith, Adam, 134, 228
Social contract
  agreement with, 164–7, 171–4
  and coercion, 45–6, 168
  constitution as, 41–3
  urban charter as, 175
Social contract theory of the state
  contemporary expositions of, 43–8
  and definition of government, 74–5
  as a fiction, 193–4
  and natural rights, 190
  as a normative theory, 3, 182–3,
    196–8
  positive vs. normative aspects,
    48–9, 216
  as a positive theory, 41–3
  and the role of government, 43–5
  and unanimity, 46–8
  and utilitarianism, 186–7
Social science, laws of, 12–13, 181–2
  vs. social engineering, 152–3
Soto, Hernando de, 19
Soviet Union, 42, 144, 176
Special interests, 97–8, 123
Staaf, Robert J., 241, 248
Status quo
  changes from, 152
  and social welfare, 218
  unfairness in, 218
Stigler, George J., 105, 227, 240

Taxation
  as theft, 8–9, 73
  as tribute, 9
Tax policy, 218

Technological change, 149
Thompson, Earl A., 234, 248
Tideman, T. Nicolaus, 244, 245
Tiebout, Charles M., 46, 93, 110, 143,
    145, 150, 174
Tollison, Robert D., 239, 242, 249
Tullock, Gordon, 27, 33, 43, 44, 45, 46,
    166, 225, 227, 231, 234, 239, 241,
    244, 245, 248, 249, 250, 255, 256,
    257, 258

Uganda, 48
Umbeck, John, 225
Unanimity
  and coercion, 4
  and constitutional rules, 44
  and Lindahl equilibrium, 116
  as a normative principle, 3, 14, 198–9
  and political feasibility, 29
Underground economy, 18–20
Usher, Dan, 235
Utilitarianism, 183–5
  compared with contractarianism,
    186–7

Vanberg, Viktor, 253
Veil of ignorance
  see social contract
  see also Rawls, John

Wagner, Richard E., 225, 252, 253, 256
War
  as the health of the state, 147–8
  as political competition, 38–9, 111
Weber, Max, 80
Weingast, Barry R., 240, 245
Wicksell, Knut, 46, 116, 198–9,
    203, 216
Williamson, Oliver E., 224, 234, 252
Willig, Robert D., 239
Wilson, Edward O., 227, 250
Wiseman, Jack, 249
Wittman, Donald, 240

Yandle, Bruce, 241
Yeager, Leland B., 26, 165–6, 186, 226,
    233, 247, 256

Zupan, Mark A., 232, 245